THE GREATEST DAY
IN HISTORY

How, on the Eleventh Hour of the Eleventh Day
of the Eleventh Month,
the First World War Finally Came to an End

NICHOLAS BEST

PublicAffairs
New York

For my grandfathers,
both of whom fought on the Western Front,
and for my grandmother,
whose brothers are still there somewhere.

Library of Congress Control Number: 2008926373
ISBN-13: 978-1-58648-640-2
First Edition
10 9 8 7 6 5 4 3 2 1

CONTENTS

fights for Serbia; General von Lettow-Vorbeck invades
Rhodesia; President Wilson loses the election; Matthias
Erzberger accepts a poisoned chalice; the Armistice
commission sets out from Berlin.

Contents

Princess Blücher tries to sleep; Ludendorff acquires a false
beard; Marlene Dietrich loathes the mob; Kurt Weill enjoys the
excitement; General Gröner studies the Armistice terms; the
Kaiser agrees to abdicate; Vladimir Lenin gloats.

Princess Blücher watches the fighting; the Kaiser steals away;
the Armistice commission discovers its whereabouts; the
Leinsters near Fontenoy; the Prince of Wales near Mons;
Howard Vincent O'Brien passes Zeebrugge; Harry Truman
hates the Hun; George Coles hears the guns in prison camp;
the Germans strip the fat from human bodies; Princess Blücher
flees; Wilhelmshaven celebrates the republic; Hindenburg
addresses the army; Corporal Hitler weeps; Maude Onions
plays the organ; Foch demands an answer; the Chancellor
responds; the Kaiser seeks asylum; President Wilson decodes a
cable; the Germans want to talk.

The Armistice signed; the fighting continues; the Canadians take
Mons; atrocity near Valenciennes; German troops raped; the RAF
stands down; Captain Glubb misses the war already; Herbert Sulzbach
hates to surrender; the Kaiser booed in Holland; Harry Truman fires
off his ammunition; George Coles in prison camp; an Australian
woman in Leipzig; Erich Maria Remarque poses as an officer;
Henry Asquith attends a funeral; President Wilson hears the news;
Americans killed in the advance; the generals refuse to call it off; the
British push on from Mons; Ernst Kielmayer longs for home; Georg
Bucher in a gas attack; fighting continues right up to the wire.

A Boer hears the news; the Grenadiers still have a score to
settle; peace in Malplaquet; euphoria nearby; the Leinsters
don't even cheer; Lessines stormed at two minutes to eleven;
the last men to die; American troops still haven't heard; Eddie
Rickenbacker watches from the air; Georg Bucher distrusts
the Americans; Octave Delaluque blows his bugle; a machine

gunner bows to the South Africans; General Pershing drinks
from a German helmet; Paris goes wild; HMS *Amazon*
still doesn't know; Dickie Dixon terrifies his mother; the
crowd mob Buckingham Palace; Winston Churchill watches
the excitement; Vera Brittain too sad to care; Olive Wells
excused her homework; Virginia Woolf emotional; Bertrand
Russell watches in wonder; Agatha Christie refuses to dance;
an Austrian internee fears another war; the bells ring in
Southwold; no tea in Liverpool; the Yanks march through
Southampton; Etonians celebrate in Windsor; pacifists
attacked in Cambridge; Napoleon III's widow exults; global
party.

Contents

Churchill dines at No. 10; King George takes another bow; bitterness at the Ritz; Siegfried Sassoon picks a quarrel; Maynard Keynes fears the economic consequences; Noël Coward has a thrilling evening; bombed children fear the fireworks; President Wilson has a ball; Harry Truman can't sleep; Adolf Hitler decides to enter politics.

LIST OF ILLUSTRATIONS

The Germans were within sight of the Eiffel Tower when their final offensive petered out. (Mary Evans Picture Library)

German gunner, killed at Villers Devy Dun Sassey on 4 November 1918. (Corbis)

Captain Charles de Gaulle. (Bridgeman Art Library/Archives de Gaulle, Paris)

Harry Truman. (Getty Images)

Sergeant-Major Flora Sandes, a British clergyman's daughter serving in the Serbian infantry. (TopFoto)

Herbert Sulzbach. (Weidenfeld Archive)

After a scratch supper at Homblières, the German Armistice delegates returned to their car for the journey to Compiègne. (Imperial War Museum)

Matthias Erzberger, leader of the German delegation. (Getty Images)

Prince Max von Baden, Chancellor of Germany for only a few weeks. (AKG-Images, London)

General Wilhelm Gröner. (Getty Images)

Philipp Scheidemann at the window of the Chancellery in Berlin. (AKG-Images, London)

View from the top of Berlin's Brandenburg Gate during the revolution. (AKG-Images, London)

Princess Blücher. (Weidenfeld Archive)

Soldiers on the Brandenburg Gate. (AKG-Images, London)

Corporal Teilhard de Chardin. (Editions Grasset)

Ludwig Wittgenstein. (Getty Images)

2nd Lieutenant George Coles. (Imperial War Museum)

The Kaiser waits for his train to arrive at Eisden, 10 November.
(AKG-Images, London)

Lady Susan Townley, wife of the British ambassador at the Hague.
(National Portrait Gallery, London)

Marshal Foch signs the Armistice for France soon after 5 a.m. on 11
November. (TopFoto)

The Canadians relax in Mons's main square on Armistice morning.
(National Archives of Canada)

The Irish Guards at Maubeuge, five minutes before the Armistice.
(Getty Images)

Patricia Carver. (Private collection)

Crowds at Buckingham Palace on Armistice morning. (Getty
Images)

Crowds at the White House, 1918. (Getty Images)

Newspaperman Roy Howard. (Getty Images/Time & Life Pictures)

Australians in Sydney's Martin Place on Armistice day. (Australian
War Memorial)

American Troops dance through the streets of Paris on Armistice
day. (Bridgeman Art Library/Archives Larrousse, Paris)

Henry Gunther, officially the last US soldier to die in the war.
(Baltimore Sun)

US air ace Eddie Rickenbacker. (Getty Images)

Bogart Rogers. (Weidenfeld Archive)

Ernest Hemingway in uniform. (Weidenfeld Archive)

Agatha Christie. (Bridgeman Art Library: Illustrated London News)

John Maynard Keynes. (Bridgeman Art Library)

Mahatma Gandhi. (Getty Images)

T. E. Lawrence. (Imperial War Museum)

Marlene Dietrich and Erich Maria Remarque. (Getty Images)

Paris showgirl Mistinguett and Maurice Chevalier. (Bridgeman Art
Library/Bibliotheque de L'Arsenal, Paris)

André Maurois. (Getty Images)

Chancellor Friedrich Ebert Greets 'undefeated' troops at the
Brandenburg Gate on 10 December. (AKG-Images, London)

ACKNOWLEDGEMENTS

Thanks to the following for permission to quote from documents at the Imperial War Museum: Mary Coles (G.T. Coles 03/58/1), Jeanne Davies (W.W. Johnstone Wilson 97/5/1), M.R.D. Foot (R.C. Foot 86/57/1), Cynthia Ford (H.M. Wilson 04/1/1), D.A. Hamilton (A.S. Hamilton 93/31/1), estate of H.W. House (H.W. House 88/56/1), P.M. McGrigor (A.M. McGrigor P399), Diana Stockford (H.C. Rees 77/179/1), Estelle Wells (Ernest Cooper P121), Miss E. Wells (Olive Wells 91/5/1) and to Richard Davies of the Brotherton Library, University of Leeds for permission to quote from S.C. Marriott's letter of 11 November 1918 in the Liddle Collection.

Thanks also to the following for permission to quote from published works: Juliet Nicolson (*Peacemaking* by Harold Nicolson, Constable, 1933), University Press of Kansas (*A Yankee Ace in the RAF* by Bogart Rogers, UPK, 1996), Random House (*The Question of Things Happening: Letters of Virginia Woolf*, Hogarth Press, 1976) Oxford University Press (*Journey from Obscurity* by Harold Owen, OUP, 1965) and Decie Denholm (*Behind the Lines* by Ethel Cooper, Collins, 1982).

Other copyright holders have been difficult to track down. They are welcome to get in touch if they wish.

Thanks too to Jane Wilson, Robin Boyd, the staff of the Documents Department at the Imperial War Museum and Pamela Clark of the Royal Archives.

'The biggest news in the history of newspapers, perhaps in the history of humanity. A scrap of news that two thousand million people – the whole world – awaited breathlessly. News that would mean to tens of millions that their sons, husbands or sweethearts would come home alive and unmaimed … News that had never before and could never again mean so much to so many people. The Armistice!'

Webb Miller, *United Press*

'The greatest day in history.'

London *Daily Express*

CHAPTER ONE

Monday, 4 November 1918

The New Zealanders were on a roll. For weeks they had been chasing the Germans across France, forcing them steadily back towards the frontier with Belgium. Ahead of them now lay the ancient citadel of Le Quesnoy, straddling the road to the frontier beyond. One final push and the German army would be out of France altogether.

Le Quesnoy stood on high ground amid rolling countryside. It had been a fortress for eight hundred years, its thick walls long familiar to the English, who had had their first taste of cannon fire there in 1346. The walls had later been strengthened by Marshal Vauban, who had remodelled the ramparts in the seventeenth century to withstand a long siege. They stood sixty feet high now, topped with gun emplacements, heavily defended by the German garrison of the town.

The New Zealanders came out of the mist in the early morning of Monday, 4 November 1918. They bypassed the town first, clearing the surrounding fields of Germans before turning their attention to the citadel. It was an easy target with modern artillery. The New Zealanders could have reduced it to rubble in no time if they had wished. But there were five thousand French civilians in Le Quesnoy, as well as the German garrison. The New Zealanders didn't want to use artillery if they could avoid it.

Some prisoners were sent in instead, to explain to the garrison that their position was hopeless. The Germans didn't doubt it, but their garrison commander was reluctant to surrender without a fight. When the prisoners failed to return, a message was dropped by aeroplane urging the garrison commander to capitulate, promising that his men would be honourably treated if they raised the white flag. When the commander still refused to parley, the New Zealanders decided to capture Le Quesnoy the old-fashioned way, by storming the bastion and climbing the walls with scaling ladders.

They cleared the walls of the enemy first, putting down a heavy barrage on the outer rampart while the storming party advanced behind a smokescreen. After some fierce fighting, the New Zealanders breached the outer walls and forced a way across to the moat. German troops threw stick grenades down on them as they circled the inner rampart, looking for a way up. The only feasible route was via a bridge across the moat. They estimated that a thirty-foot ladder on the bridge would just reach the top of the inner wall surrounding the town.

While Lewis guns swept the parapet to keep the Germans' heads down, a party of the New Zealanders' 4th battalion doubled forward with a scaling ladder. Keeping an eye out for grenades, they raised the ladder precariously against the wall. The place was ominously quiet as Lieutenant Leslie Averill began to climb. The only sound he could hear was the water gurgling in the moat as he reached the grass bank on top of the wall and peered over it into the faces of two startled Germans, who promptly ran away.

Averill fired his revolver after them and scrambled down the bank into the town, closely followed by Second Lieutenant H. W. Kerr and the rest of the battalion. Within minutes, they had gained a foothold in Le Quesnoy and were chasing the Germans along the street, egged on by the townspeople cheering wildly from their windows.

While the 4th battalion scaled the walls, the New Zealanders' 2nd and 3rd battalions were attacking from the other side of the town. Private James Nimmo and two others had been sent forward to find out what had happened to a reconnaissance patrol that had gone missing. They approached the walls cautiously, but could see no Germans as they made their way round to the gate. But the Germans were still there, as Nimmo recalled in a letter home:

'How I am alive to write this today I don't know, or at the very least I should have been in Blighty. We got into the town and were simply overwhelmed by civvies. Laughing, crying, and just about mad with joy. It was ten minutes before we could get away from them. Then two of us searched everywhere near the gate but found no Jerries. We then found out by the aid of a word or two of French and by signs that one of our boys was down the street wounded. The civvies reckoned there were no Jerries round that part so we decided to go and get him.'

The French pressed food and drink on the New Zealanders before they went. Nimmo grabbed a pancake to eat on the way as a civilian led them to the wounded man:

'Had just got a mouthful when the old boy opened out from fifty yards down the street. The civvy got one through the hand. One of my mates got one through the leg and one in the arm. There was no shelter and there was nothing for us to do but run for it. A good hundred yards. Could see the bullets hitting the cobbles in front of us, and were getting pieces of brick from behind, but neither of us got hit. Halfway along I saw a doorway and decided on a spell. I bounced into it in such a hurry that I bounced out again like a ball. I took it gently next attempt and had a few minutes in which to get my wind. Then it was a case of go again, and he opened as soon as I appeared and helped me along the final stretch. One poor little dog ran after us barking like blazes and had his leg blown clean off.'

But the fighting did not last long. The garrison quickly surrendered, knowing when it was beaten. By nightfall the town was free of Germans at last, almost a thousand of them marching meekly out of the gate as prisoners of war. Private Nimmo was sorry to see them go, because he hadn't had a chance to collect any souvenirs before they left. The New Zealanders liked wristwatches best, although revolvers and field glasses were useful too, or an Iron Cross at a pinch. Even pornography, if there wasn't anything else. The Germans always had good pornography.

Still, there would be plenty more where that came from. The Germans were giving up in thousands now, not just hundreds any more. The British army had attacked along a thirty-mile front that Monday morning, pushing forward in a vast sweep from Valenciennes to the river Sambre. Men, tanks and artillery had been in action since well before dawn. The French army was advancing too, and so were the Americans in the Argonne. All along the line the Germans were in retreat, either falling back in disarray or else running across the fields with their hands in the air, determined to surrender while they still could.

Some were still fighting, clinging tenaciously to their foxholes, but most had no more fight in them or any further stomach for the war. They just wanted the shooting to stop so that they could go home. As the day progressed and the reports came in to British headquarters, it became increasingly apparent that the German army was disintegrating at last, defeated in all but name. The Germans were ready to lay down their arms and stop fighting once and for all. It was the breakthrough everyone had been waiting for.

While the New Zealanders triumphed at Le Quesnoy, Second Lieutenant Wilfred Owen of the Manchester Regiment was leading his men forward at Ors, ten miles to the south. The Manchesters' orders were to cross the Sambre–Oise canal just above the town and dislodge the Germans from the far side. It was no easy task, with the bridges destroyed and the enemy unmoved by a preliminary bombardment which had been intended to knock them out. Owen's men reached the canal without mishap, but then came under heavy fire from the opposite bank. They returned it with interest, keeping the Germans' heads down while a party of Royal Engineers dragged a pontoon bridge of duckboards and cork floats to the water and assembled it for the crossing.

The bridge was almost ready when it was hit by shellfire. The engineers struggled to repair the damage, but were steadily picked off by the German machine guns. In response, Second Lieutenant James Kirk of the Manchesters grabbed a Lewis gun and paddled towards the enemy on one of the cork floats. He opened up from ten yards away, pinning the Germans down while the engineers completed their repairs. Kirk was wounded in the face and arm, but kept on firing until the engineers had floated the bridge across the water and reached the other side.

The Manchesters sprinted across. Two platoons made it to the far bank and flung themselves down on the German side. A third was about to follow when another shell ripped into the bridge and tore it apart again. The damage was worse this time, difficult to repair in a hurry. But if the bridge couldn't be repaired quickly, the duckboard floats could still be used as rafts for the crossing. The Manchesters launched them at once.

Owen was in the thick of the action, yelling encouragement at his men, walking up and down and patting them on the shoulder as they grappled with the makeshift rafts. None of his men knew it, but he wrote poetry in his spare time, dark little stanzas about the horrors of the war they were fighting. Owen hated the war and everything about it. He was particularly scathing about the civilians at home who justified the slaughter with absurd Latin tags about the honour of dying for one's country. Owen had seen men die in gas attacks and knew the reality:

> If you could hear, at every jolt, the blood
> Come gargling from the froth-corrupted lungs ...
> You would not tell with such high zest
> To children ardent for some desperate glory,
> The old Lie: *Dulce et decorum est*
> *Pro patria mori.*

The Germans kept up a withering fire as the Manchesters struggled. James Kirk was shot through the head and fell dead over his Lewis gun. He was later awarded the Victoria Cross for his bravery. Owen was down by the canal bank when he too was killed, although no one saw him die. The last anyone remembered, he was with his men, saying 'Well done' to one and 'You're doing very well, my boy' to another. Several people thought he had boarded one of the rafts when he was hit, but nobody could say for certain. There were too many bullets flying around for anything to be certain.

'What passing-bells for these who die as cattle?' Certainly there were no bells for Wilfred Owen as he died. The attack was called off soon afterwards and the Manchesters withdrew from the canal, taking Owen's body with them for burial in the municipal cemetery at Ors. It was a rare failure for the British on a day of outstanding success everywhere else.

While the Manchester Regiment mourned Wilfred Owen, Lieutenant Bogart Rogers of the newly formed Royal Air Force was grieving for his friend Alvin Callender, shot down a few days ago by a German Fokker. The two American pilots had been part of the British advance for the past few weeks, strafing the retreating Germans and attacking their railways and airfields whenever the weather permitted. But Callender's luck had run out at last and he had died of wounds in a Canadian field hospital. Rogers had been appointed to succeed him as a flight leader in 32 Squadron, a promotion he would have been much happier about if the circumstances had been different.

Rogers had been with 32 Squadron since May. He was a society boy from California, one of several hundred Americans who had volunteered for the Royal Air Force rather than wait for their own country to join the war. Rogers had thought it a great adventure at first, until the realities of combat had hit home. He had seen an American troopship torpedoed on the way over, with the loss of hundreds of lives. In London, he had been shaken to find women wearing khaki and British soldiers arriving at the railway stations straight from the fighting:

'You see Tommies coming in covered with Flanders mud, rifles over their shoulders and iron hats strapped to their backs, and you realise that maybe less than twenty-four hours ago they were in the front-line trenches ... I had no idea of what a tremendous affair the war is, how terrible it all is, and how the English people have worked and sacrificed.'

After a few weeks in England, Rogers had crossed to Boulogne, where he had had another shock as he watched a trainload of wounded being unloaded from the front. He had soon gone up to the front himself, and for the past six months had been flying two patrols a day over enemy territory as the British fought off the Germans' spring offensive and then attacked in their turn. He had been credited with six confirmed kills of enemy aircraft, although the real figure was undoubtedly much higher.

Rogers had almost been killed himself once when he was flying along in a daydream, thinking about England and what a nice place it was. A burst of machine-gun fire from a German plane had brought him to his senses and he had quickly taken evasive action. He found the war in the air a lonely business, with no one else to talk to and nothing audible above the sound of his own engine.

Rogers liked the English so much that he joked to his friends that he was becoming a regular Britisher, enjoying afternoon tea and drinking a toast to the king at dinner nights in the mess. He had even tried to sing the British national anthem once, until he remembered that he didn't know the words. But he remained American at heart, celebrating the Fourth of July with other Americans in the squadron and doing his best to teach the English baseball with a cricket bat.

Since 2 November, the squadron had been at La Brayelle, an airfield near Douai recently captured from the Germans. Baron von Richthofen had flown from there, his private cottage an object of fascination to the newcomers. Rogers himself was billeted in an old French chateau that the Germans had converted into a hospital. Apart from a few shell holes in one wing, it was very comfortable, much better than the officers' previous base. Rogers's room was intact except for one broken window and a cluster of bullet holes in the wall. He hoped he and his two room mates would remain there some time.

As for 32 Squadron, it had been reduced to just nine pilots and seven aircraft as the advance continued, less than half what it was supposed to be. 'There are only three flying officers in the squadron who were here when I came,' Rogers had commented in September. 'Makes one feel pretty old and experienced. It surely is hell to see them pass by. But the only way to do it is simply to forget that you ever possessed such a thing as an emotion or a nerve and carry on just as if nothing had happened. Is it any wonder that fellows go to pieces?'

By 4 November, the situation had deteriorated further with even more deaths: 'We've been having a rotten time of it, another awful scrap a couple of days ago. We were lucky to get back at all. A couple didn't. I managed to get another Hun. I'm pretty sure he was done for, but then five more chased me all over the shop. Too many!'

Afterwards, Rogers had been driven over to the aircraft depot to take delivery of a replacement aircraft and fly it back to La Brayelle. He had returned in a rainstorm, the clouds so low that he had had to fly all the way at treetop level to get the plane home. But replacement aircraft were no use without pilots, and there were far too few of those. At the present rate of attrition, Rogers was afraid that there would be no pilots left at all if the war didn't come to an end pretty soon.

On the other side of the line, Lieutenant Herbert Sulzbach of Germany's 63rd Field Artillery had been under fire all day from the French guns along the Oise–Aisne canal. The barrage had begun before dawn and had continued without let-up ever since, thousands of heavy calibre shells churning the earth around the Germans into a quagmire until it seemed to Sulzbach that there wasn't a square centimetre left untouched.

He and his men had found a cellar to hide in and were taking it in turns to man the observation post up above, but smoke from the French guns had reduced visibility to fifty yards, which was making their life very difficult. The telephone lines to the rear had been cut as well, leaving Sulzbach with no idea of what was happening anywhere else. He was worried that the French had already infiltrated the German lines and were about to overrun his position:

'What's the situation with the infantry? Nobody has any idea, and nobody knows either if the enemy aren't already behind us, because it's impossible to see anything in this mist. Are our lines collapsing, has everyone been captured and will we be too in a minute? The situation is hopeless! My batteries are still firing like mad and so far at least we have come across no retreating infantry. Now come the remaining gunners of No. 1 and No. 3 batteries carrying their firing mechanisms in their hands. The guns themselves have had to be abandoned after being overrun by the enemy. I remain at my post. Hauptmann Knigge attempts to reconnoitre new positions to the rear.'

The situation was as bad as any Sulzbach had known in more than four years of war. A civilised man from a Jewish banking family, he had enlisted in August 1914 and had been sent to the front four weeks later. As an admirer of the British, he had been horrified at the sight of his first dead Tommies in Flanders. Since then, he had seen plenty more bodies and had won the Iron Cross fighting for the Fatherland. His aim now was to keep his men in the field until the politicians could negotiate a decent peace, one that allowed the Germans to lay down their arms with honour.

During the afternoon, his batteries provided covering fire while a Bavarian regiment launched a counter-attack to recapture the 1st battalion's guns. The attack was a success and the guns were taken to the rear. Towards evening, a runner arrived with orders for Sulzbach's men to follow under cover of darkness.

They began to withdraw at 10 p.m., moving along hedges and fields to avoid the fire on the roads. Even so, they had to hit the ground every so often to escape a passing shell. Their nerves were in shreds after being bombarded all day. To add to their discomfort, the night was pitch black and raining, so dark that by midnight they were hopelessly lost.

Fortunately, they saw a light soon afterwards. It belonged to an artillery battery from a neighbouring division. Sulzbach's men were way out of position, but they were too exhausted to go any further that night. Borrowing blankets from their hosts, they lay down in a hay barn instead. Tomorrow, they had orders to continue the withdrawal towards the river Meuse, the last natural barrier available to the Germans along this part of the line. They might just make it to the Meuse if the French gunners left them alone. For now, though, Sulzbach and his men got themselves out of the rain and snatched a few hours' sleep while they had the chance.

At his flat in Berlin, General Erich Ludendorff was sitting at his desk, sunk in despair. He had been in despair for days, ever since the

Kaiser had dismissed him from his command on the Western Front. Ludendorff had been sent home in disgrace, so unpopular after the failure of his strategy for winning the war that cinema audiences had cheered when his dismissal was announced on the screen. He was still trying to come to terms with his sudden fall from grace.

Until recently, it had been a good war for Ludendorff. A master of military logistics, he had made his name against the Russians as chief of staff to Field Marshal Paul von Hindenburg. Together, they had become the most powerful duo in Germany, responsible for a policy of total war on all fronts. Overruling the political objections, Ludendorff had dictated a strategy of unrestricted submarine warfare at sea, an illegal torpedoing of civilian ships without regard for their crews, which had done much to turn American opinion against the Germans. He had been responsible, too, for the treaty of Brest-Litovsk, forcing the defeated Russians to accept peace terms so draconian that Germany's remaining enemies had seen no option but to fight on regardless.

In the spring of 1918, Ludendorff had launched a major offensive on the Western Front, aimed at capturing Paris and putting an end to the war before the Americans arrived to avenge the sinking of their ships. It had very nearly succeeded. The Germans had been able to see the Eiffel Tower through their field glasses before the tide had turned and they had been forced to pull back. Since August, however, they had been in continual retreat, with no more manpower to replenish their losses and the Americans shipping troops to France at a rate of 150,000 every month. Ludendorff's last great gamble had failed.

He himself had collapsed under the strain. For months before his dismissal he had sought consolation in the prayer book of the Moravian Brethren, thumbing through his dog-eared copy to see if the religious text for the day offered any military guidance. He had suffered a severe nervous breakdown, alternating between panic attacks and bursts of increasingly irrational optimism.

His staff had been so worried that they had arranged for a psychiatrist to visit Ludendorff's headquarters and secretly observe him at work. The psychiatrist had diagnosed overwork, prescribing a course of treatment that included the regular singing of German folk songs. But none of it had done any good. Ludendorff's nerves had gone and nothing could be done about it.

On the morning of 26 October, the Kaiser had summoned Hindenburg and Ludendorff to a meeting in Berlin to discuss the situation. Ludendorff had offered his resignation, something he had often done without expecting it to be accepted. This time, though, the Kaiser had accepted it at once and Ludendorff had found himself out of a job.

Hindenburg had half-heartedly offered his resignation as well, but the Kaiser had refused to consider it. As the two men left, Hindenburg had tried to console his old friend, only to be angrily rebuffed. 'I refuse to have any more dealings with you,' Ludendorff had hissed, adamant that Hindenburg should have insisted on resigning in sympathy. 'You have treated me very shabbily.'

Now Ludendorff was back in his flat, sitting gloomily at his desk. 'In a fortnight, we shall have no empire and no emperor left,' he had told his wife when he was sacked. The Kaiser had already left Berlin for Spa, the German army's headquarters in Belgium, ostensibly to avoid the Spanish influenza in the capital, in reality because he felt safer at Spa, surrounded by his troops. The mood in Berlin was so ugly that he might well have been assassinated if he had stayed. And if the Kaiser wasn't safe in Berlin, how much longer could the empire survive?

An Armistice was what they needed now, a few months' respite to allow the Germans to regroup and rearm, ready to resume the fight in the spring. They had no men left to fight with, but the class of 1919 would be available soon, school leavers still in training. A new army, new weapons, renewed enthusiasm for the struggle. Ludendorff was convinced that the Germans could do anything in the spring, just so long as they had a breather first, a few months of peace negotiations nicely protracted to keep the enemy at bay while they recovered their strength.

For the moment, though, Ludendorff remained at his desk in a state of catatonic shock. He said little, did less, just sat at his desk for day after day while events took their course and chaos reigned all around. His wife was very worried about him.

Ludendorff had been replaced on the Western Front by General Wilhelm Gröner . He had been in Kiev when Ludendorff was sacked, stripping the Ukraine of its remaining resources for the German war effort. Arriving in Belgium a few days later, Gröner had immediately set off on a tour of the troops to appraise the situation before making his report to the government in Berlin. What he had seen on his two-day tour had appalled him.

The German army was in no state to continue the fight much longer. The men were woefully under strength, so hungry that they were stealing oats and barley from the horses, so ill equipped that they pulled the boots off the dead and wore British jerkins because they had none of their own. Some were refusing to go into the trenches, others were slipping quietly away from the front and living rough behind the lines until the war came to an end. Those who went home on leave often didn't come back. Those who did return arrived in railway trains with 'Slaughter cattle for Wilhelm' chalked on the side, a view of the conflict identical to Wilfred Owen's.

Some of the troops were munitions workers, removed from vital war work and conscripted into the army for much lower wages. Others were trade union agitators sent to the front to get them out of the way. Still others had been prisoners of the Russians, fondly imagining that their war was over until they had been released from prison camp to fight again. Far too many of them were old men or young boys, drafted into the front line because there was no one else to fill the gap. On the rare occasions when they managed to overrun a British position, discipline had often fallen apart as the men gorged themselves on British rations and staggered about drunk rather than fight any further. It was not a recipe for success.

With time, Gröner might be able to turn the situation around, but time was not on his side. The British, French and Americans were all pushing together and the German army would collapse within days if something wasn't done to stop them. Gröner was rapidly coming to the view that the only way to stop them was to end the fighting as soon as possible and seek peace terms while the Germans were still in a position to negotiate.

Gröner was a realist, a hard-headed man of modest origins who had never been part of the high command's inner circle and did not share their distorted view of the possibilities. He came from Württemburg in southern Germany and was rare among German generals in being neither Prussian nor a gentleman. He had been excluded for years from the most prestigious military appointments because his father had been a paymaster, rather than a member of the old officer class. But Gröner was also a gifted organiser who had risen by his talents and could not be ignored forever. His time had come at last, although too late for him to do anything except take the blame for a mess that was not of his making.

What Gröner had to do now was to go to Berlin and make his report. A telegram had just arrived from Germany's new chancellor, Prince Max von Baden, asking him to come at once. If he caught the train from Spa that night, he would be in Berlin next morning. He would brief Prince Max on the position at the front, and Max would brief him on the situation at home. With rumours of trouble in Berlin and a naval mutiny at Kiel, as well as all the disasters in the field, they would have plenty to discuss when they met. General Gröner was not looking forward to it as he left Spa that Monday evening and caught the overnight train back to Germany.

At Kiel, on the Baltic, the rumours of a mutiny were all too true. The men of the German fleet were in revolt, openly defying their officers and refusing to obey their orders. They had taken over most of the ships in the harbour, hauling down the imperial flag at gunpoint and replacing it with the red banner of Bolshevism. Thousands of them were rampaging through the town, joining forces with the dockyard workers in a riot of protest and indiscipline through the streets.

The Kiel fleet had played little part in the war since the battle of Jutland in 1916. The mutiny had been triggered by a rumour that it had been ordered to sea for one last do or die battle against the British.

It was said that the officers preferred to go down fighting rather than suffer the ignominy of defeat. The sailors disagreed, seeing no point in dying unnecessarily at this stage of the war.

But their mutiny went much deeper than a reluctance to put to sea. They had been on short rations for months, fed miserably while their officers had the pick of whatever food was available. Like everyone else in Germany, the sailors were cold, tired, hungry and fed up with deprivation, sick of being lied to about a war that was never going to end. It was the war they were protesting about, the insistence of the ruling class on blindly prolonging the fight instead of negotiating the compromise peace that everyone else was longing for.

From the bridge of the *König*, moored alongside the Kaiser Wharf, Captain Karl Weniger was monitoring the events in the rest of the fleet with mounting alarm. Almost alone among the warships in the harbour, Weniger's ship was still loyal to the Kaiser and still flew the imperial flag. Weniger was a good captain with a good crew. His men could still be counted on to do what they were told. Yet for how much longer, when their comrades ashore were running amok with no one to stop them?

Several men had been killed the previous day when a patrol had opened fire on rebel sailors in the town. The survivors were howling for revenge and had the support of the garrison and townspeople. It was foolhardy, in the circumstances, to continue flying the imperial flag from the *König*. But the only alternative was to take the flag down and Weniger was damned if he was going to do that. The *König* was the Kaiser's ship and Weniger was the Kaiser's man. He would be surrendering if he took the flag down. He had decided to bide his time instead, keeping the flag flying while he waited for order to be restored in the fleet, as, please God, it surely would be, sooner or later.

Across the harbour, Grand Admiral Prince Heinrich of Prussia, the Kaiser's younger brother, was biding his time as well, keeping a wary eye on the situation from the windows of his palace in the heart of the old city. He was there with his wife and eldest son, listening apprehensively as shots echoed across the rooftops and makeshift red flags appeared on government buildings. Whatever fears Weniger had of a Bolshevist revolution were multiplied tenfold in Prince Heinrich. He was a cousin of the late czar of Russia and he could never forget what the Bolshevists had done to the czar and his family. He didn't want the same to happen to his own wife and son.

It had very nearly happened already. A party of sailors had burst into the palace and confronted Heinrich at gunpoint. They had abused him to his face, accusing him of living comfortably while they were starving. 'Do you think I eat better than you do?' he had demanded angrily. 'Yes,' one had insisted. 'You have more to eat than us. You eat and drink just like the Silesian lords.'

The sailors had been persuaded to leave after a while without doing him any harm. But the situation was deteriorating all the time and Heinrich was terrified that they would return and kill his family, just as the Russians had killed the czar. His wife was worried too, because the czarina had been her sister. What if the sailors put her son up against a wall and shot him, as the Russians had shot her nephew the czarevich? It was too awful to contemplate.

The Danish border was only sixty miles away, an easy run to the north. If the worst came to the worst, they could be there in a few hours, seeking sanctuary across the border for themselves and their son. Prince Heinrich and his wife weren't cowards and didn't want to run, but they certainly would if they had to. Better that than stay in Kiel and be massacred by a Bolshevist mob.

While Heinrich sat tight in Kiel, his brother the Kaiser was in Belgium, inspecting military units behind the lines. He was travelling on his personal train, distributing medals and making speeches at every stop, handing out cigarettes to the men lined up for his inspection. They seemed in good spirits to him, although the officers travelling with the Kaiser had noticed a marked lack of respect for him behind his back. Some of the men were even unfriendly to his face, although the Kaiser appeared not to notice.

It was a difficult time for the Kaiser. He had only been in Belgium a few days, having fled from Berlin to avoid the ever-increasing clamour for his abdication. The threat of Spanish flu had only been an excuse for leaving, as had his claim that he ought to be with his troops in the field as the war approached its climax. In reality, the Kaiser just didn't feel safe in Berlin, with revolution in the air and the newspapers calling daily for him to stand down. He much preferred to be with the army in Belgium.

The Kaiser was closely identified with everything that had gone wrong in the war, but he was determined not to abdicate if he could avoid it. He was a descendant of Frederick the Great, and Frederick the Great would never have abdicated. 'I wouldn't dream of abandoning the throne because of a few hundred Jews and a thousand workers,' he had insisted on 1 November, when the idea had been put to him by an emissary of the German government. 'Tell that to your masters in Berlin.'

The Kaiser was going to stick with it instead and see the crisis through. If all else failed and revolution did break out in Berlin, he was quite prepared to return at the head of his soldiers and hang the ringleaders out of hand, if that was what he had to do to retain his throne.

Right now, though, the Kaiser was with his men in the field. 'In Flanders, I saw delegations from the different divisions, spoke with the soldiers, distributed decorations, and was everywhere joyfully received by officers and men,' he later recalled, although his commanders had told him privately that morale was poor among the troops, especially the ones in the rear. Worst of all were the troops returning from leave at home. They often came back full of Bolshevism, only to be accused by their comrades of being blacklegs for unnecessarily prolonging the war. The discontent was spreading rapidly as morale continued to plummet.

By some accounts, the Kaiser was with some troops near his train that Monday when he heard a sudden burst of fire from not far away. Glancing up, he was just in time to see a squadron of enemy bombers swooping overhead, aiming for his train. He kept his composure, as did his soldiers, but some nearby civilians scattered, among them a panic-stricken chef in hat and apron who ran for cover as the bombers attacked.

16

Three bombs whistled through the air and exploded harmlessly nearby. They were followed by a shower of propaganda leaflets which fluttered to earth as the aircraft disappeared. The soldiers laughed as the cook sheepishly picked himself up. The Kaiser laughed too. 'Idiots!' he said, looking at the civilians. A bombing raid was no reason to panic.

Nevertheless, it might be a good idea to arm the train with machine guns, if it was going to be a target for enemy aircraft from now on. The Kaiser made a note to have it done as soon as he got back to Spa.

In Paris, the leaders of the Allied nations were meeting to discuss an end to the war. In a house on the rue de l'Université, British prime minister David Lloyd George and his counterparts from France and Italy were debating the terms for an Armistice with Marshal Ferdinand Foch and General Sir Henry Wilson. The subject had occupied them for weeks, but it had taken on a new urgency that morning with the news of the British breakthrough around Valenciennes. The politicians were meeting to finalise the precise wording of the terms that would be offered to the Germans if they decided to seek an Armistice in the next few days.

The house on the rue de l'Université was the Paris residence of Colonel Edward House, President Woodrow Wilson's personal representative at the talks. The United States considered itself an associate of Britain, France and Italy, rather than a formal ally, but with a large army in the field it nevertheless had a big say in the talks. Indeed, the peace proposals to be put to Germany were based on a fourteen-point plan outlined to Congress by President Wilson the previous January.

The mood was ebullient as the leaders talked. Turkey had stopped fighting since Lloyd George had been in Paris. So had Austria-Hungary, Germany's last remaining ally in the field. The Germans were on their own now, with no one to help them. They still had an army in France and Belgium, but they would surely accept an Armistice within a few days if one was offered to them.

The Allied ministers had been working for a long time to get the terms of an Armistice exactly right. Too lenient, and the Germans would resume the war at a later date. Too harsh, and they might refuse to sign at all. The terms the Allies had eventually decided on were harsh in the extreme, stripping the Germans of arms and territory and leaving them unable to defend themselves against any future aggression.

The terms were so stringent that Lloyd George feared the Germans might well refuse to sign. He had said as much to Marshal Foch, who had agreed with him that the Germans probably wouldn't sign. But Foch wasn't worried, because the German army was beaten in the field, so whether they signed or not made little difference in the long run. The fighting would be over by Christmas, whether the Germans liked it or not.

The meeting began at 11 o'clock and was over by lunchtime. It was agreed that President Wilson would make the approach to the Germans, telling them to contact Marshal Foch if they wanted to learn the Allies' terms for an Armistice. Lloyd George took his leave of Georges Clemenceau and the Italian premier Vittorio Orlando as soon as the discussion was over and set off back to England after a highly satisfactory few days in France.

His party travelled by train to Boulogne, where a British destroyer was waiting to take them to Dover. There was no longer much danger from U-boats, but the crossing was rough, even by Channel standards. Sir Maurice Hankey, secretary to the War Cabinet, was seasick during the voyage, as were most of the others. The sea was so bad that they had to be taken off by boat when they reached Dover.

Nevertheless, Lloyd George was in a splendid mood as they travelled through the night to London. The collapse of Austria and Turkey meant that he was bringing wonderful news home with him. He was going to see the king the next day to brief him on the Paris talks. In the afternoon, he would announce the terms of the Austrian Armistice in the House of Commons. Another few days and he would surely announce the Armistice with Germany as well. After that, he could call a general election and go to the country on his war record.

*

The Allied politicians were all agreed on an Armistice, but for General John Pershing, commanding the United States troops on the Western Front, the issue was far from clear-cut. Why, he wondered, did they want an Armistice with the Germans when the British, French and Americans were within a few days of defeating them once and for all? Why not just keep going until the German army had collapsed altogether and they had no choice but to surrender? It made little sense to stop now, just when they had the Germans on the run.

Years ago, as a cadet at West Point, Pershing had witnessed the funeral train of Ulysses S. Grant, the Civil War general who had later become US president. The general had been nicknamed 'Unconditional Surrender' Grant for his refusal to accept anything less from the defeated South. He had known what he was doing, in Pershing's opinion. The Confederates had understood that they were beaten after Grant had finished with them. The Germans needed to understand, too, if the Allies wanted to avoid having to fight the whole war again some day.

'There can be no conclusion to this war until Germany is brought to her knees,' Pershing had recently told his army. He believed it passionately. If there was an Armistice, both sides would simply stop fighting and go home. The Germans would hold their heads high, declaring that they had never been defeated in the field. But if they were forced to surrender, they would have to lay down their arms in front of their conquerors. The Allies would proceed to Berlin and march down Unter den Linden with their bands playing and their flags flying. A victory parade in Berlin was the only way to show the Germans that they had been vanquished. Anything less was folly.

Pershing had made his views known in a paper to the Supreme War Council, only to have them rejected out of hand. 'Political, not military', had been Lloyd George's judgement. 'A clear announcement of his intention to become a candidate for the presidency', had been Colonel House's. The politicians took it for granted that Pershing had ulterior motives in advocating unconditional surrender rather than an Armistice. They presumed that he wanted to ride down Unter den

Linden at the head of his men so as to become an American hero, ideally placed to seek the presidency in 1920. They didn't believe him when he insisted that his motives were purely military.

Marshal Foch understood what Pershing was saying, but did not share his concern. 'Tell General Pershing not to worry,' he had announced reassuringly. 'I'm going to get exactly what he wants from the Germans.' In Foch's view, the Armistice terms were so stiff that they amounted to a surrender in all but name and couldn't be interpreted by the Germans as anything else.

But Pershing was not so sure. Defeat in the field was the only language the Germans understood. The Allies were making a big mistake in seeking an Armistice instead of carrying on the war to the bitter end. As he travelled to the Second Army's headquarters in the Argonne for a flying visit to discuss the continuing advance, Pershing couldn't help wondering if they wouldn't all come to regret the decision one day.

At Escarmain, four miles across the fields from Le Quesnoy, the French had put a stuffed fighting cock on a pole at the crossroads. The cock was France's national emblem, a symbol of their resurgence over the retreating Germans. It had amused Private Stephen Graham of the 2nd battalion, Scots Guards as he marched past it at dawn, on his way up to the line. He thought it a bizarre sight in the middle of a war, with bagpipes playing and gunfire booming in the distance as the New Zealanders began their assault on Le Quesnoy.

The Scots Guards were part of that morning's advance, but they were not due to go into action until the next day. While the New Zealanders were busy at Le Quesnoy, the Scots were bypassing the citadel on their way to Villers-Pol, their starting point for the attack next morning.

It had been misty when they set out, but the weather soon cleared as the sun rose. Before long, they made their first halt, falling out for a cigarette beside the Sepmeries road while batteries of sixty-pounders and eight-inch howitzers bombarded the Germans from a position just behind them.

The gunners obligingly warned the troops to 'hold tight' when they were about to fire. Most of the men kept their fingers in their ears as the bombardment continued. They weren't sorry when the halt was over and they resumed their march towards the front. They soon had their first glimpse of the enemy, as Graham later remembered:

'We passed a dead German lying with his head in a pool of blood, and then batches of German prisoners carrying stretchers. The wounded of our own comrades began to come down, and told of an easy progress, stopped now and then by isolated machine-gun posts of the enemy.'

The Germans were an ill-looking lot, much the same as the ones Graham had seen the previous week in the prison cage at St Hilaire:

'Strange, unwashed, ill-shaven, dirty men in shoddy uniforms, with broken boots and weather-beaten old hats – all sorts and sizes of men, Prussians, Westphalians, Bavarians, Alsatians, different types of faces, all relieved, all "out of the war", and yet all depressed. With the failure of Germany's fortunes in the field, the last vestige of dignity seemed to have departed from the faces of the prisoners; they were creatures that once were men; human beings who had suffered three successive kinds of degradation – they had been industrialised, then militarised, and finally captured by an enemy.'

An active Christian, Graham found it hard to hate the Germans, despite having it endlessly drummed into him by the Guards sergeants that the only good German was a dead one.

The battalion reached Villers-Pol that Monday afternoon and snatched a few hours' rest before evening. They were due to attack at dawn next morning, one of many battalions keeping up the pressure on the second day of the advance as part of a concerted effort by the Allies to knock the Germans out of the war once and for all. They were given a hot supper after midnight and a tot of rum. Then, at 2 a.m. on Tuesday, 5 November, the battalion moved out again, weighed down with bombs, shovels, sandbags and all the extra kit they needed for the attack.

Scouts led the way, checking for Germans before the rest followed. The night was dark and windy, but Graham could still make out some vague shapes in the gloom, which turned out to be the bodies of men killed in the previous day's fighting. His platoon reached their start line in good time and fanned out into battle formation for the attack. They had a Grenadier battalion to their right and the Welsh Guards in support behind them.

Checking their equipment one last time, the men synchronised watches and settled down to wait for dawn. All along the line, British, French and American soldiers were doing the same, ready to press forward again next morning for the second day of what they all hoped and prayed would prove to be the last big push of the war.

CHAPTER TWO

Tuesday, 5 November 1918

A t his headquarters behind the line, General Sir Henry Rawlinson could barely contain his glee as the troops moved forward again at first light. The British had taken more than ten thousand prisoners the previous day and would have taken more if the Germans hadn't been running so fast. The Americans were through the Argonne and rapidly approaching Sedan. The French were pushing forward too, and so were the Belgians. It was a disaster for the Germans on an unprecedented scale.

All the more sweet for Rawlinson, who had seen the men under his command suffer almost sixty thousand casualties on the first day of the Somme, a catastrophe that had haunted him ever since. Rawlinson bore much of the responsibility for that failure and hated to think about it. But the Somme was more than two years ago and he had learned from the mistakes made then. British casualties yesterday had been very light by comparison. Rawlinson was in no doubt that the Germans would be forced to raise the white flag in the next few days and seek terms for an Armistice:

'Prisoners captured yesterday say the Boche will accept any terms, and I think they are right; anyway, it would have been a great mistake to tone down the terms to encourage his acceptance. Several German officers captured today were quite drunk when they were brought in. All prisoners were exceedingly glad to be captured, and in the cage there were great rejoicings as each successive batch came in, and friends met with handshakes and cheers.'

Rawlinson's problem now was how to maintain the momentum of

the advance. His troops were moving so quickly that their supporting arms couldn't keep up. The Germans systematically blew up bridges and crossroads as they withdrew, causing widespread damage which took time to repair. The nearest working railhead was now thirty miles behind the front line and the broken roads were putting an intolerable strain on the army's lorries.

Rawlinson calculated, in fact, that his men would not be able to advance more than another ten miles without calling a halt for a week while the railways were repaired. He wasn't worried, though, because the Germans were bound to throw in their hand before then. There was nothing else they could do.

Among the British troops going forward that morning was Private Hulme of the Royal Army Medical Corps. A non-combatant, he was on his way to Roubaix, just north of Lille, to help set up a casualty clearing station at the town's civilian hospital. Roubaix had only recently been liberated and the townspeople were delighted to see the British arrive, smiling and waving as Hulme's unit drove through the streets. The people had suffered dreadfully during the German retreat. A convent with 120 children in it had been deliberately blown up after the nuns failed to produce a million francs to save it. There had been other atrocities as well. The citizens of Roubaix were immeasurably relieved to see the back of the Germans at last.

The hospital was still in good shape when Hulme reached it, perhaps because it had been used by the Germans before their retreat. The staff immediately invited him in for a cup of coffee. Despite the warmth of their welcome, however, there was something in their faces that he found deeply disturbing:

'The beseeching, scared, downtrodden look of the people made me feel miserable. I was walking along the corridor when Camille met me; at the same time Jeanne and one of the kitchen girls, who had had four years of the Boche, met us . . .

'The girl wished to pass me to return to the kitchen and I stood in her way. "Permettez-moi, monsieur!" I at once stepped back and murmured "Pardonnez-moi" as I turned to her. Her eyes were fixed on me; in them I read the most abject terror, then gradually she seemed to realise she had not a German near her but a Tommy and her eyes lit up with tears of joy as I smiled at her. In those two seconds one could see the "mark of the beast" and she, for one, realised the hideousness of war.'

Hulme's officers had similar experiences when they went looking for billets in the town. Their landladies automatically provided a second bed in every room for the officer's mistress. After four years of the Germans grabbing everything they wanted, the landladies took it for granted that the British would have mistresses too. 'Oui, but he will want one for the m'selle,' was their stock response when told that only one bed would be needed in every room.

Similar stories were being reported all along the line as the British took over towns and villages that had been years under German occupation. Girls looked at them with fear in their eyes, old men stepped off the pavement to get out of their way, young boys raised their caps to the officers because that was what the Germans had required them to do. The French were free again now, but the habits of the occupation died hard. 'Everyone had that indescribable, haunted, terror-stricken look which would suddenly come even when smiling.' Hulme and his comrades saw the dread in the civilians' faces and wondered what kind of army had been there before them, that girls and little children should be so frightened of men in uniform.

As the British were advancing, so were the Americans to the east. Captain Harry Truman of the 129th Field Artillery had recently made twenty-two night marches in a row, pushing forward every evening under cover of darkness. He had gone sixty hours without sleep at one point, losing twenty pounds from an already spare frame. He had lost his spectacles as well, after riding into an overhanging branch, only to have them recovered by a kindly soldier from the rump of his horse.

Truman was a happy man nevertheless, because the war was going well for his battery. They had been in France since April without losing a single man to enemy action. If their luck continued to hold, they stood every chance of coming through the war unscathed.

They had seen plenty of fighting since they arrived, once firing over open sights as the enemy came straight at them out of the woods. A number of Truman's men had run away the first time the Germans shot at them, but they had rallied since then and had learned to stand their ground under shellfire. Truman had been a steadying influence, always leading by example. He was greatly respected by the men, who had elected him an officer when the unit was formed, although he would happily have served as a sergeant.

The unit was at Verdun now, dug in north-east of the town. The whole area was still in ruins from the great battle of 1916, as Truman had reported to his fiancée on 1 November:

'The outlook I have now is a rather dreary one. There are Frenchmen buried in my front yard and Huns in the back yard and both litter up the landscape as far as you can see. Every time a Boche shell hits in a field over west of here it digs up a piece of someone. It is well I'm not troubled by spooks.

'I walked out to the observation post the other day (yesterday) to pick an adjusting point and I found two little flowers alongside the trench blooming right in the rock. I am enclosing them. The sob sisters would say that they came from the battle-scarred field of Verdun. They were in sight and short range of Heinie and were not far from the two most famous forts of his line of defence … One's a poppy, the other is a pink or something of the kind.'

The French landscape had been a revelation to Truman during the advance, its pretty villages and meandering farm boundaries so different from the endless straight lines of Missouri, his home state. Truman hated what the Germans had done to France and wanted to see them punished for it when the war was over. If it was left to him, he would cut off their hands and feet and scalp their old men, or so he liked to claim. At the very least, the Germans should work for France and Belgium for fifty years to atone for all the harm they had done.

But the war wasn't over yet. Truman's battery was still in action, 'sending over a few shells occasionally and receiving a few'. He was in his dugout that Tuesday morning, taking the chance to censor the men's letters home before they went forward again. Some of his men were winning the war single-handed, if their correspondence was anything to go by. They were a cheerful bunch of liars and Truman was very proud of them.

Against all the rules, he had even lent money to a few men, which he never expected to see again. But if they didn't repay what they owed, they might at least get the vote out for him after the war, if he decided to run for Congress on his military record.

Further along the line, the newly promoted Brigadier General Douglas MacArthur had no plans to run for Congress, but was certainly proud of his military record. First in his class at West Point, and now the youngest general in the US army, MacArthur was a flamboyant man of thirty-eight who liked to lead from the front, brandishing a riding whip as he went into action with his men. Most of them revered him – 'he's a hell-to-breakfast baby, long and lean, kind to us and tough on the enemy. He can spit nickel cigars and chase Germans as well as any doughboy in the division' – but MacArthur had enemies as well, usually rival officers who deplored his egotism and theatrical manner.

Some of them had complained to headquarters, insisting that his disregard for the rules set a dreadful example. MacArthur routinely led attacks in person, without weapon, gas mask or steel helmet. He waved his whip at the Germans instead, an affectation that did not impress his rivals. MacArthur argued in return that how he went into battle was his affair:

'I wore no iron helmet because it hurt my head. I carried no gas mask because it hampered my movements. I went unarmed because it was not my purpose to engage in personal combat, but to direct others. I used a riding crop out of long habit on the plains. I fought from the front as I could not effectively manipulate my troops from the rear.'

MacArthur's brigade was in reserve at the moment, waiting, like Truman, for the order to continue the advance. They were fifteen miles south of Sedan, expecting to go forward again that night. The ancient fortress town on the Meuse had been the scene of a humiliating surrender in 1870, when the French army had been crushed by the Prussians at the end of the Franco-Prussian war. The French were determined to recapture the town now, to restore their national pride, but the Americans were keen to get there as well. Unless the situation changed, it was going to be a race to see who arrived first.

MacArthur was in the thick of it as always, striding about in riding breeches with a civilian scarf around his neck to keep him warm. He was still refusing to wear a steel helmet or carry a gas mask, even though he had recently been gassed without one. Image was all important to him in a war. 'It's the orders you disobey that make you famous,' he had explained to another officer, who had queried his irregular dress. MacArthur badly wanted to be famous. What else were wars for?

As expected, his brigade was ordered forward again that night, moving up through the forest towards Sedan. It was difficult terrain in the dark, with the enemy still in possession. A sniper's bullet whizzed through the trees as MacArthur advanced, blowing a hole in the sleeve of his coat and narrowly missing his arm. He wasn't ruffled, though, because a miss was as good as a mile and a bullet hole in his coat could only add to the legend.

In Bavaria, near the little town of Ingolstadt, Captain Charles de Gaulle of the French army would have given a great deal to change places with MacArthur at that moment. Instead, he was enduring another frustrating day of captivity, almost his thousandth since being taken prisoner in March 1916.

After volunteering for the Verdun front, de Gaulle had undergone a six-day bombardment during the battle, before being reinforced by a band of men in blue French helmets. Closer inspection had revealed them to be German soldiers in disguise. De Gaulle had led his own men in a bayonet charge, only to be shot in the thigh almost at once. Fainting from loss of blood, he had been left for dead by his men, regaining consciousness later to find himself a prisoner, his wound being tended by the same German he had earlier been trying to kill.

It had been too much for de Gaulle. He had always sworn the

enemy would never take him alive. After recovering from his wound, he had made repeated attempts to escape, tunnelling out of prison camp and heading for neutral territory as fast as he could go. At six foot four, however, his height made him a conspicuous sight, particularly in a stolen German uniform that barely reached down to his elbows. After being recaptured three times, de Gaulle had been sent to Fort Nine at Ingolstadt, a punishment camp for incorrigible escapers on the banks of the Danube.

The camp was an old fortress, sixty feet high, surrounded by a double moat. The inner moat alone was fifty-feet wide, an insuperable barrier to all but the most determined. The prisoners, British as well as French, were kept behind thick stone walls, a precursor of Colditz castle. Most of them were weak from months of punishment and malnutrition, although still determined to make trouble for their captors.

De Gaulle had immediately set out to escape again, yet without success. It was impossible to tunnel under the moat, because the tunnels always filled with water. The moat iced over in winter, but the Germans rowed round it in a boat, breaking up the ice so that the prisoners couldn't walk across. The only other way out of Fort Nine was through the gate and that was closely guarded. After several abortive attempts, de Gaulle had been forced to abandon the idea of escape and seek alternative ways of passing the time instead.

The British threw fancy-dress parties attended by de Gaulle's brother officers dressed as French tarts, but that wasn't for him. Aloof and austere, de Gaulle wouldn't show his legs to anyone, let alone the British. He had made few friends at Fort Nine and had been nicknamed the 'High Constable of France' by his compatriots. He preferred to make better use of his time than spend it dressing up for parties.

In solitary confinement for trying to escape, he had kept sane by reciting thousands of lines of Greek poetry which he knew off by heart. Later, he had refreshed his German so as to read the German newspapers and follow the progress of the war. By carefully studying the German communiqués and reading between the lines, de Gaulle hoped to form an idea of how the war was really going for both sides.

'But you'll only find news of German victories in those papers,' another officer had pointed out.

'Of course,' de Gaulle had replied, 'but if I read the communiqués carefully enough, I'll be able to work out what tactical mistakes the Germans have made … In these so-called victories I can see the beginnings of German defeat.'

With only the German papers to go on, de Gaulle's analyses had been reasonably successful, predicting the outcome of various offensives with a fair degree of accuracy. He had used his time at Fort Nine to make a careful study of the war, learning lessons from the conflict that might be useful to him in the future. De Gaulle had been a career soldier before the war and intended to remain so after it was over.

But he knew that the front line was where he really ought to be, fighting at the head of his men. De Gaulle was frustrated beyond measure that he was playing no part in the war as it came to an end. His promotion prospects depended on his combat experience and he hadn't seen any fighting for nearly three years.

There was a flagpole at Fort Nine, standing on a mound at the highest point. The Germans flew a flag from it whenever they had a victory to celebrate. The flag hadn't flown at all in recent months, not since the German offensive of the spring. De Gaulle didn't need to read between the lines to realise that the Germans were close to the end now, almost at their last gasp. Their army was defeated, the French were about to win the war, and here was de Gaulle, stuck in prison camp, unable to fulfil his destiny. For a man who saw France every time he looked in the mirror, the situation was intolerable.

General Gröner's train from Spa arrived in Berlin early on Tuesday morning. The city appeared calm as he drove from the station, but Gröner knew that all was not well beneath the surface. There would be a revolution within days if the crisis facing the Germans was not resolved very soon.

Prince Max, Germany's chancellor of four weeks, was still

recovering from Spanish flu. Gröner was due to see him the next day to deliver his report on conditions at the front. Meantime, he had other people to see, ministers from the civilian government which had recently replaced the military administration as a necessary prelude to peace. Gröner shared the new government's desire for peace, but as he went to see the ministers he was very much afraid that there would be no meeting of minds as to how it might be achieved.

The stumbling block was the Kaiser. The new government wanted the Kaiser to abdicate, arguing that there could be no peace in Germany until he went. The Kaiser was loathed by too many people to stay on. But the government's view was not shared by the German army. To the officer corps, at least, a Germany without the Kaiser was unthinkable. The officers were adamant that he must stay.

Gröner said as much at the meeting. As the ministers listened in silence, he told them that the supreme command at Spa would not countenance the Kaiser's abdication under any circumstances. Every last soldier in the German army had sworn an oath of loyalty to the Kaiser as their sovereign warlord. It was out of the question for the army to desert him now.

To reinforce his words, Gröner had brought a message for the ministers from Field Marshal von Hindenburg, his chief at Spa. The message was uncompromising in tone:

'The field marshal has ordered me, on the question of the Kaiser's abdication, to tell you in his own words that in his opinion it would be the act of a scoundrel for him to desert the Kaiser; and that, gentlemen, is my opinion too, and the opinion of every soldier with a sense of honour … If the agitation against the Kaiser is not stopped, the army's fate is sealed. It will simply break up. Among the soldiers who will then stream back home all the bestiality of human nature will break out.'

That was the choice facing the German government. There could be no peace with the Kaiser and no army without him. It was a dilemma they would soon have to resolve.

In Kiel, Captain Karl Weniger had spent a very uneasy night aboard the *König*, wondering what the morning would bring. There was still chaos ashore, with sailors running amok and officers fleeing the city any way they could, even stealing bicycles in their haste to escape. Weniger wasn't sure how much longer his ship could hold out with a sea of Bolshevist flags all around.

He didn't have to wait long to find out. A mob stormed the *König* soon after first light, outraged that the imperial colours had been raised again at the break of day. They presented Weniger with a stark ultimatum: he could lower the colours by noon and replace them with a red flag, or he and his crew would suffer the consequences.

Weniger held a hurried conference with his officers and those of the men who were still loyal. The officers were game for a fight and so were the ship's after-guard. Weniger decided to stand his ground and defend the imperial flag.

Led by Lieutenant Wolfgang Zenker, the *König*'s after-guard took up their positions by the halyards. The stand-off continued for two hours until the mob lost patience. Taking matters into their own hands, they rushed the ship en masse, bullets ricocheting off the gun turrets as the two factions fought for control of the halyards.

Zenker was shot and killed, Captain Weniger crouching over him as he died on deck. Lieutenant Commander Bruno Heinemann was shot as well, taken below to die later. Weniger himself was hit several times but did not die. Severely wounded, he just had time to shoot one of his attackers before collapsing. The mutinous sailors stepped over his body and began to pull the imperial flag down. It had flown proudly aloft at the battle of Jutland. Now it came fluttering to the deck and was replaced with a home-made banner of blood-red, symbol of the Bolshevist revolution.

The shootings were the last straw for Prince Heinrich at the palace. He had been assured by Kiel's naval governor that the situation was under control, but it didn't look like that from the windows of the palace. Heinrich knew that he and his family would be next, if the mob was on the rampage. It was time for them to escape.

Heinrich waited until dark before making his move. As soon as it was safe, he and his family slipped out of the palace in a chauffeur-driven car and fled the city. Heinrich and his son wore hats pulled down over their faces to conceal their identity. The car itself sported a red banner in support of the revolution. Avoiding the main roads, they put Kiel behind them and disappeared into the darkness, heading for Denmark in the north.

The car was halfway to Eckernförde when it was flagged down by some sailors clustered around a broken-down truck. Without recognising Heinrich, the men asked where the car was going. Two of them decided to hitch a lift to Eckernförde. Before Heinrich could stop them, they had jumped onto the running board and were standing over him as the car moved off again.

Were they Bolshevists who would kill Heinrich as soon as they realised who he was? Or loyalists who hadn't yet spotted the car's red banner in the darkness? Heinrich didn't wait to find out. It was impossible to see exactly what happened in the dark, but according to some accounts he produced a gun, shot one of the sailors and was about to shoot the other when the man hastily jumped off.

Behind them, the sailors at the truck ran for their rifles. They loosed off a few rounds as the car disappeared. Ducking down, Heinrich yelled at his chauffeur to step on the accelerator. The car zigzagged away, speeding into the night. It vanished as quickly as it had come and did not stop again until it reached the borders of neutral Denmark, far away to the north.

While Prince Heinrich fled for his life, staff officers at the Grand Hôtel Britannique, the German army's supreme headquarters at Spa, were planning a glorious death for his older brother. They were studying a map of the front line, looking for a good place for the Kaiser to die at the head of his troops. The idea was for him to go into battle and fall for the Fatherland, thus avoiding the embarrassment of being forced to abdicate against his will. It was a suitably German solution to a very German problem.

The idea had been General Gröner's originally. Just before leaving for Berlin, he had taken Field Marshal von Hindenburg aside and put it to him that if the worst came to the worst the Kaiser could always go to the front and seek a hero's death at the head of his soldiers. It would solve all sorts of problems if he fell bravely in battle instead of abdicating in disgrace and being forced ignominiously into exile. Gröner had been quite blunt about it:

'He should go to the front, not to review troops or to hand out decorations, but to look for death. He should go to some trench which is right in the middle of the action. If he were killed, it would be the finest death possible. If he were wounded, the feelings of the German people would completely change towards him.'

Hindenburg had been horrified at the idea, appalled by the very suggestion. But he hadn't absolutely vetoed it. Instead, he had allowed a few trusted officers to begin the staff work for the Kaiser's death in the field. They had the map out now and were choosing a place for their supreme warlord to die. It wasn't as easy as it sounded, with the front line shifting by the hour and the roads so choked with debris that the Kaiser might not be able to get there anyway.

The officers were also looking for volunteers to accompany the Kaiser on his last great adventure. Younger officers felt that older officers should volunteer. Older ones felt that the whole idea needed further thought. The only point they could all agree on was that if the Kaiser did decide to seek a soldier's death, it would have to be by Thursday at the latest, because there was bound to be an Armistice after that.

In France, the Armistice could not come too soon for Lieutenant Herbert Sulzbach and his gun batteries. They were continuing their long withdrawal, working their way back under cover of darkness while the French continued to pound them with heavy artillery. It was not a pleasant experience in the cold and wet:

'We ride through the pitch-dark night, you can't see your hand in front of your eyes! The roads are soft from twenty-four hours of rain. The French are shelling us with the nastiest conceivable low-trajectory guns and bombarding all the roads to the rear with heavy-calibre artillery at irregular intervals. We can't avoid the roads with our columns and guns, so we just have to endure the barrage; it was truly awful, because we were already at the end of our tether with our nerves from yesterday, worse than ever before. We also have to lay obstacles for the enemy, and yet again all the crossroads behind us have to be blown up, heavy trees felled and all the bridges blown into the air. The delays on the tightly packed roads are a real nusiance, because we're all very anxious to get to our new position.'

To add to their troubles, the Germans were also being attacked by French civilians, francs-tireurs who sniped at them as they withdrew, picking off stragglers with their rifles. Sulzbach had been outraged to learn that two soldiers from the 154th Regiment had been shot in the back as they passed through a village. He decided on reprisals to discourage further attacks. Forming up his guns in the dark, he waited until 4 a.m., then shelled the village with sixty rounds from each of his batteries while the French were still asleep.

For Private Graham of the Scots Guards, the day had begun with a barrage just before dawn, a softening up of the enemy positions beyond Preux au Sart. It had been followed by a rapid advance as the Guards went forward, taking their first objective at twenty to seven and their second at ten past eight. They were delayed for a while by a machine gun in a cemetery, but were approaching Bermeries by 9 a.m., probing the outskirts as their tanks went ahead to roust out the enemy:

'At 12.30 the village was still held by Germans. Tanks were, however, exploring the position, followed by our advance companies. A further German retirement occurred, and Bermeries proved empty of the enemy. An enemy line was located four hundred yards beyond it, in the low scrub alongside an orchard. At 1.30 a sharp encounter took place between one of our companies and a number of German machine-gunners. The enemy was in deep slits, and his positions cleverly hidden. It took about an hour altogether to locate him certainly and dispose of him. Our men made a bayonet charge, and all the Germans were either killed, wounded, or taken prisoner.'

That was the end of the day's fighting for the Scots Guards, although the German artillery kept up an indiscriminate bombardment for the

35

rest of the afternoon. With the roads so badly damaged, it was much easier to fire off their ammunition than carry it away. They weren't aiming at anything in particular, just shooting in the general direction of the British. The weather deteriorated too, making life miserable for Graham and his comrades as the daylight began to fade.

'The men wallowed in mud all night, and it rained and rained, never ceased raining. The German artillery was very active, though firing largely at random. There were a number of casualties from stray shells. The last men to fall in the war fell, as it were, by accident; strolling back from the line towards headquarters; they were being brought back to Bermeries for a few hours' rest, and were lighting cigarettes and chatting in little knots when two heavy shells came in their midst, tore one man's face off, ripped up another's stomach, and the like.'

The Welsh Guards suffered too, following immediately behind the Scots. The Welsh were due to take over the lead the next morning and were moving up accordingly. A company was sheltering in a barn when it received a direct hit about midnight. Thirty men were killed or wounded, the rest badly shaken. The Germans might be in retreat, but the war wasn't over yet.

For Captain John Glubb of the Royal Engineers, the day had seen no fighting, although plenty of clearing up. The engineers' job was to follow the infantry and mend the roads quickly so as to keep the advance flowing freely. Glubb was at Fontaine-au-Bois, leading his men through the same driving rain that was soaking the Guards to the north. They weren't enjoying the weather but were happy enough otherwise, singing cheerfully as they marched up the road towards the Forêt de Mormal:

> Oh it's a lovely war.
> Form fours! Right turn!
> How shall we spend all the money we earn?
> Oh, oh, oh it's a lovely war!

Glubb had ridden into the forest the previous day on a long reconnaissance to see what work needed to be done. The enemy appeared to have melted away like snow, but they had left a few bodies behind, as Glubb had been quick to notice:

'At a crossroads, there was a shell hole in the middle of the road and a young German soldier lying on the edge of it. His helmet had rolled off, his face was snow-white and a stream of blood flowed from the top of his head. He looked so young and innocent, scarcely over sixteen I should think. I am afraid the Boche army is in much the same state as ours, all children or old men.'

Advancing the next day, Glubb's sappers had made swift progress through the forest, overtaking their own infantry by the time they reached Noyelles. There was still no sign of the Germans, although they had destroyed the bridge over the stream before retreating. Glubb watched as the British infantry arrived and began to climb across the debris in single file:

'They were, of course, all like drowned rats, with their waterproof sheets hanging shining over their shoulders. Two Frenchmen were standing on the far side of the stream, helping our fellows to scramble up. Our boys were laughing, and all of them thanked the Frenchmen for giving them a hand. I heard one of the Frenchmen say to the other, "Mon Dieu, mon ami, quelle différence après les Boches!"'

It was too late to mend the bridge that night. Glubb decided to go back before dark and return with the pontoon wagons next morning. All being well, they would have a temporary bridge in position by the end of the day, strong enough to keep the traffic moving in pursuit of an increasingly elusive enemy.

In the United States it was election day. The people had gone to the polls for the first time since President Woodrow Wilson had taken them into the war. The president himself was not up for re-election, but his fellow Democrats were contesting seats in both houses of Congress. They were waiting nervously for the nation's verdict on the president's handling of the war.

Wilson had been careful never to make any promises about

keeping America out of the war when he ran for re-election in 1916. Unfortunately, others had made the promise on his behalf. He was worried that the Democrats were about to pay a price for it at the polls. German-Americans certainly weren't going to vote Democrat after what had happened. Nor were the Irish, if it meant supporting an English war. Wilson feared that he might lose control of Congress just when he needed all the help he could get in the difficult days that lay ahead as he attempted to create a new political order in Europe.

It would have been very different if the war had been over by now. If the Germans had given up last week, or even yesterday, Wilson would have been on top of the world, his party assured of a landslide victory at the polls. But the Germans hadn't given up. They were still in there, still fighting, not in the least sensitive to the needs of the Democratic Party. It was enough to make a politician despair.

Wilson was quietly confident that the Democrats would win, nevertheless. And even if they didn't, he had just had splendid news from Europe to compensate. A telegram had come from Paris confirming that the Allies had finally agreed the Armistice terms and wanted him to invite the Germans to the negotiating table. Wilson had promptly done so, sending a message to Berlin via the Swiss embassy instructing the German government to approach Marshal Foch if they wished to hear the terms. He was on his way to a Cabinet meeting now to tell them what he had done.

The Cabinet all stood up as Wilson entered the room. It was obvious to everyone that a load had been taken off his mind with the news from Europe. David Houstoun, his agriculture secretary, thought Wilson was looking 'well and happy' as he came in, less strained than he had been for a long time. Franklin Lane, his secretary of the interior, thought so too. 'He is certainly in splendid humour and in good trim – not worried a bit. And why should he be, for the world is at his feet, eating out of his hand! No Caesar ever had such a triumph!'

Yet there were still plenty of problems facing the president. His most immediate concern was the Bolshevist revolution that was threatening to engulf Germany. According to a recent dispatch, it was being funded by Jewish conspirators in Russia, who had deposited ten million dollars for the purpose in Swiss banks. The Bolshevists' aim was the overthrow of the German government. They might well succeed if they weren't stopped soon. If they succeeded, months of chaos would follow and there would be no legitimate government for the Allies to negotiate with to end the war.

But they hadn't succeeded yet. Wilson's note must have reached Berlin by now. If the German government acted at once to make peace, they might still be able to retrieve the situation before it was too late.

CHAPTER THREE

Wednesday, 6 November 1918

In Berlin, as Wednesday dawned, Prince Max von Baden was acutely aware of the need to make peace in the next few days. As Germany's chancellor for the past four weeks, nobody understood better than he did that the country was on the brink of collapse, incapable of continuing the fight much longer. There would be revolution soon if there wasn't peace first. Max didn't want revolution any more than President Wilson did.

Still groggy from Spanish flu, the German chancellor was a sensible man, a cousin by marriage of the Kaiser yet very different in character and temperament. He was a Prussian general of liberal convictions, who favoured a British-style constitutional monarchy rather than the unyielding autocracy of the Kaiser. He had been advocating a compromise peace for years, in the belief that half a loaf was better than wholesale slaughter. He had bitterly opposed the policy of unrestricted submarine warfare that had made Germany so many enemies and brought America into the war. Max was a man the Allies could do business with, which was why he had been appointed Germany's first parliamentary chancellor on 3 October. The Germans needed a leader without blood on his hands to represent them in the hard talking that lay ahead.

President Wilson's telegram had not yet officially reached Berlin, but the details had been leaked and Max had them in front of him as he sat waiting for General Gröner to arrive for their morning meeting. The details did not make for happy reading. True, the Allies were offering the Armistice that the Germans so badly needed, but it was clear that the terms would be dreadful, far worse than the Germans had been hoping for. 'Compensation by Germany for all damage done to the civilian population of the Allies and their property' would be enough to bankrupt the economy on its own, let alone any other conditions as well.

General Gröner brought little comfort when he arrived. The two men went into the chancellery garden to talk in private. They rapidly agreed that the situation at home was as dire as it was in the field. The Germans couldn't go on as they were. They would have to cross the lines with a white flag and seek an Armistice. They had no other option.

'But not for a week at least?' Max suggested. The German army needed time to regroup before they started to negotiate.

Gröner shook his head. 'A week is too long.' He was worried that the home front might collapse if they delayed any further. Kiel had already gone and the mutiny was spreading to other ports. Bavaria was in a state of anarchy, on the brink of declaring itself a republic. The rest of Germany would follow if the Bavarians repudiated their monarchy. The quickest way to defuse the tension was to seek an Armistice. They could always reject it later, if the terms proved unacceptable.

'Not before Monday, anyway?' Max ventured.

Gröner shook his head again. 'Even that is too long to wait. It has to be Saturday at the latest.'

He sat in on the Cabinet meeting that morning and told the ministers what he had just told Max, that an Armistice was an immediate necessity. He had the same message for the trade union and Social Democratic Party leaders who arrived to see him at midday.

Friedrich Ebert, the SDP's working-class leader, would have been the people's choice for chancellor if it had been put to a popular vote. He agreed that the Armistice commission must set out at once and repeated his insistence that the Kaiser must abdicate as well to forestall a revolution. Gröner demurred, reminding him that there could be no army in the field without the Kaiser, because the men would refuse to go on fighting without their supreme warlord at their head. He reminded Ebert, too, that the Kaiser's sons had all pledged themselves to refuse the regency if their father was removed against his will.

Ebert remained unmoved. The Kaiser had to go at once, in his opinion. He and Gröner were still arguing about it when Philipp Scheidemann, Ebert's SDP colleague, was called away to the telephone. It was some time before he returned. When he did, his face was white with fear:

'Gentlemen, further discussion of the abdication is pointless. The revolution is in full swing! Sailors from Kiel have seized control in Hamburg and Hanover. This is no time to sit around talking. This is the time for action. Otherwise, we might not still be in these same chairs by this time tomorrow!'

It wasn't just Hamburg and Hanover. It was Lübeck, Rendsburg, Ratzeburg, Flensburg, Cuxhaven, Brunsbüttel and a host of similar places as well. The sailors from Kiel were heading in all directions, rallying the workers, joining forces with local garrisons across the country, seizing control in the name of the people. They intended to do for Germany what their Soviet counterparts had already done for Russia.

At Wilhelmshaven, hundreds of sailors from the naval base had gathered for a protest march through the town. Among them was Richard Stumpf, an ordinary seaman from the *Wittelsbach*. Like most of his comrades, Stumpf wasn't really a Bolshevist, but he had been caught up in the general excitement as the men hurried ashore for the demonstration. He wanted to be part of it, if only to register a protest after so many months of starvation rations and indifferent treatment from their officers.

Almost all the other men from the *Wittelsbach* were there too. Their officers made no attempt to stop them as they went ashore. Nor did the armed marines at the Old Port barracks. Instead, the marines gave three cheers as the sailors swept past them, rallying men from other ships to their cause. Stumpf was with them as the procession wound its way through the docks, accompanied by a band:

'At the Peterstrasse we were met by a forty-man patrol led by an officer. The men joined us with their weapons. It was very amusing to watch the lieutenant when he suddenly realised that he was all alone. Because of the music we received large reinforcements from all directions. I thought at first that we would release the sailors imprisoned in the gaol. But I soon realised that we didn't have any leadership. The crowd was just being driven along by sheer mob instinct.'

At the marine barracks, an elderly major tried to hold the mob back with a pistol as they broke down the gates. Stumpf watched uncomfortably while the sailors overpowered him:

'He was immediately disarmed, hands reaching for his sword while others tried to tear off his epaulettes. My sympathy went out to this man who was bravely trying to do his duty. Disgust at the brutality rose in my throat. I felt like shaking the man's hand.'

The crowd was several thousand strong by the time it moved towards the Torpedo Division, but Stumpf wasn't sure if he still wanted to be part of it:

'I observed a gradual increase in bestiality. Every woman was greeted with whistles and coarse remarks. Red cloths waved aloft. Instead of a banner, someone was carrying a red bed-sheet on a pole. It was hardly a great honour to march behind this dirty rag. Since it was the first day of our new-found freedom, however, we were prepared to ignore these minor objections.'

From the Torpedo Division, the crowd moved on to the navy's headquarters building, where a deputation presented Admiral Günther von Krosigk with a list of grievances. Krosigk had earlier planned to disperse the crowd with cold steel, but the size of the demonstration persuaded him otherwise. He decided to concede their demands instead.

Within half an hour, a preliminary agreement had been hammered out. Krosigk offered the same concessions already made to the sailors at Kiel: food committees, equal rations for officers and men, less rigid discipline, a more streamlined procedure for the hearing of complaints. He retained control of naval matters, but conceded almost everything else the mob had been asking for.

There was a roar of approval when the concessions were announced. The mob dispersed soon afterwards, their leaders hurrying off to form a Council of Twenty-One to take over the running of Wilhelmshaven. The council was led by Bernhard Kuhnt, a rabble-rousing stoker who had been a local secretary of the Social Democratic Party in civilian life. On behalf of the people, Kuhnt immediately claimed command not only of the city, but also of the naval docks, Helgoland and the High Seas Fleet as well.

That wasn't all. The mob didn't know it, but once Kuhnt had control of Wilhelmshaven he intended to move into the surrounding countryside, taking over the whole province of Oldenburg and forcing the Duke of Oldenburg to abdicate. After that, Oldenburg would be declared an independent republic within the new Germany. And then, if all went according to plan, Stoker First Class Kuhnt would become Oldenburg's first president.

In France, the unrest had reached the German front line, although few soldiers took much notice of it. Red flags and political speeches were the province of barrack-room lawyers rather than the men in the trenches. But the unrest had certainly affected troops in the reserve areas behind the lines. There was plenty of Bolshevism among them, as surgeon Stefan Westmann had noticed:

'On every street corner one could find the prophets of this faith with red cockades on their caps and red flags in their hands. Many of them were former ammunition workers who had gone on strike and been put into uniform and drafted into the army. The front-line fighters were not very enthusiastic about this kind of talk, and they beat up the agitators. But more and more red-guardists arrived and tried to set up "soviets" of soldiers. A supply column passed through our little township with red flags on their carts. A few seconds later a platoon of infantry seized the drivers, gave them a thorough hiding, and tore down the flags.'

Westmann himself had little time for politics. A part-qualified medical student, he had been commissioned into the medical corps and was serving as a probationary surgeon in a field hospital near the

Belgian border. Others might riot in the streets, but Westmann was too busy with his patients to bother about anything else.

Until recently, some of his patients had been French civilians without a doctor of their own. Westmann hadn't charged the French for his services but had accepted gifts of rice instead, which the French got from the Red Cross. He sent the rice back to his family in Berlin, who were desperately short of food. The Royal Navy's blockade was so tight now that babies all over Germany were dying of malnutrition.

But this cosy arrangement with the French had come to an end and Westmann's unit had orders to move out that morning. They were to pull back across the border into Belgium. The whole hospital was to be packed up and the patients transported to the rear by ambulance.

The ambulances failed to arrive, so the patients were loaded into carts instead and taken by horse to the nearest railhead. Luckily for them, a hospital train had steam up and was about to leave for Germany. The patients were quickly put aboard, but there was no room for Westmann and the hospital staff to go with them. They had no choice but to continue the retreat on foot.

Westmann's riding boots were worn out and impossible to re-place, but he had managed to scrounge a pair of French army boots from his orderly, who had got them from God knows where. He was glad the new boots fitted well, because it looked as if he was going to spend the rest of the war on the march.

Still with their carts, the hospital staff took the road to Belgium. Thousands of other Germans were doing the same, retreating in good order with their units towards the frontier. Quite a few Frenchwomen were going too, girls who had slept with the enemy and knew that they would be beaten up by their own people and have their heads shaved if they stayed.

Some had children with them, little blond bastards who would be stigmatised for life because of who their fathers were. Westmann knew of one German soldier who had managed to get a Frenchwoman pregnant and her daughter as well. Others had doubtless done the same. It was all part of the price that had to be paid when hitherto sensible nations went to war.

*

While Westmann retreated into Belgium, Lieutenant Herbert Sulzbach and his gun batteries were continuing their withdrawal towards the river Meuse. They had spent the night at Etroeungt, just south of Avesnes, chatting with French civilians who could scarcely contain their excitement at the knowledge that the Germans would be gone for good the next day. The French were delighted to see the back of them after four years of occupation. Sulzbach had every sympathy for them:

'What a heavenly feeling it must be for the patriotic French. Tomorrow at this time they'll be free, free after four and a quarter years! We can understand how they feel.

'High on the church tower the white flag is fluttering! I am deeply moved at this sign of our traditional decency. We're showing the enemy that there are French civilians here from several villages, so that they don't endanger their own people with artillery fire. We push on in the afternoon. I say goodbye to the civilians with the words *"Gardez un bon souvenir des Allemands!"*.'

Sulzbach's men joined the retreat towards the east, an endless column of troops and guns slogging through the mud towards the river. It rained again that night, another long downpour in the murk. Sulzbach was glad of it, because the French air force couldn't fly in bad weather. It was unpleasant enough having to retreat in the mud without being bombed from the air as well.

At Semeries, he called a halt for the night. The village was tiny, its population more than doubled in the past few days with a sudden influx of German soldiers and French evacuees. Sulzbach had to search some time before finding any shelter for his men. Eventually he discovered one last floor that hadn't been claimed by anyone else. A hundred of his men promptly flopped down side by side, glad to be out of the rain at last. Beside them slept ten elderly French civilians who hadn't been able to find anywhere else either.

In Flanders, the rain had begun as drizzle at dawn and grew steadily worse as the day wore on. Captain Frank Hitchcock of the 2nd battalion, the Leinster Regiment was thoroughly miserable as he marched his company of Catholic Irishmen up the road towards the river Scheldt. They hadn't seen any Germans for days, although the Germans had certainly been there recently. With their usual efficiency they had blown up all the bridges, forcing the Leinsters to make lengthy detours through the mud and wet,

The landscape was depressing as the Leinsters advanced, a mix of bleak mining towns, desolate fields and neglected, broken-down farms. The people seemed glad to see them, despite the weather. They turned out to watch as the Leinsters came past, the women in shawls with ragged children, the men in workmen's blue blouses and peaked caps. Hitchcock's troops had fallen out for a ten-minute rest in a wet ditch when a woman emerged from the cottage opposite and put a chair out for them in the rain. For Hitchcock, her kindness was the only bright spot on a march that didn't get any better as the day progressed:

'The further we advanced, the more desolate the landscape seemed. At one point we came on a particularly revolting sight – half a dozen barefooted women tearing off flesh from a mule, which had been killed some days previously in the advance. They had pulled the skin off the quarters, and with knives and forks were cutting off chunks, and putting them into handkerchiefs. They were ravenous with hunger.

'We billeted in a meagre little farm, the men being accommodated in damp and smelly barns in an adjacent farm. The peasants were poor, scantily clad, and hungry-looking, and the children were delighted with the pieces of biscuit given them by the men.'

While his soldiers settled down, Hitchcock learned that he had been detailed to lead one of the platoons across the river Scheldt when they attacked in a day or two. The procedure was routine for Hitchcock, something he had done many times before, except for one intriguing detail. His orders contained an extra set of instructions headed 'Prisoners under White Flag' and referring him to the appropriate section in Field Service Regulations. It must mean that the war would be over soon if the high command was expecting the Leinsters to deal with prisoners under white flags.

*

In the newly liberated Serbian town of Cuprija, Sergeant Major Flora Sandes of the Serbian army was in no doubt that the war was already over in all but name. An Irish clergyman's daughter, she had been with her regiment when it liberated Cuprija a few days earlier and had seen the Austrian army fleeing from one end of the town while the Serbs entered it from the other. The Austrians had ceased hostilities soon afterwards and requested an Armistice. The Bulgarians were beaten as well, which left just a sprinkling of Germans in the field, military units more interested in getting home in one piece than in prolonging the war.

Flora's regiment had continued the advance and was probably in Belgrade by now. She would have been with them if it hadn't been for an attack of Spanish flu. Instead, she was still in Cuprija, convalescing well but unable to rejoin her regiment for a while. The local hospital was in chaos, overwhelmed with soldiers dying of flu. No one else was doing anything about it, so Flora had taken command and was dosing the men with medicine originally prescribed by a French vet for the horses.

Hers had been an unconventional war. She had gone out to Serbia in 1914 as a volunteer nurse, although she knew little of nursing. But the Serbs had retreated so rapidly at first that the wounded had had to be left behind and Flora had had very little to do. She had drifted into the Serbian army instead, picking up a rifle at a moment of crisis and keeping hold of it after the crisis had passed. She had known how to ride and shoot since she was a child and was happy to dress as a man in the army. She had once fooled a girl in a brothel who had sat on her knee for quite some time before realising that Flora was a woman.

But the men in her regiment all knew she was a woman, if only because she didn't strip to the waist when the order came for shirts off in pursuit of body lice. Flora bathed by herself in the river instead, and had once been surprised by a German battery which dropped shells all around her as she hurriedly ducked behind the riverbank. It was her habit to recite Tennyson's poem *The Charge of the Light Brigade* to herself in moments of stress. She had been in the Albanian town of Durazzo when it was bombed by the Austrian air force and had been appalled to see Italian troops scuttling down a storm drain in their haste to escape. She felt that the Italian army fell considerably short of Tennyson's military ideal.

Her own moment of truth had come on a hillside in Macedonia, when her regiment had been attacked at dawn by the Bulgarians. Fixing her bayonet, Flora had joined the counter-attack up the hill, creeping from rock to rock in mist so thick that visibility was restricted to a few yards. The Bulgarians' machine guns had kept the Serbs pinned down for a while until a strangulated bugle call had urged them on again:

'A moment's hesitation, a "now or never" sort of feeling, and we scrambled to our feet and raced forward, and I forgot everything else except the immediate business in hand. As we flung ourselves on our faces again a group of Bulgars emerged out of the mist, not ten paces above us, and, dodging behind the rocks, welcomed us with a volley of bombs. They were almost on top of us, and it was actually our close quarters that saved us, for they threw the bombs over and behind us instead of into our faces.

'I immediately had a feeling as though a house had fallen bodily on the top of me with a crash. Everything went dark, but I was not unconscious for I acutely realised that our platoon was falling back. I heard afterwards that every single one of them had been wounded by that shower of bombs. One had his face split from nose to chin, another an arm broken, but none, except myself, had actually been knocked out.'

One of the grenades had exploded against Flora's revolver, which had shielded her from the full force of the blast. Even so, her right arm had been smashed and she had shrapnel wounds all over her back and side. Her comrades dragged her away 'like a rabbit flung into a poacher's bag', desperately hauling her through the snow before the Bulgarians could catch up with them. There would be no mercy if they were taken prisoner. The Bulgarians were routinely savage to their captives. Ten Serbs caught in the same action were found next day with their throats cut, killed as soon as they had surrendered.

But Flora survived, albeit with 'half a blacksmith's shop' still inside her. After a recuperative trip to England, and an abortive attempt to visit the Western Front, she had returned to the Balkans and rejoined the Serbian army as the tide turned in the Serbs' favour. She would have been with her regiment now, marching triumphantly into Belgrade, if it hadn't been for the Spanish flu.

Instead, she was stuck in Cuprija, running the hospital there because no one else was up to the job. As well as Serbs, she had a hundred French soldiers under her care, some of whom had broken into the hospital's storeroom and stolen their comrades' trousers, which they had sold to buy wine. Flora had responded by putting an armed sentry on the door with orders to shoot to kill. She noted happily that there had been no more thefts of trousers after that.

In Northern Rhodesia, thousands of miles from the battlefields of Europe, General Paul von Lettow-Vorbeck of Germany's East African command was leading his men towards Kajambi, an isolated mission post in the middle of nowhere. The Germans might be in retreat everywhere else, but von Lettow and his mainly black troops were still advancing steadily, moving deeper into British territory every day.

Von Lettow had been in command of Germany's East African troops ever since the war began, fighting a much larger British force without any help from home. Cut off from Germany with no possibility of resupply he had held off the British for four long years, threatening Kenya at first, then retreating through German East Africa into Portuguese territory, then back again and across the border into Northern Rhodesia. His orders had been to tie up as many British troops as possible, so that they couldn't be released for service on the Western Front. He had carried them out to the letter.

But his men were weary now, desperately short of everything they needed to continue the fight. The admiralty in Berlin had tried to send them a Zeppelin from Bulgaria with fifty tons of arms and ammunition, but it had turned back at Khartoum after the British had sent it a faked message saying von Lettow had surrendered. His men had learned to tap rubber from trees instead, making paraffin from copra and quinine from cinchona bark, improvising most of what they needed rather than give in to the British. Yet how much longer could they keep going, with no news from Germany and little idea of what was happening in the outside world?

Von Lettow had captured some English newspapers on 18 October and learned of Bulgaria's surrender. He knew, too, that Cambrai, St Quentin and Armentières had recently fallen to the enemy. But that might just mean that the Germans were shortening their line in the west to strengthen their defences. Positions could be given up for all sorts of sensible reasons. It didn't necessarily follow that Germany was on the brink of defeat.

Yet the situation was not looking good as von Lettow's troops arrived in Kajambi on the Wednesday morning. They had been well received by local Africans, glad to see the back of the British, but they were running short of ammunition and were losing their native porters as well. Thirty-three had deserted in a single day rather than go any further into Rhodesia. Kajambi wasn't much of a place either, although von Lettow did appreciate the architecture:

'The Catholic mission station there consists of wonderful, spacious and massive buildings. The missionaries had fled, quite unnecessarily. In the nuns' house there was a letter for me from a Catholic nun. She was a native of Westphalia, and as a fellow countrywoman appealed to my humanity. She would certainly have spared herself many discomforts if both she herself and the other people attached to the mission had remained quietly at their posts. We should have done as little to them as we had done earlier to the old English missionary at Peramiho.'

At midday, von Lettow heard rifle fire to the north-east, probably about two hours' march away. He guessed that his rearguard was being attacked by a British patrol. His men would fight the British off, as they always did, and tomorrow they would continue their advance towards Kasama, a British base to the south. There were bound to be stores at Kasama, supplies of food and ammunition. The British had set up depots all along the road to resupply their own forces. But if the

51

Germans managed to get there first, the stores would be theirs for the taking and it would be the British who would have to go without.

In Washington, the results of the US election were in and they were not good news for the Democrats. President Wilson's party had lost control of the Senate by one vote and the House of Representatives by forty-five. It was a disaster for the Democratic Party and a great rebuff for Wilson personally.

The Germans and Irish were not the only ones who had voted against him. Large numbers of blacks had too, and women and farmers and businessmen. The war had upset all sorts of people in different ways. Wilson's mistake had been to make the election personal, claiming in an appeal to the voters that a Republican victory would be interpreted in Europe as a vote of no confidence in his leadership. He had placed his neck on the block and the American people had duly swung the axe. They didn't like what was going on and they had made their objections plain at the ballot box, casting their votes against Wilson's party all across the nation.

Joe Tumulty, Wilson's secretary, told him that the people didn't know what they were doing, didn't understand the difficulties that Wilson faced in trying to build a new order in Europe. Wilson agreed. It might have been different if the Democrats had been able to tour the country, meeting the people face to face and making speeches to explain why they needed their support. But that had been impossible with Spanish flu everywhere. Wilson himself had made very few public appearances during the campaign and remained a remote figure to most Americans, an austere academic more interested in hobnobbing with Europeans than pitching horseshoes in Kentucky. The people had voted accordingly.

So now Wilson's hands were tied, just as Andrew Johnson's had been after the Civil War. He would continue with his strategy, but it wouldn't be easy with both houses of Congress lost to the opposition. Wilson's plans for a new world order included a League of Nations, or some such name, an international talking shop for countries to settle their differences diplomatically rather than by going to war. It was an excellent idea in principle, but Wilson knew he would have trouble selling it to his fellow Americans. Among the tribunes of the people who had just been elected to Congress, plenty were boneheaded enough to reject the notion if Wilson put it to them. They couldn't see beyond their noses, some of them.

But Wilson was still president. He would battle on. 'You may be sure that the stubborn Scotch-Irish in me will be rendered no less stubborn by the results of the election,' he insisted to his colleagues. He had a meeting of the War Cabinet that afternoon and was seeing the trade union leader Sam Gompers at five. After that, he was spending the evening at Keith's Theatre. His people knew where to find him if they had any good news for him from Europe.

In Berlin, it had been a day of frenzied activity as Prince Max and his Cabinet sought to contain the revolution sweeping the country. The unrest was spreading by the hour, although it had not yet reached the capital. The authorities were taking steps to make sure it never did. Troops had been quartered at strategic points across the city and large guards placed at the railway stations of Rathenow and Neustadt an der Dosse. Orders had been given for all sailors arriving in Berlin to be arrested on sight. Police and army commanders in the city reported that their forces remained loyal and could be relied upon in a crisis. Max just hoped they were right.

He shared Friedrich Ebert's view that the Kaiser had to abdicate at once as part of the solution to the problem. There was still time for the Kaiser to step down voluntarily if he acted fast. The crisis could yet be averted if he only had the sense to take the advice he had been given and jump before he was pushed. But sense had never been the Kaiser's strongest point.

Even more urgently than the Kaiser's abdication, Max needed someone to lead the Armistice commission across the Allied lines to negotiate a ceasefire. His first ministerial choice, Konrad Haussmann, had refused point-blank, pleading exhaustion after his recent lightning trip to Kiel. Max's second choice, Matthias Erzberger, wasn't keen either. A former schoolmaster, Erzberger headed the Catholic

Centre Party in the Reichstag and was a bitter opponent of the policies that had brought Germany to rack and ruin. He had long advocated a negotiated peace, sensible discussions by sensible men getting together around a table. But he didn't want to be one of those men himself.

The job was a poisoned chalice, as both Max and Erzberger well knew. Erzberger would be committing political suicide if he put his name to what was effectively Germany's surrender. With the German army still a force to be reckoned with in France and Belgium, millions of his fellow countrymen would never forgive him.

Yet somebody had to do it. 'Pale with shock', Erzberger had allowed himself to be persuaded at the Cabinet meeting that morning. He had agreed, at any rate, to travel with the Armistice commission to the army's headquarters at Spa, where he would discuss the situation with Field Marshal von Hindenburg before coming to his final decision. He needed time to think it over before giving his answer. Among other things, he was still mourning his son, an officer cadet who had just died of Spanish flu.

The train for Spa was due to leave at 5.05 p.m. General Gröner was going to be on it. Erzberger agreed to join him, along with the other members of the commission. As to who the other members were, Erzberger had no idea, because their names had yet to be decided. Nobody else wanted to destroy his career either.

The commission needed formal credentials to present to the Allies when they arrived at their lines. Erzberger rang the chancellery at three to inquire about the documentation and was referred to Herr Kriege, head of the foreign ministry's legal department. Kriege complained that no one had consulted him about any of this, pointing out that his department had never had to draft the paperwork for an Armistice before and didn't know the form. 'The entire course of world history knows no precedents for the kind of document required,' he told Erzberger. He wasn't even sure if it was the ministry's job, since they had no powers to authorise the signing of a military Armistice.

'There are no precedents in your files for a world war either,' Erzberger retorted tartly. He told Kriege that he had to have the documents in his hand by 5 o'clock, in time for the train to Spa.

While Kriege grumbled, Erzberger found out who else was going with him to Belgium. The Armistice commission was supposed to consist of high-ranking statesmen, to demonstrate that Germany was no longer being run by the Kaiser and his army, together with an admiral and a field marshal to represent their respective services. But the admirals and field marshals had proved just as reluctant to get involved as the politicians. They had all quietly distanced themselves from any talk of an Armistice, pretending instead that Germany's impending humiliation had nothing to do with them. Nobody wanted to go with Erzberger if he could avoid it.

After a great deal of arm-twisting, some names had finally been put forward. General Erich von Gündell was one. He still nominally headed the commission that had been set up in October to prepare the ground for the Armistice, although the Allies were unlikely to accept a negotiating team led by a military man. Count Alfred von Oberndorff, a career diplomat and a friend of Erzberger's, was to represent the foreign ministry. In the absence of the top brass, the navy was to be represented by Captain Ernst Vanselow and the army by Major General Detlev von Winterfeldt, an obscure divisional commander whose father had helped draw up the terms for France's humiliating surrender at Sedan in 1870. The final shape of the commission was not to be decided until they got to Spa, but it was obvious from the names going forward that none of Germany's most important leaders wanted anything to do with it.

With a heavy sense of foreboding, Erzberger set out for the train. Kriege had promised to have the credentials waiting for him at the station, but they weren't there when he arrived. He refused to travel without them, delaying the train's departure and pacing the platform impatiently until they turned up. Count Oberndorff joined him at 5.10 and at 5.15 a messenger appeared at last from the ministry, bearing two documents giving Erzberger full power to negotiate an Armistice, subject to the approval of the German government. The messenger also brought him a private note from Prince Max: 'Obtain what mercy you can, Matthias, but for God's sake make peace.'

Erzberger joined General Gröner and the others aboard the train. A minute later, it had left the station and they were on their way to Belgium. As soon as they had gone, Max issued a press release to announce their departure:

PEACE AND ARMISTICE NEGOTIATIONS.

In order to put a stop to the bloodshed the German Delegation for the Conclusion of an Armistice and for the opening of Peace Negotiations has today been appointed and has started its journey westwards.

Max added an appeal to the German people to remain calm and avoid any further civil disturbances. He was hoping the announcement of peace negotiations would defuse the situation across Germany and kill all talk of revolution, and perhaps even of the Kaiser's abdication as well. The next few days would show whether he was right or not.

CHAPTER FOUR

Thursday, 7 November 1918

While Erzberger and the others travelled through the night, the lights still burned at the Hôtel Britannique, German supreme headquarters at Spa. Field Marshal von Hindenburg's staff were working late, frantically preparing the ground for the Armistice commission's arrival the next morning.

Their first priority was to contact the Allies to let them know what was happening. It was already past midnight when Hindenburg sent a telegraph message to his opposite number in the French army. The message named the members of the German commision, told Marshal Foch that they would arrive at the Allied lines by car, and asked to be informed by wireless where Foch wanted them to go. 'In the interests of humanity', Hindenburg also requested a temporary ceasefire when the commission appeared, to allow them to cross the Allied lines in safety.

An hour later Hindenburg had a reply, relayed from the new radio transmitter on top of the Eiffel Tower:

To the German Commander-in-Chief:

If the German plenipotentiaries wish to meet Marshal Foch and ask him for an Armistice, they will present themselves to the French outposts by the Chimay-Fourmies-La Capelle-Guise road.

Orders have been given to receive them and conduct them to the place arranged for the meeting.

Chimay to Guise was a stretch of the front line straddling the Belgian border, ninety miles from Spa. With the roads so bad, it would take all day to get there by car. There would be very little time to waste when the Armistice commission arrived. They would have to move fast if they wanted to be safely across the French lines by nightfall.

It was raining when the train pulled in to Spa at 8 a.m., the same grey, drenching rain that had been bucketing down for days. Erzberger and the others hurried across the platform to the cars waiting to take them to the Hôtel Britannique. Their mood was even grimmer than when they had left Berlin. They had stopped at Hanover during the night to send a radio message to Marshal Foch saying that they were on their way. While the message was being sent, General Gröner had studied the sailors lounging around the station, bands of undisciplined mutineers who had taken control of the town and no longer saluted officers or acknowledged any authority except their own. He had been deeply disturbed at the sight.

At the hotel, the delegates braced themselves for the ordeal ahead. Erzberger was still in two minds about whether to lead the Armistice commission himself, but was talked into it by Admiral Paul von Hintze, who told him frankly that there was no realistic alternative. The Allies were not willing to negotiate with the Kaiser or his army. They would only deal with civilian representatives of the German government, and that meant Erzberger. There wasn't anyone else.

Reluctantly, Erzberger agreed to take over the formal leadership of the commission from General von Gündell, who was only too glad to stand down. After confirming his decision by telephone with the chancellery in Berlin, Erzberger prepared to set out for the French lines. Hindenburg came to wish him luck before he left. With tears in his eyes, the field marshal took Erzberger's hand in both of his:

'Hindenburg told me that this must be the first time that politicians rather than soldiers negotiated an Armistice. But he agreed with this entirely, especially since the supreme command no longer issued political directives. The army required an Armistice above anything else. He said goodbye with the following words: "May God go with you, and see that you succeed in attaining the best that can still be secured for our Fatherland.'"

A convoy of five cars was waiting to take them across the lines. Accompanied by two army captains who had volunteered their services as interpreters, the commission set off at midday. Erzberger rode in the first car with his friend Oberndorff. The others followed, sticking close together as their convoy headed out through the streets of Spa.

The rain was still falling as they left and the road was slippery and wet. They had hardly cleared the town when Erzberger's car failed to negotiate a narrow bend and drove straight into the side of a house. The second car drove into the back of the first and both were written off in a shower of broken glass. Nobody was hurt, but it could hardly have been a more disastrous start to the journey.

The delegates were badly shaken as they contemplated the wreckage. Count Oberndorff was not alone in thinking it a bad omen, but Erzberger hastily reminded him of the old German proverb that broken glass brings good luck. Rather than waste time returning to Spa, he decided to press on in the remaining three cars. The luggage was transferred and the delegates climbed back in. A few minutes later, they had put the crash behind them and were picking up speed again, heading unhappily for the front line and their appointment with destiny.

As soon as it had been confirmed that they were on their way, Marshal Foch gave orders for a local ceasefire to come into effect when Erzberger's delegation reached the French lines. Elsewhere, though, he ordered the fighting to continue unabated, in case the Germans tried to take advantage of the lull. It was possible that the Germans were just trying to buy time with the Armistice negotiations while they regrouped their army. In a message to General Pershing, Foch made it clear that they were not to be trusted at this critical juncture:

The enemy may spread rumours that an Armistice has been

signed in order to deceive us. There is nothing in it. Let no one cease hostilities of any sort without authorisation from the Commander-in-Chief.

Pershing didn't need to be told. He disapproved of the Armistice anyway. His men were advancing towards Sedan, hoping to capture the town before the French. They weren't about to call a halt now.

Owing to a mix-up in the orders, one of Pershing's divisions had crossed another's boundaries during the night, leading to widespread confusion as they encountered each other in the dark. From the heights south of Sedan, Brigadier Douglas MacArthur hurried forward as soon as it was light to sort out the problem before anyone was killed. He hadn't gone far when he was intercepted near Beau-Ménil farm by a patrol from the other division, which took one look at his forage cap and civilian scarf and concluded that he must be a German spy. The patrol captured him at gunpoint, to their consternation and MacArthur's professed amusement after the misunderstanding had been cleared up.

'As I finished talking to Lieutenant Black I noticed that one of the soldiers in the patrol was looking at me in a rather wistful way. I was smoking a Camel cigarette and presumed he was envying me what was then a rare possession at the front – American tobacco. So I offered him one from the rather dilapidated pack I was using. He thanked me and as he lit it said, "I was thinking, if you had just a' bin a Boche general 'stead of an American one we would all of us got the DSC."

'I laughed and gave him the pack saying, "If you don't get a medal in any event you do get a packet of cigarettes." He grinned and blurted out, "To tell the truth, sir, I would rather have the cigarettes than the medal." As they disappeared down the hill he was the rear point of the patrol. He turned and waved his musket and I raised my cap to him as he disappeared in the morning mist.'

MacArthur learned afterwards that the man was killed later that day, fighting at the gates of Sedan.

*

While the Americans advanced towards Sedan, Father Pierre Teilhard de Chardin of the French army was marching through the Haute Saône on his way to Citers. As chaplain to a combined Moroccan regiment of Zouaves and Tirailleurs, Teilhard had said Mass before the regiment set out that morning and was busy now turning over various ideas in his mind as he marched, gathering his thoughts for a paper he was planning to write about the Resurrection and the flesh of Christ.

Teilhard had been an intellectual before the war, studying for the priesthood in Jersey after the Society of Jesus had been obliged to leave France. He had moved to England in 1908, where an interest in human palaeontology had brought him to the Piltdown dig in Sussex. Teilhard had played no part in the discovery of Piltdown Man but had later unearthed an eye-tooth at the site, a triumph for which he had been commended in the Geological Society of London's quarterly journal. Thereafter, he had returned to France, joining the army in December 1914 and volunteering for duty as a stretcher-bearer on the Western Front.

Rather than don the kepi and sky-blue uniform of a Frenchman, Teilhard had insisted on wearing the same red fez and khaki as the Moroccan Muslims who made up the bulk of the regiment. He had endeared himself to the Moroccans by refusing promotion to captain, arguing that he would do better to remain a corporal among the men. He had been quite fearless under fire, enduring the gas at Ypres and the horrors of Verdun without turning a hair. He had once crawled into no-man's-land after dark to retrieve the body of a captain from under the nose of a German machine-gunner, reappearing at dawn with the dead man on his back. He thought nothing of holding a Mass under shellfire and had been awarded both the Croix de Guerre and the Médaille Militaire for his courage in the face of the enemy.

But that was all in the past now, as Teilhard's regiment marched cheerfully towards Citers. They had been on the move for several days without seeing any Germans. The Haute Saône was a quiet sector of the front, close to the Swiss border, virtually untouched by the war. The leafless woods seemed beautiful to Teilhard as he strode along with the rest:

'We've been continuing to make our way on foot northwards, through lovely country, quite new to me. We're advancing leisurely in short stages. No one here has the slightest idea what they have in store for us.'

Ahead of them lay Alsace, a little slice of France along the Rhine which had been seized by the Prussians in 1870 and had remained in German hands ever since. They would be there in a few days, if nobody stopped them, liberating their fellow countrymen after a wait of almost half a century. A stain on France's honour would be avenged at long last, and then Father Teilhard would be free to return to his real work. Once he had written his religious paper – 'The Spiritual Power of Matter' seemed a good title – he was planning to read for a natural science degree at the Sorbonne, specialising in the mammalian stratigraphy of the French lower Eocene.

As Teilhard de Chardin marched through the Haute Saône, Captain Frank Hitchcock and four NCOs of the Leinster Regiment were cutting across a beetroot field towards the river Scheldt. They were on their way to Moen to reconnoitre the village before the Leinsters took it over from a Territorial battalion of the Queen's Westminster Rifles.

Shrapnel was bursting overhead as they went and the going was very heavy in the mud. The ground was so waterlogged that they had to make a wide detour to reach the village. With heavy equipment on their backs and soil clinging to their boots, Hitchcock and the others were exhausted by the time they reached the Westminsters' command post in a derelict farm building on the outskirts of Moen:

'The village was being subjected to heavy shelling, and there were groups of inhabitants watching the "crumps" bursting with great curiosity (Moen was new to war!). I was supplied with a guide, and we headed off across a swampy stretch towards a thick clump of trees which surrounded the chateau where company HQ was situated. A fairly heavy bombardment was going on and the Boches were search-ing Bossuit, the chateau and its approaches. Several high explosive crumps landed unpleasantly close in the marshy soil, making great upheavals of earth.

'We entered the chateau grounds by a back entrance and, passing through the stables, came out in front of a beautiful medieval castle, with grey turrets, and surrounded on three sides by a moat. I found the company commander of the Territorial unit in the dark, spacious kitchen, the only safe place. All its windows had been barricaded up with sandbags on the outside, as protection against back-bursts. The chatelain had decamped when the fighting started, leaving his furniture and china for the use of either Briton or Boche.'

The company commander was down with Spanish flu, but did his best to brief Hitchcock while shells continued to fall into the moat. A soldier then took Hitchcock forward to inspect the troop positions along the river Scheldt. Less than twenty yards wide, the river had been deepened by Marshal Vauban in 1706 and turned into a line of defence, one of many similar lines across the Flemish countryside. It had been spanned with a temporary bridge of duckboards and metal drums, allowing a British observation post to be established on the far bank. Hitchcock went across to inspect the position, then made his way back to the chateau, where the rest of his company was arriving to relieve the Westminsters.

Shells were still raining down as Hitchcock led his men to their positions. The firing was intense but only spasmodic, which suggested to Hitchcock that the Germans were just getting rid of their ammunition before retreating. They had made a dreadful mess of the chateau's front drive, pockmarking it from end to end with shell holes and fallen tree trunks.

The Germans had made a mess of the village as well and were still shelling it that evening as Hitchcock blundered along in the dark, carrying rations for his men. If past form was anything to go by, the Germans would continue to fire all night, loosing off a few rounds every now and then to make sure nobody got any sleep. But at least the village had cellars for Hitchcock's men to shelter in, even if they didn't get much rest. It was almost like the Ritz after what they had been used to in the past.

*

In Wilhelmshaven, the revolution was gathering pace as the sailors from the North Sea Fleet met for another day of demonstrations. They were joined this time by thousands of civilians and dockyard workers, ordinary people marching in a long procession towards the main square. There were even a few minor officials among them, and some deck officers without their swords. Very few of the protesters were Bolshevists, but they were happy to march behind the red banners for the moment, showing solidarity with the workers. It was the only way to make their voices heard.

Seaman Richard Stumpf had decided not to join the march, but was a fascinated spectator as the crowd assembled in the square. A speaker in a flowing cloak stood up and announced that the Reichstag deputies had been taking bribes from food speculators and war profiteers. Another accused the mayor of refusing to help a soldier's wife with five children. A third called for the overthrow of the Kaiser and all the federal princes. To Stumpf's disgust, a show of hands revealed that fully half of the crowd wanted to see the Kaiser deposed, even though the sailors had all sworn an oath of loyalty to him as head of state. This was too much for Stumpf. He left soon afterwards and returned angrily to his ship.

He was still aboard some time later when he heard a terrific noise outside. Curious, Stumpf didn't have to wait long to find out what was happening:

'Someone stuck his head through the door and bellowed: "All hands to receive rifles and ammunition!" I stopped the first man I met and asked "What's going on? Why the rifles?" "Treason," he gasped, trembling with rage. "The loyalists are firing on us at Rüstringen!" Someone else shouted, "The 10th Army Corps is marching against us. We shall shoot them down like dogs!"'

Stumpf went with the others to find out what was happening. He was horrified to see sailors emerging from the armoury with rifles and bayonets:

'I said to myself: this means blood will be spilled. These people are absolutely insane. The streets were like a madhouse. Armed men ran through the gates from all directions. There were even a few women dragging cases of ammunition around. What lunacy! Is this the way it has to end? After five years of brutal fighting, shall we now turn our guns against our own countrymen? Since even the most stable and reasonable men I saw were in a state of semi-hysteria, only a miracle could prevent a disaster.'

But a miracle did occur. The same revolutionary committee that had spread the rumour about the loyal soldiers now sent men round in cars and on bicycles to announce that it had all been a false alarm. No one was coming to attack them. There was nothing to worry about at all.

Stumpf learned later that the committee had deliberately invented the rumour to justify the seizure of arms. It was a disgraceful thing to do, in his opinion, quite inexcusable. The committee was playing with fire, issuing weapons to the men. Wilhelmshaven was calm again that evening, but for how much longer, now that everyone had guns in their hands and the genie was out of the bottle?

In Cologne, the situation was even more alarming as sailors from Kiel mingled with soldiers from the garrison, brandishing red flags and chanting revolutionary slogans along the Hohestrasse. Mayor Konrad Adenauer watched in horror, powerless to do anything as a lawless mob rampaged through the streets, ripping the epaulettes off any officer unwise enough to cross their path.

The sailors had arrived by the trainload from Kiel despite Adenauer's best efforts to keep them out of the city. He had pleaded with the local army commander and the head of the rail network, but neither had been prepared to take responsibility for preventing the sailors' arrival in Cologne. The men had spilled out of the railway station and spread in all directions, rapidly overwhelming the city centre. Prisoners had been released from the military gaol and soldiers wearing red cockades had taken up positions at every intersection and public square. They had been joined by factory workers from Cologne, thousands of angry demonstrators crowding the Neumarkt and calling for a soviet of workers and soldiers to overthrow the old

65

regime and take over the running of the city.

It was all too much for mayor Adenauer. There was a battery of field artillery in the courtyard of the Apostelgymnasium, his old school. Adenauer telephoned the army commander and asked why the gunners hadn't been ordered to fire on the mob. He wanted them to start shooting at once. A few rounds of artillery fire over the people's heads would surely bring them to their senses, if nothing else would.

The commander disagreed. Firing into the mob wasn't the answer. The gunners would simply kill a few people and enrage the rest. His men would be torn limb from limb if they fired into the mob. The commander politely declined Adenauer's request and told him that he was going to withdraw his men to barracks instead.

With no one else to turn to, Adenauer was forced to admit defeat. The newly formed Workers' and Soldiers' Council was holding an inaugural meeting that afternoon in Cologne's town hall. Biting the bullet, Adenauer decided he would have to negotiate with the revolutionaries in order to keep the city's administration running smoothly.

After talking to them all afternoon, he managed to secure a number of concessions, not least of which was that the red flag would not be allowed to fly from the town hall. It wasn't much, but at least it meant that Konrad Adenauer was able to stay on as mayor, holding the city together in the difficult days that lay ahead.

In Munich, capital of Bavaria, eighty thousand people were gathered on the Theresienwiese, the vast open space where the annual Oktoberfest was held. They were listening to Kurt Eisner, a firebrand politician, haranguing them from the podium.

Eisner was from Berlin, clever and Jewish, with a long history of left-wing agitation. He had been imprisoned at the beginning of 1918 for organising a strike of munitions workers against the war. The authorities had released him in October in the hope of defusing the situation, but Eisner had continued to rally people against the war. His aim now was the overthrow of the Bavarian monarchy, the toppling of the whole rotten regime in favour of a new Bavarian republic, with himself as prime minister.

Scanning the faces of the crowd, Eisner knew that this was the moment to seize the city and take over the administration. As in Cologne and elsewhere, the people were all for it, their mood increasingly militant as Eisner egged them on. They stood listening excitedly as he called them to arms:

'Spread out across the city! Occupy the barracks! Seize the arms and ammunition! Win over the troops! When you've done that, make yourselves the masters of the Government!'

Eisner's speech was electrifying. As soon as he had finished, one of his supporters leapt up in his place.

'Comrades, our leader Kurt Eisner has spoken. There's no need for any more talking. Follow us!'

The crowd needed no further urging. With a loud cheer, tens of thousands surged forward, following Eisner towards the Guldein school, which had been requisitioned by the army as a temporary arms depot. The officers there could do nothing to stop them. Instead, they stood back and watched helplessly as the mob shoved them aside and grabbed all the guns and ammunition they could lay their hands on.

From the Guldein school, the crowd headed north, occupying the Maximilian Kaserne barracks and other army installations at gunpoint. While they did so, Eisner set up his headquarters in the Mathäserbräu, one of Munich's best-loved beer halls. The beer flowed freely as the crowd voted Eisner full powers to take over the apparatus of state and establish a republic forthwith.

From the Mathäserbräu, revolutionary troops fanned out across the city to seize government buildings in the name of the people. Carrying red banners, they shouted 'Republic!' and 'Down with the dynasty!' as they went. King Ludwig III of Bavaria heard them from his palace and knew, with a sinking heart, that Munich was on the brink of revolution. He had suspected it since early that morning, when the palace guards who protected him had failed to show up for work.

Ludwig was an old man, not much loved by his people, but not hated either. He was strolling uneasily in the English Gardens near the palace when one of his aides came rushing up to tell him that his life was in danger with the mob on the rampage. The aide advised him to go back to the palace, but not by the main entrance because a crowd was gathering there to demand his abdication. Ludwig returned by the back entrance instead, making his way unobtrusively to the royal apartments, where he locked himself in with his family, intending to sit tight until the crisis had passed.

He was still there when two of his ministers came to see him after dark. They brought bad news. The king's safety could no longer be guaranteed, because there were no longer any troops in the city loyal to the royal family. The ministers thought Ludwig should leave Munich at once, taking his family with him, before the mob stormed the palace and killed them all.

The Wittelsbach dynasty had an estate near the Austrian border. Ludwig decided to go there immediately with his wife and four daughters. Pausing only to grab a box of cigars, he sent for his chauffeur, only to discover that the man had defected to the revolution and there was no one to drive them out of Munich. Nothing daunted, Ludwig decided to hire a car instead. At 9.30 that evening, he and his family took some trusted servants and left Munich in a convoy of three vehicles, heading for their family estate in the south.

'You can take care of your own filth now,' Ludwig was said to have shouted to the mob as he left. The convoy cleared Munich without mishap but hadn't gone much further in the fog when Ludwig's car skidded off the road and ran into a potato field, where it became stuck in the mud. After failing to pull it out, Ludwig's servants trudged across the fields in search of help. They found a couple of soldiers in a farmhouse and persuaded them to haul the car out with their horses. It was 4.30 in the morning by the time the task had been completed and the convoy went on its way again.

Ludwig arrived safely at the family estate, only to discover that Eisner had taken control of parliament the previous night and Bavaria was now a republic. The king was a wanted man. His sole remaining option was to continue south and flee across the Austrian border before the revolutionaries caught up with him. It was an undistinguished end to seven hundred years of monarchy in Bavaria. It was also the death knell for all the other monarchies in Germany, because none of them could hope to survive now that Bavaria had become a republic.

The events in Bavaria were still unfolding as American journalist Roy Howard travelled on the overnight train from Paris to the Atlantic port of Brest. As head of the United Press agency, Howard took a close interest in the news from Germany, but it was the Armistice that preoccupied him during his journey across France. Howard had seen Prince Max's press release from Berlin before he set out. He assumed from the wording that a truce would follow in a matter of hours, perhaps even during the night while he was still on his way to Brest.

Howard's train arrived soon after nine on Thursday morning. He went at once to the American military headquarters in the town, where his suspicions about an Armistice were all but confirmed by a contact at the intelligence office. Nothing had been said officially, but the rumour in Brest was that an Armistice had indeed been negotiated overnight and the terms agreed between the parties. The Germans had thrown in the towel at last. The war was over.

Howard could hardly believe his luck. For technical reasons, Brest was the best possible place in France for sending a news flash to New York. It only needed a moment to send a cable across the Atlantic from Brest, whereas it could take up to seven hours along the land-lines from anywhere else in France. The biggest scoop of the war and if he sent it now Howard would have a head start over his rivals in Paris, perhaps even as much as half a day. The right journalist in the right place at the right time! Legends were made of this.

First, Howard had to confirm the story. He spent the rest of the morning racing from one place to another, trying to get the cor-roboration he needed. Everyone in Brest had heard the rumour, but no one could confirm it for certain. Howard lunched with General George Harries, the senior American officer in the town, but

69

Harries couldn't confirm it either, although he was pretty sure it was true.

Harries assigned Major Fred Cook, a journalist in civilian life, to escort Howard around Brest in search of someone who could help. At ten past four that afternoon, still without confirmation, they went to see Admiral Henry Wilson, who commanded all the US naval forces in France. The navy's band was playing in the square outside as Howard accompanied Cook up five flights of stairs to the landing at the top:

'As we entered the admiral's office we were greeted by Ensign James Sellards, Admiral Wilson's personal aide, secretary and interpreter. Sellards immediately ushered us into the inner office, where Admiral Wilson was standing by his desk holding in his hand a sheaf of carbon copies of a message. The bluff old sailor's greeting to Major Cook, even before I could be introduced, was: "By God, Major, this is news, isn't it?" and without waiting for a reply or giving Cook an opportunity to make an introduction, the admiral barked at a young orderly who had followed us into the room: "Here, take this to the editor of *La Dépêche* and tell him that he can publish it – and tell him to put it on his bulletin board. And here, take this copy to that bandmaster; tell him to read it to the crowd – both in English and French – and then tell him to put some life into that music!"'

As the sailor departed, Major Cook asked the admiral what the news was. The band outside had changed its tune and was playing 'There'll be a hot time in the old town tonight' as the admiral told him the Armistice had been signed. Cook asked incredulously if the news was official. The admiral said it was. Heart thumping, Howard asked if the admiral had any objection to his filing the story, if it was official. The admiral had no objections at all.

'Hell, no. This is official. It is direct from GHQ via the embassy. It's signed by Captain Jackson, our naval attaché at Paris. Here's a copy of what I have just sent to *Dépêche*. Go to it.'

Howard needed no further urging. Taking the stairs at a leap, he raced across the square to the cable office. The censors there had already heard the news and were out in the street celebrating, but an operator was quickly found and the cable sent. By twenty past four that afternoon, the greatest newspaper scoop of the century was scorching along the wires to New York and all points beyond:

URGENT ARMISTICE ALLIES GERMANY SIGNED ELEVEN SMORNING HOSTILITIES CEASED TWO SAFTERNOON SEDAN TAKEN SMORNING BY AMERI-CANS.

Howard spent the rest of the afternoon in a delirious haze, unable to believe his good fortune. The scoop every newspaperman in the world wanted, and he had got it! The scoop of the century! From New York it would go to the four hundred newspapers across North and South America that took UP's service and from there across the rest of the world as well. By the same time tomorrow there wouldn't be anybody on the globe who didn't know the war was over, courtesy of newspaperman Roy Howard in Brest, France, the man who filed the stories that other reporters could only dream about.

It was another two hours before Howard discovered that someone in Paris had got their wires crossed and no Armistice had been signed. To add insult to injury, the Americans hadn't taken Sedan either.

By then it was far too late to recall the cable. The damage had already been done. Howard's story had gone out at 4.20 on a dark French afternoon, but it was still only a minute to midday when it arrived at the UP offices in New York. In California, it was even earlier, the beginning of a new day. Across the international date line, it was already next morning in the Pacific. Australians heard the news on their way to work and began celebrating at once, so enthusiastically in Sydney that all places serving alcohol had to be closed by two in the afternoon to prevent the party getting out of hand.

In New York, extra editions of the newspapers were on the streets by 1 o'clock. All over the city, people abandoned their offices and flooded the streets from Fifth Avenue to Washington Square. The Stock Exchange closed and Wall Street was festooned from end to end with ticker tape. Flags waved, complete strangers kissed each other, and from the windows of the Hotel Knickerbocker, Enrico Caruso gave an impromptu rendering of 'The Star-Spangled Banner' to an ecstatic crowd below. The mayor stood on the steps of City Hall to announce a public holiday for the city's employees, most of whom had already taken one and were out dancing in the streets. Shops closed as well, their owners pausing long enough to scrawl 'Too happy to work today. Come tomorrow' across the windows before rushing off to join the fun.

In Washington, the city was so crowded by lunchtime that the streetcars couldn't move, their passengers abandoning their journeys and jumping off instead to join the party. Whistles blew, sirens hooted across the city, and several bands played outside the White House as the crowds stormed the grounds, calling for the president. Edith Wilson rushed to the Oval Office and begged her husband to come to the portico to greet the people. Wilson refused, knowing that he would have heard about it by now if the Armistice really had been signed. His wife understood, but still couldn't contain herself, Armistice or no Armistice:

'As the day lengthened the excitement grew, and I simply could stand no longer having no part in it. In an open car I picked up Mother and my sister Bertha at the Powhatan Hotel, thinking we would drive down Pennsylvania Avenue and watch the crowds. No sooner was the car recognised than the throngs surged around us. I was glad that I had come out, to take my place among all the other Americans who had stood behind their president during the war. My only regret was that he was not there.'

In fact, Wilson later relented and showed himself briefly to the crowd, although his misgivings about the celebration remained. They were shared across the Atlantic, where British newspapers had the story but declined to make much of it without further corroboration. The news leaked out anyway and a few people in Britain exulted, although most remained wary, having been disappointed too often before.

In Cuba, they had no such scruples, a crowd cheering in Havana even though Cuba wasn't in the war. And in Argentina, with a considerable German population, the crowds in Buenos Aires divided into two distinct factions as the news spread, each celebrating the end of the fighting in different ways and for different reasons.

But it was in France and Belgium that the story had the most immediate impact. For the men on the front line, it could mean all the difference between life and death if the war was over and there was no fighting any more.

Private Darryl Zanuck of the US Army's Buckeye Division was preparing to go into action for the first time when the false Armistice was announced. His unit had been ordered forward to the Lys–Scheldt canal, where the Germans were mounting a last-gasp defence. Sixteen-year-old Zanuck could not conceal his disappointment when his unit was told to stand down. He had been longing to kill a Hun before the war came to an end. He knew he would never have the chance now.

Zanuck might still have been at school in Nebraska if two European recruiting posters hadn't caught his eye. The first had been Lord Kitchener's 'Your country needs you', which had been widely circulated in the United States. The second had been a French poster of a German soldier savagely cutting the breast off a half-naked Belgian woman. 'Please save me!' she had cried, and Zanuck had heeded the call. Fourteen at the time, he had volunteered at once for the US Army, only to be rejected at first. Lying about his age, he had eaten heavily and drunk gallons of water to increase his weight before successfully reapplying.

In England, Zanuck had been sent to the south coast for final training before shipping over to France. He had been surprised to discover that the war was clearly audible from across the sea:

'Every night we heard distant firing on the Western Front. Then one night we were put on a train to Southampton and went across the English Channel at night by boat. We were packed in like sardines. Body against body. Awful!'

At Brest, Zanuck had had another surprise when the train arrived to take them up to the line. It had been full of wounded Americans evacuated from the fighting:

'Jesus Christ, three hundred guys, with arms gone, holes in their chests. They were staring at us. My first real shock. This was war where they were killing people. The guys were pushed out of the train and we were pushed on.'

Zanuck himself had seen no fighting and never would now, if the war was over. But he had twice been wounded, once when a rifle exploded during target practice and once when he tripped over a rock. Neither incident had anything to do with the Germans, yet they entitled him to wear two wound stripes on his uniform, which would impress the girls back home. Zanuck had written a letter about his experiences that had been published in *Stars and Stripes*, the US Army's newspaper.

He was thinking of becoming a writer when he went back to America – perhaps even a movie writer, because there was bound to be a demand for movies about the war once the troops had come home and the dust had settled. But it would have been nice to have had some combat experience as well, if only to brag about it to his friends in Nebraska, who were all still at school.

In Rouen, well behind the British lines, Lieutenant J. B. Priestley had aspirations to be a writer too, once the war was over. Unlike Zanuck, though, he wasn't sorry when the false Armistice was announced. Priestley had done his share of fighting over the past three years and had nothing left to prove.

Priestley had last seen action in September, somewhere beyond Péronne. Still suffering the effects of a German gas attack, he had fortified himself with several tots of rum before going forward at dawn, only to feel distinctly queasy as he advanced towards the enemy in the mist:

'After ten minutes – and you may put it down to gas, rum or carelessness, just as you please – I had lost the whole battle, which I could hear all round me but could not see. I was wandering about, befogged inside and out, entirely alone. But I must have been more or less advancing, not retreating, for a figure came looming up through the whiteness, and I saw it was a German and waved my revolver at him. After all, he was not to know that I had been on two revolver courses and never could hit anything.

'He was a lad about sixteen, who ought to have been several hundred miles away, putting his school-books into a satchel. He raised his arms, poor lad, and made gibbering noises. I tried to look a little less idiotic than I felt, and pointed sternly in what I hoped was the direction of the British and not the German army, and off he trotted, leaving me alone once more in the mist, wondering where to find the battle. I never did catch up with it. My head going round, too short of breath to move any further, I took a rest in a shell hole, where I was found by a couple of stretcher-bearers.'

After a short spell in hospital, Priestley had been classified as B2, unfit for active service but still capable of other work. He had been sent to the Labour Corps depot at Rouen, where he spent his days in an old factory building auditioning conjurors and female impersonators for the entertainment units behind the lines. Priestley was working as a glorified talent agent when news came of the supposed Armistice. The depot's commanding officer ordered champagne for the entire officers' mess that night. He was livid to find himself stuck with the bill when the report was denied just after the last of the champagne had been drained.

Further north, it wasn't until half past nine that the Armistice rumours reached Cayeux, near the mouth of the river Somme. Private Fen Noakes of the Coldstream Guards was in his hut at No. 5 Convalescent Camp, preparing for bed, when he heard distant cheering from the other side of the compound:

'At first it was greeted with sarcastic laughter and a few ironical counter-cheers, but the sound increased, and presently the throbbing of a drum mingled with the shouting. At that, the noise in the hut was suddenly silenced. Men gazed at each other with eager, questioning eyes. "Can it be?" was the unspoken query – "It is!" and with a simultaneous movement, everybody huddled on their clothes and poured out on to the parade ground.

'On all sides, the other huts were disgorging their occupants and in a few minutes the huge open space was black with excited men. The rumour and the cheering spread like a conflagration: "Germany has surrendered!" and the whole eight or ten thousand of us yelled ourselves hoarse. With one accord, the whole throng burst into unanimous song:

> Take me back to dear old Blighty,
> Put me on the train for London town;
> Drop me over there, any blooming where:
> Birmingham, Leeds or Manchester –
> Well, I don't care ...

'Backwards and forwards we swayed, arms linked, shouting, cheering and singing. The uproar was indescribable, and it never occurred to us to doubt the truth of the rumour. I remember thinking: "This is the happiest moment of my life. I must fix it in my memory forever!"'

One of the men grabbed a box of Very lights and began shooting them into the sky. The bugler sounded 'Last Post', the signal for lights out in the huts, but the troops invaded the power house and prevented the dynamo attendants from switching off the electricity. Some of the wilder spirits emptied a fire bucket over the regimental sergeant major and tried to release the defaulters from the guardroom. Then they broke out of camp and headed into Cayeux to celebrate in the town.

Noakes did not go with them. Still recovering from the effects of mustard gas, he was beginning to have doubts about the Armistice, since no official announcement had been made. Others had doubts too. They began to drift back to their huts, making their way disconsolately to bed.

It wasn't until the next day that their suspicions were confirmed and they heard that there had been no Armistice. Roy Howard in

Brest had sent a second cable to New York as soon as he had realised his mistake, but it had been delayed on the way and had taken forever to arrive. Howard's scoop had turned out to be the biggest embarrassment of his career. For the rest of his life, his friends never stopped pulling his leg about it.

The Armistice was no laughing matter to Matthias Erzberger and the German commission as they drove from Spa towards the French front line. The rain-clouds matched their mood, so low and grey that it was almost dark in the middle of the afternoon. They passed thousands of German soldiers going the other way, exhausted men withdrawing in good order, yet with little fight left in them. The roads were a morass, littered with broken vehicles and the abandoned detritus of war. The German army in retreat was not a pretty sight.

The roads were so bad that it was well after dark before the commission came anywhere near the front line. They were still in Belgium, approaching Chimay, at six that evening. Trélon lay just across the French border, but the local military commander told them they couldn't go any further that night because the way forward was impassable. His men had felled trees and laid mines across the roads to delay the enemy advance. No one had told him the commission was coming that way.

Exasperated, Erzberger grabbed a field telephone and asked the corps commander at Trélon for help. The commander was desperately short of men – one of his divisions was down to 349 against a nominal 16,000 – but agreed to send a pioneer detachment to clear the road. The work was quickly done in the dark and Erzberger's convoy reached Trélon at 7.30.

They conferred briefly with the corps commander, who was horrified to hear of the trouble in Kiel and Munich. He begged Erzberger not to mention it to anyone, not even his officers. The timetable agreed with the French had already expired, so the commander decided to send some officers forward to negotiate an extension to the ceasefire before Erzberger's convoy followed on behind.

The commission left the German lines somewhere near Haudroy.

The leading car flew a large white flag and carried a soldier with a trumpet on the running board to warn the French of their arrival. As they passed the last German outpost, Erzberger's car was stopped by a German soldier who spoke in the same Swabian accent as himself.

'Where are you going?' the soldier asked.

'To negotiate an Armistice,' Erzberger told him.

'Just the two of you are going to do that?' The soldier was impressed.

The convoy drove out slowly into no-man's-land. For Erzberger, the journey was every bit as melancholy as the one he had made three weeks earlier to say goodbye to his dying son. He was reminded of Schumann's song 'The Two Grenadiers', about Napoleonic troops returning in shame from Russia to France, knowing that their country had just lost a cataclysmic fight. The parallels did not bear thinking about.

The soldier with the trumpet blew the ceasefire repeatedly as the Germans moved cautiously forward. They had gone about 150 yards into no-man's-land when they saw their first Frenchmen, troops of the 171st Infantry Regiment, who appeared in the fields with lanterns and waved the convoy to a halt. Sergeant Maître was at a forward observation post as the Germans arrived:

'Suddenly, at exactly half past eight in the evening, while a card game was going on, a call was heard in the distance and then soon much nearer till it was loud and clear near our command post ... "They wouldn't run over us, would they?" Captain Lhuillier cried out. Standing on the running boards of the car were two Boches, taking it in turns to sound the ceasefire with a silver bugle at least five feet long, like a Jericho trumpet. While one was blowing, the other was waving a large white cloth as a flag of truce.'

General von Winterfeldt got out to identify himself. Captain Lhuillier immediately took command, replacing the German trumpeter on the running board with Corporal Sellier, one of his own buglers. Lhuillier joined the convoy and directed it to La Capelle, a couple of miles behind the lines, which the French had reoccupied only that afternoon. They hadn't even had time to remove the German army signs, still visible in the headlights as the convoy drove through the rain.

At La Capelle, the Germans were formally received by Major Le Prince de Bourbon-Busset, a man of royal blood, on behalf of General Marie-Eugène Debeney. Winterfeldt apologised to the prince for the Germans' late arrival. 'We are prepared to sign one of the most shameful capitulations in history,' he confessed. 'We have no choice, because of the revolution. We don't even know if there will still be a Germany tomorrow.'

The prince had little sympathy. There were still plenty of French around who remembered their own capitulation of 1870, the Prussians swaggering into France as if they owned the place, Winterfeldt's father among them. The boot was on the other foot now.

French troops had little sympathy either, although they were more inclined to be chatty. 'Finie, la guerre?' they asked hopefully, as a crowd gathered around the German cars. Some even applauded the delegates before trying to scrounge cigarettes from them. But they were out of luck because the Germans didn't smoke.

At the Villa Francport, the Germans had their photographs taken before being transferred to a fleet of French cars for the journey to the nearest railhead. It was a long drive in the dark. They stopped on the way to have a scratch supper at Homblières, General Debeney's headquarters near St Quentin. When they emerged again, they found that a crowd of sightseers had gathered around their cars to watch history in the making.

'Nach Paris!' one of the crowd mocked, as the Germans got back in. But the Germans weren't going nearly as far as Paris, not even under a flag of truce.

CHAPTER FIVE

Friday, 8 November 1918

It was the middle of the night as the Armistice commission left General Debeney's headquarters. Erzberger shared a car with the Prince de Bourbon-Busset. The roads were so bad that Erzberger kept losing his spectacles as they jolted along. He complained to Bourbon-Busset, who told him to blame the German army for the state of the roads, not the French.

They drove for what seemed like ages through a desolate wasteland of ruined villages and abandoned houses. The landscape was a revelation to Erzberger, who had not hitherto been anywhere near the fighting. Comparing notes later, the delegates wondered if the French had deliberately taken them on a circuitous route through the ruins to soften them up for the negotiations that lay ahead. Erzberger remembered one village in particular:

'Not a house was still standing. One ruin after another. The broken buildings seemed ghostly in the moonlight. There was no sign of life anywhere.'

The Germans didn't even know where they were going, because the French refused to tell them. It wasn't until they arrived at the railhead beyond St Quentin that Bourbon-Busset relented a little.

'Where are we?' Erzberger asked.

'At Tergnier.'

Erzberger looked around. 'But there aren't any houses here.'

'True enough,' Bourbon-Busset conceded. 'Yet there *was* a town here once.'

It was 3 o'clock in the morning, French time. A company of

chasseurs was waiting at the ruins of the railway station. The men came smartly to attention and presented arms as the Germans emerged from their vehicles, picking their way across the rubble to the train.

As they climbed aboard, General von Winterfeldt noticed a huge hole beside the track.

'Delayed action,' Bourbon-Busset told him. 'It exploded three weeks after the German army left. I hope there aren't any others under our train. I wouldn't want to see you blown up, or me either.'

Winterfeldt was embarrassed. 'It must have been an isolated incident,' he insisted. 'The High Command never sanctions that kind of behaviour. It's very regrettable.'

He joined the others on the train. It had been specially assembled for the German delegation. Its *pièce de résistance* was the saloon, a magnificent railway carriage from 1860 that had once belonged to the emperor Napoleon III. The saloon was upholstered in green satin, decorated with golden Napoleonic bees and monogrammed with the imperial *N* surrounded by laurel leaves. Napoleon III had been humiliated by the Prussian army at Sedan, defeated in war and forced to relinquish his throne. Now that it was the Germans' turn to surrender, the French had brought his coach out of retirement to add to their despair.

The windows were shut and the curtains drawn so that the Germans couldn't see out. They asked where they were going, but the French still wouldn't say. It didn't matter much anyway. The delegates were offered brandy as the train pulled out of the station. Then they settled down to sleep in their clothes, getting what rest they could before arriving at their final destination, wherever that might be.

While the Germans travelled uncomfortably through the night, Marshal Foch and the rest of the Allied delegation were waiting for them in the Compiègne forest, north of Paris.

The forest was an odd choice for an historic meeting. A more obvious place would have been Foch's headquarters at Senlis, much nearer Paris. But Senlis was too accessible for Foch's liking, an easy trip for journalists and sightseers from the capital. The town had been held briefly by the Germans in 1914. They had shot the mayor and several other hostages before retreating, an outrage not forgotten by the locals. There would have been ugly scenes if the German delegation had arrived there now, caps in hand, asking for peace.

Compiègne was a better bet all round. It was much more isolated, a dark and gloomy forest surrounded by military sentries, cut off from the outside world. A railway cutting concealed in the woods near Réthondes station had been used by the French artillery to bombard the Germans. The cutting could be used for the peace negotiations too, far away from the prying eyes of journalists and other undesirables.

Foch and his staff had arrived from Senlis on Thursday evening, travelling on a train much like the Germans'. It had two sleepers, two second-class passenger coaches, and a dining car with a large table in it for the negotiations. Foch and the others had spent the night aboard the train and were ready and waiting when their German counterparts arrived to join them at 7 a.m.

The German train pulled up a hundred yards across the tracks from the French. The curtains were opened and the Germans looked out to see a forest all around. They still didn't know where they were and the French still wouldn't tell them. They hadn't been there long when they received a visit from General Maxime Weygand, Foch's chief of staff. He told them that if they wanted to meet Foch, the marshal would be ready to receive them on his train at 9 a.m. precisely. The Germans confirmed that they would be there.

They walked across on the wooden duckboards connecting the two railway spurs. Vanselow and Winterfeldt wore service dress, but Erzberger and the diplomat Oberndorff were in civilian clothes, more than a little crumpled after their journey.

Erzberger was their leader, a common little man in spectacles, about as far removed from the Prussian officer class as it was possible to be. There had been a couple of dozen army officers at Spa deputed to accompany him to the negotiations, but Erzberger had declined their services, knowing full well that the Allies had had enough of the German army and wanted to deal with civilians instead. Erzberger was certainly a civilian, but he did not impress as he arrived at Foch's train. For all his political astuteness, he lacked the presence that came naturally to Germans of the upper class.

The delegates were shown to the dining car by General Weygand. The car had telephones, a map of the front line, and a large conference table with four place cards on either side. Weygand motioned them to the German side and went to fetch Foch, who was waiting for them in the next carriage.

The marshal wasn't long in coming. He was accompanied by Vice Admiral Sir Rosslyn Wemyss, Britain's First Lord of the Admiralty, who was representing the Allied navies at the negotiations. Erzberger noted with surprise that there were no Belgian, Italian or American representatives with them. Just a French soldier and a British sailor, staring at the Germans with distaste.

For their part, Foch and Wemyss noted sourly that the German army and navy were represented by Winterfeldt and Vanselow, officers of decidedly subordinate rank. They understood the reason for it only too well. Quite apart from protecting their own careers, the German supreme command wanted the Armistice to be a political affair, something for which the armed services could not be held in any way responsible.

The atmosphere was stiff and tense as Foch entered. He and Winterfeldt knew each other well from Winterfeldt's time as military attaché in Paris before the war, but Foch showed barely a flicker of recognition as he asked to see the delegation's credentials. The documents were handed over and Foch took them back to the other carriage to examine them with Wemyss and Weygand. The documents were in order, but it did not escape their notice that Erzberger and his colleagues had no powers to sign an Armistice. Anything they agreed still had to be authorised by the government in Berlin.

Back in the dining car, Foch asked the Germans why they had come. 'What do you want of me?' he demanded.

Erzberger said they had come to hear the Allies' proposals for an Armistice on land, sea and in the air, on all fronts.

'I have no proposals to make,' Foch answered.

Puzzled, the Germans conferred over the translation before trying again. Oberndorff said they wouldn't stand on ceremony. They just wanted to know the conditions for an Armistice.

'I have no conditions to offer,' Foch told them.

Still puzzled, Oberndorff produced President Wilson's last note to the Germans and read out the relevant part in English. The note stated clearly that Foch had been authorised by the US and Allied governments to communicate Armistice terms to Germany's accredited representatives.

Foch agreed that he could certainly communicate terms if the Germans wanted to ask for an Armistice. Were they formally asking for one?

The Germans said they were.

Having established that to his satisfaction, Foch told them that Weygand would now read out the Armistice conditions. Rear Admiral George Hope, Wemyss's deputy, was watching as the Germans braced themselves for the terms:

'Erzberger was very nervous at first and spoke with some difficulty, the general awfully sad, the diplomat very much on the alert, and the naval officer sullen and morose.'

The Germans' mood worsened visibly as Weygand read out the Armistice conditions. There were thirty-four clauses in total, each more draconian than the last. All occupied lands were to be given up, including Alsace and Lorraine; all cash and gold reserves were to be returned to their rightful owners; all German territory west of the Rhine was to be occupied by the Allies, and some to the east as well; all German ports were to remain blockaded until a peace treaty had been signed. Ten thousand lorries were to be delivered to the Allies within fourteen days, together with 5,000 locomotives, 150,000 railway cars in good condition, and more heavy artillery, machine guns and fighter aircraft than the German armed forces still possessed. The treaty of Brest-Litovsk was to be annulled and reparations paid for war damage, even though the Allies' terms would effectively cripple the German economy for a generation to come. With a host of other demands as well, the proposed Armistice wasn't just a disaster for the Germans, it was a catastrophe beyond their wildest imaginings.

The blood drained from Winterfeldt's face as Weygand spelled out the details. Count Wolf-Heinrich von Helldorf, one of the German interpreters, was openly tearful by clause five, the one that dealt with the occupation of Mainz, Cologne and Coblenz, the main crossing points of the Rhine. Marshal Foch sat 'still as a statue', occasionally tugging at his moustache to relieve his emotions. Wemyss toyed with his monocle. Erzberger couldn't speak French, so didn't yet know the worst, but he could see from his colleagues' faces that it was pretty bad.

There was a stunned silence after Weygand had finished. Erzberger was the first to break it. Without commenting on the Armistice terms, he asked Foch for an immediate ceasefire, pointing out that Germany was on the brink of a Bolshevist revolution. The trouble would quickly spread to the rest of Europe if the German army didn't put a stop to it. But the German army couldn't put its own house in order if it was fighting the Allies as well. It was in everybody's interests for a ceasefire to come into effect at once.

Foch shook his head. He told the Germans he wasn't about to ease the pressure on them now:

'At the moment when negotiations for the signing of an Armistice are just being opened, it is impossible to stop military operations, until the German delegation has accepted and signed the conditions which are the very consequence of those operations. As for the situation described by Herr Erzberger as existing among the German troops and the danger he fears of Bolshevism spreading in Germany, the one is the usual disease prevailing in beaten armies, the other is symptomatic of a nation completely worn out by war. Western Europe will find a way of defending itself against the danger.'

General von Winterfeldt spoke next. He read out a note from the German supreme command also requesting a ceasefire on humanitarian grounds. Foch listened politely but remained adamant. If the Germans wanted the killing to stop, then all they had to do was agree the Armistice terms. The sooner they did that, the better it would be for everyone.

Foch gave them seventy-two hours to make up their minds. The deadline was set for 11 a.m. on Monday, 11 November. If the German government hadn't agreed the terms by then, the war would go on and they would have to fight to the bitter end.

Erzberger was aghast. Seventy-two hours wasn't nearly long enough. The German government was split between Berlin and Spa. He couldn't possibly consult people in both places and have a definitive response within seventy-two hours. He asked at once for a twenty-four hour extension to give him time for a proper consultation with the authorities at home.

Foch wouldn't listen. The deadline remained Monday, 11 a.m. The Germans could take it or they could leave it. They would take it, if they knew what was good for them.

Returning to their own train, the Germans conferred hurriedly. The first thing they had to do was transmit the Armistice conditions to the German government. Foch had offered them a radio link to Berlin and Spa, but wouldn't allow them to broadcast the details *en clair*. They could send the thirty-four clauses in code, but that would take hours. In any case, they hadn't brought the necessary ciphers with them. The details were too important to discuss over the telephone. The only real option was to take them by hand, sending a messenger back across the lines to deliver the full text in person to supreme headquarters at Spa.

At 11.30, Winterfeldt returned across the duckboards to send a radio message to Spa. It was from Erzberger, giving notice of the Monday deadline and warning the German government that there was to be no ceasefire in the interim. Full details of the Armistice proposals would follow by hand:

A German courier bearing the text of the Armistice conditions has been sent to Spa, there being no other practical mode of com-

munication. Please acknowledge receipt and send the courier
back as soon as possible with your final instructions.

The courier was Count von Helldorf. He was twenty-two years
old, a captain in the German cavalry. He had volunteered his services
as an interpreter to accompany the Armistice commission from Spa.
Now he volunteered to go back again, crossing the front line for the
second time in just over twenty-four hours.

Helldorf set off at lunch time. He was accompanied as far as the
French front line by his fellow aristocrat the Prince de Bourbon-
Bisset. As before, arrangements were made for a local ceasefire to
allow Helldorf to cross the lines in safety. This time, though, the arrangements were all on one side, because the German army refused
to have anything to do with them.

Helldorf arrived at the front to find his fellow countrymen 'firing
like the devil', taking no notice of his white flag or the bugle calls for
a ceasefire. Perhaps the order hadn't reached them, or perhaps they
didn't approve of the Armistice. Whatever the reason, the Germans
wouldn't stop shooting. They wouldn't let Helldorf across, and without going across he couldn't deliver the Armistice conditions to Spa.
Instead, he was forced to remain where he was, cursing impotently
on the French side of the lines while bullets whizzed over his head
and the hours to the deadline ticked steadily away.

A few miles to the north, Lieutenant Herbert Sulzbach was still
in action near Felleries, firing desultorily at the French to keep
their heads down while his gun batteries prepared for yet another
withdrawal after dark. This time they were to cross the border into
Belgium. Another few hours and the 63rd (Frankfurt) Field Artillery
Regiment would be out of France for good.

Sulzbach was sorry to go. He had come to love France over the
past four years, even if the love wasn't reciprocated. It grieved him
that the French hated the Germans so much, even though he understood the reasons for it well enough.

The French were castrating stragglers now, falling on the Germans with kitchen knives and hacking off their manhood before they had a chance to escape. Civilians were the main offenders, French villagers with four years of occupation to avenge. They were still shooting Germans, too, becoming increasingly bold as the invaders' grip weakened. Sulzbach had ordered his men to remain on high alert for the rest of their time in France, taking no chances as they prepared to slip away in the night:

'The French civilians understand perfectly well what is happening and would love to shoot another one or other of us. We have therefore been ordered to keep the sharpest discipline on the march and to leave no one behind. From now on, none of the men can go anywhere on their own or be billeted on their own and the wounded are not to be left alone and defenceless even for a moment. Every wounded man is to be taken with us no matter what the circumstances.'

It was 5 p.m. when Sulzbach's men received orders to begin pulling back. The rain was pouring down as usual, the roads a quagmire as the troops withdrew in the dark. The news from home was bad as well: Austria in chaos and a revolution in Kiel, according to the latest reports.

The only ray of hope was the Armistice commission. It was said to have crossed the lines yesterday, making contact with the French near La Capelle. Like everyone else in his unit, Sulzbach was longing for an end to the war, just so long as it could be achieved with honour. 'Peace without humiliation' was his hope now. Anything else would be too awful to contemplate after everything they had been through during the past four years.

From the loft window of his farmhouse on the Scheldt, Captain Frank Hitchcock of the Leinsters had spent the morning studying the ground ahead, preparing for the advance that night. He could see German troops across the river, shooting at the British from some buildings behind a line of willows. Their machine guns had been busy all day, peppering the farmhouse with bullet holes as they traversed back and forth across the brickwork.

The house was already a mess from the shelling, with crucifixes, broken mirrors, ladies' underwear and books scattered at random all over the floor. Hitchcock's men took little notice. They were nice and comfortable in the cellar, emerging only at intervals to dig up a few more potatoes from the garden. They remained quite happily where they were until nine that evening, when Hitchcock ordered them up for the advance.

The company was to cross the river by the pontoon bridge in front of the chateau. As they marched up the village street, the men bumped into a section of Royal Engineers who had arrived too late to build them a proper bridge. As well as being dark it was bitterly cold, a night for staying in by the fire instead of blundering about in the gloom while shells continued to whine overhead.

The pontoon bridge was looking decidedly rickety as Hitchcock examined it. Swollen by all the rain, the current was pushing so hard against the bridge that the central section had bent and the duckboards were under water. Hitchcock sent his heavily laden men across one by one, telling them to move quickly because the duckboards would sink further if they hesitated. One man didn't listen and promptly disappeared up to his knees in water, dropping his ammunition panniers as he did so. Hitchcock was the last man to cross, relieved that his men had all reached the other side safely without losing any of their eight Lewis guns.

Fanning out, they advanced towards a farm building across the mud. The building looked deserted, but they couldn't tell for sure. Hitchcock tried the door and found it locked. The gate to the farm-yard was locked too. Hitchcock continued round until he came to a wire fence on the other side:

'With my batman I climbed this fence, and jumped into a stag-nant manure pond. Down I went, wallowing up to my waist into this slimy, smelly water, my servant being somewhat luckier. We crawled out soaked, stinking like polecats, and cursing like blazes to the inner door of the farm, to find chalked across the door the words "Goodbye, Tommy" in English – the last pleasantry of the retiring enemy.'

They continued to advance until they reached the next village. Company HQ was set up on the outskirts while a patrol went forward to reconnoitre the rest of the village. When it returned, one of the sentries opened fire with his Lewis gun, killing Privates Kane and Bousfield instantly and wounding two others. It was a ghastly mistake, but there was no time for recriminations, no time to do anything except keep on going. They still had ground to cover in the dark.

'We took up our position in another farm, and very nearly surprised some Jerries having a meal, as they decamped leaving most of their repast on a table in the cellar. It was freezing hard, and being soaked through I was chilled to the bone, so I took off my clothes, bar my shirt, which stank most dreadfully. Sergeant Rochford lent me his greatcoat, which, as he was a tall man, fitted me admirably. I found a pair of civilian boots with elastic sides in the farm. Thus attired, with sergeant's chevrons on my arm, I visited the outposts. The remainder of the company slept in a straw barn.'

Cold, wet, covered in slime. Two men dead from friendly fire. The Leinsters were across the Scheldt at last.

Behind the lines, their progress was being followed by no less a personage than Lord Curzon, one of the five members of Lloyd George's War Cabinet. He was on a visit to General Sir William Birdwood's headquarters in Lille, monitoring the day's events as the German army withdrew all along the front and the British chased after them across the river.

Curzon and Birdwood knew each other from their time in India, where Curzon had been the viceroy and Birdwood a former adjutant of his bodyguard. The great man's arrival in Lille had been preceded by a reputation for overweening arrogance unrivalled in the British Empire, but Curzon had turned out to be much nicer in person than Birdwood's staff had expected. Captain Alick McGrigor, one of Birdwood's aides-de-camp, was impressed:

'Lord Curzon arrived in the evening and stayed the night. He was most pleasant and affable and not at all pompous as everyone says he used to be when viceroy. We got some indication of the Armistice terms from him and, by Jove, they are a big pill for the Boche to swallow, the forty kilometre or so stretch the other side of the Rhine to be occupied is pretty humble pie for him, though the general opinion seems to be that he will now take any terms.'

As to exactly when the Armistice would come, Curzon couldn't say for sure. But the British were across the Scheldt now, encountering very little resistance as they pushed on. They would be in Tournai tomorrow. The French and Americans were advancing too, taking advantage of the increasing chaos as the German army disintegrated into Bolshevism. The end couldn't be more than a few days away.

On the Italian front, the war was already over. The Austro-Hungarian army had collapsed and the fighting had stopped five days ago. Three hundred thousand Austrian soldiers had surrendered to the Allies. The rest were streaming back across the mountains, heading for home as fast as they could go.

Cecil Cox of the Honourable Artillery Company had been halfway across the river Tagliamento when he heard the news. An officer had ridden up at midnight on Sunday to tell them the war was over. The men had found it hard to believe at first, particularly at midnight in the middle of a river. But over it was, and they were slowly coming to realise that they had all fired their last shots in anger.

Cox was happier about that than most. A reluctant soldier from the first, he had been 'a number in uniform' since 1917, conscripted for a war that clashed heavily with his Christian principles. He had done his basic training in England, practising with his bayonet at the Tower of London before going to France with the rest of his platoon. Luckily for him, Cox had come down with German measles before the end of his training and the platoon had gone ahead without him. Cox learned later that every single one of them had been killed at Passchendaele.

He had followed them to France soon enough and was with his regiment one day when they came across a man tied to a gun wheel in the middle of a field. The regiment came to an immediate halt, refusing to march any further until the man was taken down. A few weeks later, Cox was part of a detachment ordered to fire on some mutinous Canadian soldiers. Without hesitation, they had all refused to do so. They were there to kill the enemy, not their friends.

Cox had been sent to Italy in October 1917, part of a division dispatched to the Italian front to stiffen the Italians' morale. The Italians were not enjoying the war, as the Honourable Artillery Company quickly discovered. The troops had disembarked from their train and were forming up outside the station when they were suddenly pelted with tomatoes and rotten eggs by an angry crowd yelling at them to go home and stop prolonging the war. Cox had been interested to read in the English newspapers later that the Italians had actually been strewing their path with flowers of welcome.

Marching for a hundred miles, the Honourable Artillery Company had made its way to the front line high in the mountains of northern Italy. Cox had seen plenty of fighting over the past twelve months and had lost several friends to enemy action. He himself had had a narrow escape when a shell landed between his legs without doing him any damage beyond a few bruises. He had been so drunk once after a night raid on the enemy trenches that he had remained teetotal ever since, promising himself he would never touch another drop as long as he lived.

The early hours of 24 October 1918 had found Cox north of Venice, moving up through the darkness for the final big push across the river Piave. The Honourable Artillery Company had been detailed to capture the Grave di Papadopoli, a big island in the middle of the river. The river was flooded and they had crossed in six-man boats, losing numbers of men to shellfire as they struggled ashore in the rain.

A couple of Cox's friends had been killed, but the northern end of the island had been taken and the men had dug themselves in while the enemy machine-gunned them in the dark. Cox had fallen asleep as soon as he had finished digging his hole, waking at dawn to find it full of water.

'The next day, we had orders to advance. Going out over the island, I saw a young German coming towards me and at that moment I just could not murder him and lowered my gun. He saw me do so and he followed suit, shouting "What the hell do you want to kill me for? I don't want to kill you." He walked back with me and asked had I anything to eat? At once, the relief inside me was unspeakable and I gave him my iron rations and my army biscuit.'

The two men went their separate ways and the fighting continued. Another of Cox's friends had been killed the next day, calling for his mother as he died in Cox's arms. A few days after that, the Austrians had raised the white flag and the whole dreadful business had come to an end at last. Nobody in the Honourable Artillery Company would miss it one bit.

They were on their way home now, marching down from the mountains. After two weeks of very little sleep, Cox could barely keep his eyes open as they passed a regiment of Americans coming the other way. The Yanks were new to Italy, fresh off the boat. They had never fired a shot in anger, but that didn't stop them pulling British legs as they came past. 'Ah, boys,' they shouted cheerfully. 'We've won the war for you.'

Cox was so tired he couldn't even raise a smile

On the other side of the line, Lieutenant Ludwig Wittgenstein of the Austrian army's mountain artillery had been a prisoner since Sunday, one of thousands of Austrians forced to surrender when the Italian army had reoccupied Trento, north of Verona. There had been a misunderstanding about the timing and terms of the Armistice. The Austrians had assumed that they would be allowed to go home if they laid down their arms. Instead, hundreds of thousands had been taken prisoner, a haul so large that the Italian army was having serious problems feeding and accommodating them all.

Wittgenstein had had a curious war. As a Cambridge man, he had never been in any doubt which side would win. 'We cannot get the upper hand against England,' he had insisted from the start. 'The English – the best race in the world – *cannot* lose. We, however, can lose and shall lose.' Nevertheless, Wittgenstein had abandoned the summer holiday he had been planning with David Pinsent, the English boy he loved, and had joined the Austrian army in August

1914, motivated not so much by patriotism as a desire to do something unintellectual and dangerous. War qualified on both counts.

He had ended up in Italy via stints as a latrine orderly, train engineer and searchlight operator on a patrol boat on the Vistula. He kept a Bible with him, which he read in Latin because it was more of a challenge, and treasured his letters from Pinsent, who had been found medically unfit for active service in the British army and had got a job as a test pilot instead. 'I wonder whether he thinks of me half as much as I think of him', Wittgenstein had asked himself when they were first apart. He had been so pleased once to receive a letter from his friend that he had kissed it in his excitement.

But David Pinsent was dead now, killed in a flying accident in May. Wittgenstein had won a medal fighting the British on the Asiago plateau, but he had been so distraught when he heard of Pinsent's death that he had contemplated suicide for weeks. He was still dreadfully upset. David Pinsent, his country's enemy, had meant everything to him.

To add to his troubles, Wittgenstein was now a prisoner of the Italians, held with thousands of others while their captors wondered what to do with them. On his last leave in Austria, he had left behind several battered notebooks that had spent much of the war in his kitbag. He was glad his work hadn't been captured by the Italians, because he intended to have it published as soon as he got home. The *Tractatus Logico-Philosophicus* was ground-breaking in its field, the fruit of all Wittgenstein's intellectual musings during four years of war. He was going to dedicate it to David Pinsent.

In Munich, the Democratic and Social Republic of Bavaria had come into being overnight with fireworks in the sky and sporadic outbursts of shooting across the city, which had continued into the small hours. The king had vanished from his palace and a provisional Workers', Soldiers' and Peasants' Council had been set up in the parliament building. The newspaper that morning carried an appeal for calm from Kurt Eisner, but the shooting had begun again at first light. Several army officers had been killed at the Bayrischer Hof and there were reports of looting in the city. Soldiers had been selling their rifles and throwing their uniforms away before heading for home with no one to stop them.

In Poschingerstrasse, author Thomas Mann learned of the night's developments from his mother-in-law, who telephoned at breakfast time to find out if the family was all right. The railway station had been occupied during the night and no trains were running. There were few trams either and most shops were shut. From the garden of his house, Mann heard more gunfire during the course of the morning, while his daughter played in her pram. He had been inclined to dismiss the revolution the previous day. He realised now that it was more serious that he had first imagined.

At midday, he slipped out of the house to find out what was happening. In Pienzenauerstrasse, he read a proclamation from the new council, signed by Eisner, prohibiting looting and calling on the workers to form a civil guard. He saw soldiers waving a red flag and heard people calling the king a 'stupid bumpkin' and a 'bloodthirsty tyrant'. There was no bread in the shops, but the Manns had two days' supply at home and some flour as well, so they would be all right for a while, so long as their house wasn't looted.

Back at home, the Manns spent the afternoon preparing for the arrival of the mob, which was expected at any minute. Mann's Jewish wife Katia and his older children cleared most of the food out of the pantry and hid it in different places around the house. Mann himself prepared a little speech against the mob's arrival:

'Listen. I'm neither a Jew nor a war profiteer nor anything else that's bad. I'm a writer who has built this house with money earned by the sweat of my brow. In my drawer there are two hundred marks. Take the money and divide it between yourselves, but please don't destroy my possessions or my books.'

In the event, the mob never arrived. There was more shooting at teatime, but not as much as before. Orders were given for all bars in Munich to close at seven that night, to be followed by a curfew on the streets at nine. The new council was moving rapidly to assert its authority over the city.

Mann was happy to see order restored, but with Bruno Frank and Wilhelm Herzog sitting on the council with Eisner, he was worried that both Munich and Bavaria were now being run by Jewish journalists, a situation that clearly wouldn't last for long. Herzog, in particular, bothered him. He couldn't stand the man:

'A slimy literary hack like Herzog, who let himself be kept for years by a film actress. A moneymaker and businessman before anything else, with the big city shit-elegance of the Jew boy, who would lunch only at the Odeon Bar, but never bothered to pay Ceconi's bill for partially patching up his sewer-grate teeth. That is the revolution! The leaders are almost exclusively Jewish.'

The Jews would have been wiser to take a back seat, in Mann's view. They were only storing up trouble for themselves by overthrowing the monarchy and fomenting revolution. The German people wouldn't tolerate Jewish leaders for long, that was for sure. Men like Eisner and Herzog were too clever for their own good.

In Bayreuth, renegade Englishman Houston Chamberlain shared Mann's view of the Jews. They were the ones to blame for Germany's collapse. They were in the pay of the English, bribed to destabilise the country. Hadn't Lloyd George said that if the Germans couldn't be defeated from outside they would have to be defeated from within? It was the Jews who were doing it, funded with English gold.

Chamberlain was the nephew of Field Marshal Sir Neville Chamberlain. His own father had been a British admiral, but he himself had lived in Germany for most of his adult life. He had taken German citizenship and was married to the daughter of the composer Richard Wagner. He was in little doubt that the Germans were the greatest people on earth, a master race whose manifest destiny was to rule the rest of the world. He had said as much in his book *Die Grundlagen des neunzehnten Jahrhunderts*, which had been widely admired in Germany. The Germans very much liked this excellent English idea of the Teutonic peoples making slaves of everyone else.

But the revolution was a puzzle. Chamberlain couldn't explain what was happening in Germany unless it was the Jews who were responsible. How else could the greatest nation in the world have been defeated, if it hadn't been betrayed from within? Look at the British spies in Germany! Look at the Jews! They were the same people. The British were using the Jews to do to the Germans what they hadn't been able to do to them on the battlefield.

From the chancellery in Berlin, Prince Max had no view on the Jews but was nevertheless following the events in Munich with dismay, particularly the abrupt disappearance of King Ludwig from his palace. He was afraid the same thing would happen to the Kaiser if he didn't abdicate soon of his own accord.

Max had a report on his desk that warned of dire consequences if the Kaiser didn't step down while he still could:

'There can be no doubt that Bolshevism will for the moment get the upper hand all over the country, unless indeed the popular government is able to deploy the necessary loyal troops. And that is unthinkable until the question of the Kaiser has been dealt with. The widespread complaint: "The Kaiser is to blame!" provides common ground between the insurgents and the troops who are expected to put them down. We shall see wholesale desertions, even by troops who have proved their loyalty at the front.'

How to get through to the Kaiser? He was in Spa at the moment, surrounded by a protective bubble of elderly courtiers who never told him anything he didn't want to hear. Max's chief of staff had been on the phone to Spa repeatedly, urging the Kaiser's people to talk some sense into him. He had reminded them that the government would fall if the Kaiser didn't go, because the coalition parties were pledged to resign if he stayed. The Kaiser's people had listened, but there was little they could do. The Kaiser was determined to continue as German emperor and nothing would change his mind. He considered it his sacred duty to remain at his post.

Spa had been a watering hole before the war, a popular destination for European royalty. The Kaiser was quartered just outside the town in the Villa Fraineuse, a big old house that had once belonged to

Queen Marie Henriette of Belgium. The villa had been modified for his arrival with a bomb-proof room and an emergency exit in case he needed to leave in a hurry.

He was not a happy man as he presided over that morning's meeting with his generals in the villa's garden room. As well as the calls from the chancellery, he had a very gloomy assessment of the situation from General Gröner, just back from Berlin. Gröner's assessment was much the same as Max's, but the Kaiser did not want to hear it. He was determined not to abdicate. He owed it to his people to stay on instead and save Germany from the rising tide of Bolshevism that was threatening to engulf them all.

The Kaiser had an alternative proposal to make. While Hindenburg, Gröner and the other generals listened uneasily, he outlined it to them. Instead of abdicating, he intended to ride back to Berlin at the head of his army, recapturing on the way those cities that had gone over to Bolshevism. Once in Berlin, he planned to restore order in the capital, executing the ringleaders of the revolution and machine-gunning his own palace if necessary, if that was what it would take to restore order. Strong leadership was what Germany needed now, strong leadership above all else. The Kaiser meant to supply it.

Hindenburg and Gröner could not hide their misgivings. After four years fighting the rest of the world, the Kaiser was now proposing to turn his army on his own people. It would mean civil war if he went ahead. It was not a decision to be taken lightly.

But the Kaiser was not deterred. He knew what had to be done. As the meeting broke up, he told General Gröner to begin the necessary planning for a march on Berlin. Gröner nodded, yet without intending to do much about it. The Kaiser was living in a world of his own if he thought he could march on Berlin now.

There was a guest for lunch that day, a visiting general from Holland. An aide asked if the Kaiser wanted to put him off in the circumstances, but the Kaiser said no. Johannes van Heutsz was a former governor of the Dutch East Indies and had been in Spa since Tuesday on a fact-finding visit to German HQ. The Kaiser would be happy to meet him for lunch.

Van Heutsz was officially a representative of the Dutch army, but he was almost certainly an emissary of the Netherlands' Queen Wilhelmina as well. She and the Kaiser knew each other of old. Wilhelmina was a good sort, calm and sensible, like her people. The Kaiser had once boasted to her that he had guards in his army two metres tall. She had replied that Holland would be three metres deep if she opened the dykes. Wilhelmina had kept her country firmly out of the war, while offering her good offices to both sides in the search for peace. It had not escaped her attention that if for any reason the Kaiser decided to skip the country in a hurry, the nearest neutral border to Spa was Holland's, just twenty miles to the north.

It would be very embarrassing for Holland if he did decide to seek asylum. The Germans would come after him, calling for his head. So would the Allied powers, wanting to try him for war crimes. The last thing the Dutch needed was the Kaiser on their doorstep, seeking protection from his enemies.

That was why General van Heutsz was in Spa. He was there to sound out the Kaiser over lunch and assess his intentions. If the Kaiser was thinking of leaving for Holland any time soon, then the Dutch wanted to be the first to know about it.

Lunch was hardly over when the telephone rang again. It was Prince Max's office again, demanding the Kaiser's abdication. There was a general strike planned for Berlin the next morning, a mass demonstration of workers converging on the Reichstag in a concerted attempt to force the Kaiser's departure. The only way to prevent a revolution in Berlin was for the Kaiser to stand down voluntarily before the Bolshevists took the law into their own hands. If he did stand down, there was still a chance that the monarchy might be saved, a regency established until one of his grandsons came of age and succeeded to the throne in his place.

But the Kaiser didn't want to know. Safe in Spa, far away from the capital, surrounded by fawning courtiers, he had no intention of surrendering his throne, now or at any time. He knew his duty. It was to remain at the helm and be an inspiration to his people. There was nothing more to be said.

Exasperated, Prince Max decided to ring the Kaiser himself. At eight that evening, with an aide at his elbow taking notes, Max spoke down the line to Spa. He did not mince words. Abandoning the niceties of royal protocol, he was perfectly blunt in what he said. He spoke to his kinsman in language the Kaiser had rarely heard before:

'The advice I have sent Your Majesty by Herr von Hintze I now give you as a relative. Your abdication has become necessary to save Germany from civil war and to fulfil your mission as the peacemaking emperor till the end. The blood would be laid upon your head. The great majority of the people believe you to be responsible for the present situation. This belief is false, but it is held. If civil war and worse can be prevented through your abdication, your name will be blessed by future generations ...

'Disorders have already occurred. It might perhaps be possible at first to put them down by force, but once blood has flowed the cry for vengeance will everywhere be heard. The troops are not to be depended on. At Cologne power is in the hands of the Workers' and Soldiers' Council. At Brunswick the red flag flies from the palace. At Munich the republic has been proclaimed. At Schwerin a Workers' and Soldiers' Council is sitting. Nowhere has the army been any use. We are heading straight for civil war. I have fought hard not to admit it, but the position today is untenable. Your abdication would be received with universal relief and welcomed as a liberating and healing act.'

There was more, but the Kaiser still wasn't listening. He didn't want to hear this. Max was a weak man, far too ready to panic at the first sign of trouble. This was no time to panic, with the enemy at the gates. The Kaiser waited until Max had finished, then spoke in his turn:

'Unless you have something else in mind in Berlin, I intend to return with my troops after the Armistice has been signed. I will fire on the city if that is what has to be done.'

The Kaiser was deluding himself. Even as he spoke, Bolshevist rebels from Cologne were on their way to Spa to arrest him. They were already at Aix-la-Chapelle, only twenty miles away. A particularly reliable division sent to head them off and retake Cologne had just mutinied instead, disobeying their officers and setting off for home. The Kaiser couldn't depend on anyone any more.

While Prince Max was on the phone to the Kaiser, reinforcements were moving into Berlin, quietly taking up positions around the city in readiness for trouble the next morning. A heavily armed column of infantry and light field artillery had come in through the Halle gate and was marching towards the heart of the city. The men were veterans of the Eastern Front, tough-looking troops who had been fighting Russian revolutionaries for the past few months and were no lovers of Bolshevism. They were on their way to the Alexander barracks, where they were to stay the night before being deployed on the streets the next day.

Their arrival was welcomed by most Berliners, terrified of what the morning might bring. The revolution still hadn't reached the capital, but it was bound to arrive next day if the mass demonstration went ahead. Train services had been suspended to prevent an influx of troublemakers and the government offices on the Wilhelmstrasse had closed early as a precaution. A crowd of thousands had swirled around the Brandenburg Gate for hours, waiting idly for something to happen. From her house next but one to the gate, Princess Blücher had kept a watchful eye on them, all too aware that the Blüchers would be a prime target for attack if the mob began to riot. Even with fifty policemen based in the stables behind their house, the Blüchers had been advised to stay indoors and keep a low profile until the situation had calmed down again. It was not a good time to be upper class in Berlin.

Evelyn Blücher wouldn't have been in Berlin at all if the choice had been up to her. With four brothers in the British army – one of them killed at Ypres – and three brothers-in-law in the Royal Navy, she was English to her fingertips, the granddaughter of Lord Petre. Her husband was a descendant of the Blücher who had led the Prussians at Waterloo. They had been living in England at the outbreak of war, with every intention of remaining there for the duration. But the authorities had decided otherwise and the Blüchers had been forced to join a trainload of anglophile Germans sent home via Harwich and the Hook of Holland. They had been guaranteed safe passage across the North Sea, although no one had told the Royal Navy, which had shelled their ship, fortunately without success.

The Blüchers had been in Germany ever since, longing for an end to the war between their two countries. Evelyn yearned for a British victory, but she had plenty of sympathy for her German friends who had suffered so much for so little purpose. She had seen the Germans badly misled by their leaders, lied to that victory lay just around the corner even as the country was collapsing on all fronts. It was the leaders who were to blame for the war, not the ordinary people of Germany:

'My personal feelings of dislike and bitterness towards the men who have perpetrated so many brutal deeds during these four years is counterbalanced somewhat by sorrow for the good and brave men of this land who have sacrificed so much for false ideals, and at the sight of a great country crumbling into ruins, destroyed by the culpable ambition of a few self-seeking men. My feelings are shared even more intensely by other Englishwomen married to Germans, who are all more or less pained at the downfall of a nation which has offered so much to the world, and whose fundamental feelings and attitude towards life in general are more in harmony with our own than those of any of the Latin races.'

Evelyn Blücher belonged to an odd little coterie of Englishwomen married to Germans. Among them were the Princess Münster and the Princess Pless, Earl De La Warr's daughter, who had once startled some British prisoners on the Somme by flinging her arms around them and giving them a big hug. The three women had devoted themselves to the welfare of British prisoners of war, using whatever influence they had to ameliorate conditions in the prison camps. They had been delighted when twenty-nine British officers had managed to tunnel out of Holzminden, one of the more unpleasant camps.

They only wished the rest had done the same.

But most of Evelyn Blücher's friends were German, civilised people whose world was collapsing around them as the revolution approached the capital. Her husband had just come back from Unter den Linden, where he had seen lorry-loads of armed soldiers being driven towards the palace. The word on the street was that the Kaiser would shortly return to Berlin by train. The Socialists intended to intercept the train and take him prisoner, but without murdering him. For that at least the Blüchers could be grateful, because if the Kaiser was murdered, there was no telling which of them would be next.

At the Opera House, unbelievably amidst all the turmoil, the Royal Berlin Orchestra was giving a concert. Even as the troops moved into position, a large audience had braved the unrest on the streets to come and hear Richard Strauss conducting Beethoven's *Overture to Egmont*.

The music was carefully chosen. Beethoven had composed it to accompany Goethe's tragedy about a Dutch nobleman resisting Holland's Spanish oppressors. The nobleman died, but the play ended on an upbeat note with a triumphant celebration of freedom over adversity, a release from strife brilliantly underpinned by Beethoven's music. The score mirrored perfectly the times they were living in. Even Kurt Eisner, a noted critic as well as a Bavarian revolutionary, spoke of the *Overture* as a new beginning for mankind.

Strauss conducted with his usual panache. He was calm, almost nonchalant in his movements, with none of the exhibitionism of lesser conductors. Outside, soldiers with machine guns stood guard along Unter den Linden, but inside all was perfectly civilised as Strauss presided with his customary composure. The audience was appreciative, savouring the moment while it lasted. Whatever else happened in Germany, the Germans would always have their music. No one could take that away from them. The Germans had the best music in the world.

No Wagner, though. Not just now.

*

At the front line, Captain von Helldorf still hadn't managed to cross to the German side with the Armistice terms. He had waited almost five hours in the dark, while messages flew in all directions, but still his own people wouldn't let him through. They continued to ignore bugle calls and white flags, blazing away indiscriminately at anything that moved. There wasn't a thing Helldorf could do about it except sit helplessly and wait, hoping that someone, somewhere would knock some sense into his compatriots before the deadline expired and his mission was over before it had even begun.

At Compiègne, General von Winterfeldt was considering alternative arrangements in case Helldorf couldn't get through. If the worst came to the worst, the details might have to be taken by air. Captain Hermann Geyer, the Germans' other interpreter, could take them with a French pilot. The plane would have to carry two white streamers as identification markers to prevent it being shot down. One way or another, they would get the Armistice terms through to Spa. It beggared belief that they hadn't managed to do so already.

At Spa itself, General Gröner was working on the Kaiser's plan for a march back to Berlin after the Armistice. He had sent out orders summoning fifty senior officers for a meeting next morning. The officers had been chosen from a representative sample of the troops still in the field. Hindenburg was going to explain the situation to them and ask what they thought of the Kaiser's proposal. It could not succeed without the support of the soldiers under their command.

As midnight passed and Friday turned to Saturday, all fifty officers were on their way to Spa, struggling along the bad roads in the dark. They had been given no reason for the summons. Most assumed that they had been ordered to headquarters to discuss the possibility of an Armistice. They would have been surprised to learn that they had been summoned instead to discuss the Kaiser's ambitions for retaining his throne after the war was over.

CHAPTER SIX

Saturday, 9 November 1918

While the officers struggled through the dark, Field Marshal von Hindenburg lay awake in his room, unable to get to sleep. He slept well as a rule, but the light in his room was seen to go on and off many times as he tossed and turned, wrestling with the problem of the Kaiser's abdication. Hindenburg was no great admirer of the Kaiser, but he remained a fervent monarchist. For him the emperor of Germany was still 'All Highest' or 'Most Gracious Kaiser, King and Lord'. He would rather die than see the emperor step down and Germany become a ramshackle collection of independent republics.

Yet even he was beginning to wonder how much longer the Kaiser could go on, with the home front in turmoil and the fighting troops no longer to be trusted. Much against his will, he was coming round to the view that the Kaiser might indeed have to abdicate for his own safety, if not the greater good of the country.

It was a bitter pill for Hindenburg to swallow. He had been with the German empire from the very beginning. As a young Guards officer, he had been at Sedan in 1870, watching from his horse as Napoleon III was taken prisoner from the battlefield in a cloud of dust. He had been at Versailles for the formal proclamation of the German empire a few weeks later, saluting the new Kaiser in the Hall of Mirrors while soldiers from all parts of Germany did homage to their liege lord. And he had been with the army when it entered Paris, riding down the Champs Elysées with a hussar friend while the French looked the other way and pretended they hadn't seen anything.

Hindenburg had also been in Paris for the Commune, the first stirrings of Bolshevism as the defeated French turned on each other and fought to establish a new social order. There had been no quarter on either side as the French tore into one another. Hindenburg had watched from a hotel window in St Denis while government troops surrounded Montmartre and stormed the rebel stronghold, bayoneting their own people with far more ferocity than they had ever displayed on the battlefield. He had seen a nation destroyed by civil war and the memory had haunted him ever since. Hindenburg was terrified the same thing was about to happen to Germany.

He rose early after his restless night. He was due to address the officers summoned by General Gröner at nine that morning. He wanted a private word with Gröner first, to tell him that he had changed his mind about the Kaiser's abdication.

Gaunt and red-eyed, Hindenburg found Gröner in his office. He told him not only that the Kaiser should go, but that he should probably flee the country at once to avoid becoming a hostage or worse. They must tell him so when they saw him later that morning.

Gröner was shocked at the volte-face. He was coming round to the same view himself, but he was surprised at Hindenburg. The old warhorse had always been adamant that the Kaiser had to stay. Now he was saying he had to go. In effect, Hindenburg had taken the momentous decision to put his duty to his country before his allegiance to his monarch. It was a seismic event.

Gröner would have liked to discuss it, but now was not the moment. The army officers had arrived for the meeting at the Hôtel Britannique and were waiting for Hindenburg in the dining room. In the event, only thirty-nine of the fifty had made it in time. The rest had been held up on the way, delayed by the chaos on the roads as the front collapsed and the Germans retreated all along the line.

The officers all stood up as Hindenburg entered the room. He was a legendary figure to most of them, the victor of Tannenberg. They listened intently as he gave them a swift rundown of the situation, beginning with the revolution breaking out all over Germany, of which they knew little, and moving on to the demands for the Kaiser's abdication. He told them that the Kaiser proposed to march back to Berlin with his army, a journey that would take two or three weeks at least since the railways couldn't be relied on any more. The supply problem would be enormous and there would be trouble with the Bolshevists along the way. Hindenburg did not say what he thought of the plan, but his silence spoke volumes.

The picture he had painted was so depressing that nobody could think of a thing to say when he had finished. Instead, there was 'a silence as of a tomb; not a word, not a whisper', punctuated only by one of the Kaiser's aides dabbing his eyes with his handkerchief.

Hindenburg didn't linger long. He and Gröner were due at the Villa Fraineuse for their meeting with the Kaiser. In their place, they deputed a staff officer to conduct a poll of the thirty-nine officers and ask them two key questions on the basis of what they had just heard. The first was: 'Would it be possible for the Kaiser to regain control of Germany by force of arms, at the head of his troops?' The second: 'Would the troops march against the Bolshevists in Germany?' On the answers to those two questions would the future of the monarchy depend.

While the officers mulled over their responses, Hindenburg and Gröner drove the one and a half miles to the Villa Fraineuse. They didn't speak during the journey. Hindenburg was in the grip of deep emotion, struggling to get a hold of himself as he went to meet his Kaiser. He knew what had to be done, but he wasn't looking forward to being there when the Kaiser was told to his face that he had to abdicate because his beloved army was no longer loyal to him. It was more than Hindenburg could bear.

The Kaiser was waiting for them in the villa's garden room. He had had more bad news from Berlin overnight: telegrams announcing the deposition of various German kings and grand dukes and warning him that the country was about to find itself without a chancellor or a government. Having ordered General Gröner to begin the preparations for the march back to Germany, the Kaiser was hoping to hear from him that the situation was well in hand and they would soon be on their way to Berlin to put the situation to rights. But something in the generals' faces told him it wasn't so.

The Kaiser asked for a report. Hindenburg began to speak, but couldn't find the words. With tears in his eyes, he made a veiled request to resign instead. As a Prussian officer, bound by centuries of military tradition as a vassal to his liege lord, he couldn't stand in front of the Kaiser and tell him to abdicate. It wasn't something a Prussian could legitimately do.

Gröner could, though. He wasn't Prussian. Quietly and unemotionally, he told the Kaiser that a march back to Germany was out of the question. It wasn't a case of suppressing an insurrection any more. There would be civil war if the Kaiser tried to lead his troops back to Germany. With much of the Rhineland in Bolshevist hands, the fighting would begin as soon as he crossed the border.

Gröner didn't say what the Kaiser should do instead. He was very careful not to mention abdication. But it was obvious from what he had said that abdication was the Kaiser's only remaining course. There was nothing else left.

Other officers disagreed. General Friedrich von der Schulenburg, who had arrived at Spa that morning, challenged Gröner's analysis, arguing that the situation could still be retrieved. He insisted that the Kaiser could still go home at the head of his troops, restoring order city by city. People would rally to him, once they knew he was coming.

That was what the Kaiser wanted to hear. He perked up as Schulenburg spoke. But Gröner wasn't having it. He had come to the villa to tell the Kaiser the truth and that was what he was going to do. Facing up to the Kaiser, he gave it to him straight:

'Sire, you no longer have an army. The army will return to Germany as an organised force under the orders of its generals, but not under those of Your Majesty. The army is no longer with Your Majesty.'

There was a sharp intake of breath around the room at Gröner's words. Nobody ever spoke to the Kaiser like that. Outraged, he struggled for a moment to control himself. 'The Kaiser's eyes flashed with anger and his body stiffened', according to one of his courtiers. Then he turned on Gröner in fury:

'I shall require that statement from you in writing, confirmed by all my army commanders. Have they not taken the military oath to me?'

Gröner shrugged. Schulenburg took him to task, insisting that no German soldier of any rank would desert the Kaiser in the face of the enemy. It was unthinkable that a German soldier would disgrace himself like that.

But Gröner remained unmoved. He knew where the truth lay. 'I have other information,' he replied stonily.

Even as he spoke, there was a telephone call from Berlin to say that the troops in the capital had deserted and the situation was completely out of hand.

The Naumburg jägers had gone first, the ones who had marched in through the Halle gate the night before. At a meeting that morning they had queried their orders, asking what they were doing in Berlin. They weren't prepared to shoot at their own people, if that was why they had been brought in. If there was to be a mass demonstration that day, the Naumburgers would rather join forces with the demonstrators than fire on them. They weren't in the army to gun down their own kind.

The jägers at Kupfergraben barracks had gone next and then the men guarding the Kaiser's palace. They were all refusing to move against the demonstration, asserting that they would mutiny against their officers before they opened fire on the people. The remainder of the Berlin garrison had followed, the Northern Reserve, the Jüterbog artillery and the rest, all of them taking their cue from the jägers and refusing to bear arms against the people. It was their duty to avert civil war by supporting the people instead.

The demonstration itself was still in the early stages, thousands of factory workers gathering in the northern suburbs and forming up for a march on the city centre. Some were Bolshevists and some were Social Democrats, but most were just fed up with the war, determined that the Kaiser must go if that was the only way to bring it to an end. An ultimatum for his abdication had already expired with no word from Spa. If the Kaiser wouldn't step down of his own accord, then the workers would take matters into their own hands and force him to go. Long columns of them were beginning to move towards the city centre, headed by a mass of women and children bearing placards saying 'Brothers, don't shoot!' The demonstrators were not looking for violence, but they were quietly resigned to it if violence couldn't be avoided. They could see no other way of bringing the nightmare to an end.

At his desk in the chancellery, Prince Max learned of the soldiers' defection with dismay. He had been afraid it might happen. His people had been on the telephone to Spa repeatedly since breakfast, insisting that the Kaiser's abdication couldn't be put off any longer. It wasn't a matter of hours any more, but minutes. Max had to have the Kaiser's decision at once if he was to save Berlin from revolution.

The Kaiser's staff had responded by continually promising that a decision was imminent. The Kaiser was still thinking it over, working out his best course of action. 'Events are taking their course,' they kept telling Berlin. 'You must wait a little.' There would be an answer by and by.

But Max couldn't wait any longer. Tens of thousands of protesters were coming his way, all of them prepared for violence if there was no alternative. There would be fighting in the streets if he didn't take action now. People would be killed outside his window. He had to have an answer at once or it would all be too late.

While Berlin trembled, Matthias Erzberger and the other German delegates were spending a fraught morning aboard their train in the Compiègne forest, putting their objections to the Armistice terms in writing. It was a laborious exercise, but they had little else to do until they received a response from the government in Berlin.

The good news was that Captain von Helldorf had managed to cross the German lines at last. According to German radio, he had crossed safely in the night and was on his way to Spa with the Armistice details. The Germans were claiming that it had been an exploding ammunition dump that had delayed him, not his own people firing at him.

For the moment, though, there wasn't much happening at Compiègne. The German delegates were having one-to-one discussions with their opposite numbers, but the discussions didn't take long and the Allied representatives still had plenty of time on their hands. Once they had read the newspapers and gone for a walk in the woods, there was nothing else to do except stand around and talk. Admiral Wemyss decided on a sightseeing trip instead.

Taking a car, he drove to Soissons. The French had recaptured the town in August after heavy fighting. Wemyss was expecting devastation, but nothing he had heard prepared him for the reality:

'Truly a dreadful sight – not one single house is habitable. The cathedral is literally torn in two. Going through the streets gave one the impression of visiting Pompeii.'

Clause nineteen of the Armistice terms dealt with the payment of reparations for war damage. It was clearly going to be a very large item.

South of Cadiz, a British battleship was on her way to Gibraltar. Surrounded by a protective screen of destroyers, HMS *Britannia* was making steady progress down the southern coast of Spain. Another few hours and she would anchor in the bay at Gibraltar, her crew tidying themselves up and trooping down the gangway for some well-earned leave ashore. After a long time at sea, and with the end of the war in sight, they were greatly looking forward to spending some time ashore.

Ahead of them, just coming up on the port side, they could see the distant outline of Cape Trafalgar, scene of the most famous naval action in British history. The cape was an emotive sight to the men of the *Britannia*. There had been a *Britannia* in Nelson's fleet, sailing three ships behind HMS *Victory* in the dash for the French line. As they saw Cape Trafalgar now, so had their predecessors in 1805. The French had been routed at Trafalgar and Britannia had ruled the waves ever since, the ships of the Royal Navy keeping the peace across the oceans of the world for more than a hundred trouble-free years.

The Germans had done their best to challenge the Royal Navy in 1916, but to no avail. The Battle of Jutland might have been hailed as a German victory if the German fleet hadn't scuttled back into harbour immediately afterwards and never come out again. The Royal Navy had continued to rule the waves, seeing off the U-boat menace and maintaining an ever-tighter blockade of North Sea ports, quietly throttling the German economy until the Germans no longer had the raw materials to continue the struggle. The British army had stopped the Germans on the Western Front, but it was the Royal Navy that had deprived them of the means to fight.

Now HMS *Britannia* was steaming south, heading past Trafalgar as the sun came up over the Spanish hills. She was a distinctive sight as she ploughed through the water, with close-set funnels and big gun turrets at the corners of the superstructure. Her destroyers sailed with her, proud to be part of her battle group, proud to be sailing past Trafalgar with all the connotations of courage and good seamanship that the name implied. The war was won and the destroyers belonged to what was still the finest navy in the world. Everyone aboard knew it. The king's ships were at sea.

From the periscope of U-boat 50, Kapitanleutnant Heinrich Kukat studied the *Britannia*'s unusual superstructure and knew that he was looking at a pre-Dreadnought battleship of the King Edward VII class. She would make a good target if he could get past her destroyer escort. Kukat gave the word and the submarine slipped carefully forward, manoeuvring into position for a crack at the British battleship.

It had been a difficult few days for the men of U-50. They had been at the far end of the Mediterranean when Germany's Turkish allies had stopped fighting, followed soon afterwards by the Austrians. With no friends in the Med any more, they had been ordered to make the long voyage back to Kiel, with instructions to seek internment in Spain if Kiel proved impossible. They had slipped through the Strait of Gibraltar the previous night, terrified that the Royal Navy would catch them on the surface and sink them before they had a chance to crash-dive. Now they were submerged off Cape Trafalgar and there was HMS *Britannia* in their sights, creaming forward with her destroyers as the sun came up on a new day.

U-50 fired three torpedoes. One missed, but the other two struck home. The *Britannia* stopped dead in the water, but remained afloat. When Kukat raised his periscope to see what was happening, the *Britannia* turned her guns on him, blasting the sea all around until the submarine was forced to dive again and slink away underwater.

It took the *Britannia* three hours to go down. Her destroyers came alongside and took the crew off before the end. About fifty died. Some of them were buried in the naval cemetery at Gibraltar, just as their predecessors had been in 1805.

On land, the British were faring rather better as Canadian troops advanced further into Belgium. The Canadians had already taken Valenciennes and Jemappes and were moving up through the outskirts towards the big coal town of Mons, marching past places that the British hadn't seen since the beginning of the war. Tomorrow or the next day, Mons would fall and the town from which Britain's 'contemptibly little' army had so famously retreated in 1914 would be in Allied hands once again. It was good to be back.

The Canadians had had a wonderful hundred days since the beginning of August. They had done nothing but go forward since the big breakthrough at Amiens, chasing the Hun from one place to the next and pushing ever onward with little to stop them. They had faced up to the worst that the Germans could do to them and had acquitted themselves with distinction. The Canadians knew it and were proud of it. In their eyes, Great Britain was the mother country and they were her lion cubs. They had given the old country every reason to be proud of them since their arrival in France.

The Canadians had a distinguished visitor attached to their headquarters as they went forward. Edward, Prince of Wales, was a young Grenadier officer, banned from the front line in case the Germans took him prisoner, but following the war as closely as his position as heir to the throne allowed. He had been with the Canadians for almost a month during the advance, visiting different units every day and witnessing mounds of German dead on the battlefield. He had had a good time and was sorry that his stint with the Canadians was almost up. 'I like these old Canadians more and more the longer I'm with them and they are all so nice to me and so easy to get on with … I don't think I've spent such a pleasant month since the war started.'

But the war wasn't over yet. The Germans were still contesting the ground as the Canadians advanced. As his platoon approached Mons, Captain Charles Smith, an Iroquois Indian from Cayuga, near Niagara Falls, spotted a party of Germans preparing to detonate a road mine before the Canadians arrived. Smith led the charge and overwhelmed the Germans just as they were igniting the fuse.

Shortly afterwards, he personally captured a German machine gun as well, a spectacular double for which he was later awarded the Military Cross. The medal came just in time for Smith, because his elder brother already had an MC from the Somme. Their father, a Six Nations chief in Ontario, would be delighted to learn that the second of his warrior sons now had the same medal for gallantry as the first.

On the Belgian coast, Howard Vincent O'Brien, an artillery officer attached to US intelligence, was on his way to the newly liberated town of Ostend. With the enemy in full retreat, the Americans were worried that German agents might slip across the Dutch border into Belgium to make trouble during the Armistice negotiations. O'Brien had been sent to assess the threat and report back to American HQ.

He and his men had left Calais early that morning and were in Dunkirk by 10 o'clock. With rumours of an imminent end to the war, O'Brien was hoping that their journey would prove unnecessary, but although they inquired at every stop, nobody had any news of an Armistice. They continued into Belgium along the coast road and were soon driving through country that had recently been occupied by the Germans. O'Brien's notes on the journey made sobering reading:

'Stark bones of what once were homes, tumbled about, and fields looking as if giant had stamped on them, and spit afterward. Country of marshes and shattered footbridges and rusty barbed wire, marking furthest advance of German civilisation. Miles without sign of life, human, animal, or vegetable. Silence that weighed like heavy pack. Marvelled that man could ever have lived there, let alone fight for four years ...

'Many stories of German occupation. Holes in shoes mark of distinction for female Belges. Not honourable to be well dressed. Too many – *caractère légère* – whose first dislike of Hun had somewhat abated ... such had not wanted for shoes. Boche trickery. Sent his own planes to bomb Ostend and blamed it on British. Fake exposed by discovery of unexploded Boche bomb.'

After several stops on the way, it was seven in the evening by the time O'Brien and his companions actually reached Ostend. They found the town still reeling from the German occupation:

'Little chambermaid, extremely pretty, acted scared as rabbit. Landlady explained – no reason to feel comfortable in presence of officers, and we first Americans town had seen ... Pathetic how cowed everybody is, particularly women. Frankly astonished at our mild demeanour.'

Happily, the Belgians soon began to relax. They all had stories to tell and were longing to do so now that they were free again. A waiter in the hotel dining room pointed out a broken mirror on the wall and told O'Brien that a German soldier had shot it up just for fun. Others added that the Germans had looted everything of value before they left, stealing furniture, rugs and pictures and sending it all back to Germany in packing cases. They had even taken the door knobs and the brass fittings on the wall, all the mattresses, everything they could carry. The worst offender had been the German military commander, a prince of royal blood who should have known better. He had taken everything he wanted and sent home trainloads of paintings and crockery for his personal use.

O'Brien was struck, too, by the way everyone hurried to salute him when he appeared, civilians hastily doffing their caps, as required by the Boche. The German invaders had thought nothing of putting people in prison for not showing them enough respect. But they had won little respect from the Belgians over the past four years. All they had done instead was make enemies of them for a lifetime to come.

At Spa, the results of the officers' poll had been delivered to the Villa Fraineuse. Only about thirty of the thirty-nine officers had been interviewed so far, but a strong consensus had already emerged. The Kaiser had no chance of regaining control of Germany at the head of his troops. Nor would the troops march against the Bolshevists at home. It was the end of the line for the Kaiser, so far as his army was concerned.

There was a long pause after the findings had been announced. Then the Kaiser asked gloomily if the army would return to Germany in good order without him. Gröner had no doubt that it would, but Schulenburg disagreed. A third officer thought that the army would certainly go home in good order and would be happy for the Kaiser to come too, provided that he was no longer in command and didn't require them to do any more fighting.

While they were discussing it, the telephone rang. It was Prince Max's office again, demanding the Kaiser's abdication. Max was adamant that if he didn't have the Kaiser's abdication within the next few minutes, Berlin would fall to the revolution.

Reluctantly, 'his lips pinched and bloodless, his face pale, as though he had aged in a moment by several years', the Kaiser bowed to the inevitable. He told his officials to prepare a statement indicating that he was ready to abdicate as emperor of Germany if it was absolutely necessary in order to avert civil war, adding that he intended to remain king of Prussia. He would hand command of the German army to Hindenburg if he did abdicate, but would himself remain with his Prussian troops. It wasn't all that Max had asked for, but it was as much as the Kaiser was prepared to concede. Having made the decision, he left the details to his officials and went off bitterly to lunch.

While the Kaiser continued to procrastinate, the revolution in Berlin was fast approaching the city centre. Upwards of a hundred thousand

protesters were converging on the government and Reichstag buildings, with more arriving every minute. Instead of blocking their path,
the soldiers brought in to stop them were reversing their weapons to
show that they wouldn't fire, then joining in the march. There was no
stopping the revolution now that it had started.

At the chancellery, Prince Max could wait no longer for the
Kaiser. He knew, even if they didn't in Spa, that the Kaiser's abdication must be announced at once if he was to avoid the humiliation
of being publicly deposed. When no word came from Spa, Max took
matters into his own hands. He issued a press release to the Wolff
telegraph agency announcing the Kaiser's immediate abdication, as
both emperor of Germany and king of Prussia. Max added that the
crown prince would relinquish all rights to the succession, and that
he himself would resign the chancellorship in favour of the populist
Friedrich Ebert of the Social Democrat Party as soon as the abdication had been effected.

Max issued the press release without consulting the Kaiser. The
Wolff agency published it at once and the news was on the streets by
lunchtime.

At the Villa Fraineuse, the Kaiser's officials did not complete the
drafting of his abdication as emperor until two in the afternoon.
After the Kaiser had reluctantly signed it, Admiral von Hintze went
to telephone the text to Berlin, only to discover that he was too late.
Prince Max's press release had already gone out. The Hohenzollerns
had been consigned to history.

Appalled, Hintze asked for the Kaiser to come from the drawing
room. The news was broken to him in private. Then Count Hans von
Gontard broke it to everyone else, breathing heavily as he did so, 'his
teeth chattering as though in a cold sweat, and with tears streaming
down his cheeks'.

The Kaiser reacted with predictable fury. 'It's a betrayal!' he
ranted. 'A shameless, disgraceful betrayal!' He didn't know who
was behind the press release, but he could guess. It was obviously
the work of Prince Max. No one else could have authorised such an

announcement. It was Max who had done this to him. His own kins-man stabbing him in the back!

The Kaiser wasn't going to stand for it, that was for sure. Reaching for a telegram pad, he immediately began to draft a rebuttal. He hadn't abdicated, at least not as king of Prussia. Max had no right to put the words in his mouth. The Kaiser would issue a reply announcing that he was still legally king and intended to remain so, despite what had been said in the press release.

He was supported by Count Schulenburg. 'It's a *coup d'état*,' Schulenburg told him. 'Your Majesty must not yield to such an act of violence.' The count thought the Kaiser should go at once to his army and stay with them. He would be unassailable if he was with his army. No one could depose him there.

Other advisers were not so sure. For better or worse, the news of the Kaiser's abdication was already on its way around the world. It would be almost impossible to retract now that it was in the public domain.

The Kaiser abandoned the telegram pad after a while, retiring instead to an armchair by the fire. He sat silently smoking cigarette after cigarette while he struggled to come to terms with what had happened. No longer an emperor, not even a king any more. It took a while to get used to.

At 3 o'clock he roused himself and announced what had to be done. The villa was to be prepared for a siege. It was to be stocked with arms and ammunition, food, water, mattresses, everything necessary for a prolonged confrontation. The men of the Kaiser's guard battalion were to be billeted in neighbouring houses, ready to fight to the last man in defence of their monarch. If the Bolshevists at Aix-la-Chapelle were coming to get him, or the revolutionaries from Berlin, or even the soldiers in Spa who were said to be wavering, the Kaiser would go down fighting at the head of his personal troops. Much better that than surrender meekly to his fate, as everyone seemed to want him to do.

A while later, he was quietly told that not even the Kaiser's guard battalion could be relied on any more. The officers could no longer guarantee the loyalty of their men.

*

From their house just north of the Brandenburg Gate, Princess
Blücher and her husband had watched all morning as carloads of
soldiers and sailors drove past and the crowds gathered for the demonstration in the centre of Berlin. The Blüchers had stayed indoors,
expecting trouble at any moment, but it wasn't until after lunch that
the pace began to hot up:

'At about 2 o'clock a perfect avalanche of humanity began to
stream by our windows, walking quietly enough, many of them carrying red flags. I noticed the pale gold of young girls' uncovered heads,
as they passed by with only a shawl over their shoulders. It seemed
so feminine and incongruous, under the folds of those gruesome red
banners flying over them. One can never imagine these pale northern
women helping to build up barricades and screaming and raging for
blood.'

The news of the Kaiser's abdication was already on the streets.
The Blüchers had heard it from their butler, who had rushed in after
lunch to tell them. Despite her dislike of him, Evelyn Blücher couldn't
help feeling sorry for the Kaiser now that he was finally going. But
her feelings didn't appear to be shared by the crowd outside. From
what she could see, the mob was delighted to be rid of the emperor at
last.

'There could hardly have been a greater air of rejoicing had
Germany gained a great victory. More and more people came hurrying by, thousands of them densely packed together – men, women,
soldiers, sailors, and, strangely enough, a never-ceasing fringe of children playing on the edges of this dangerous maelstrom, and enjoying
it seemingly very much, as if it had been some public fete day ...

'In between the dense masses of the marching throng, great
military motor lorries, packed with soldiers and sailors waving red
flags and cheering and shouting vehemently, forced their way, the
occupants apparently trying to stir up the strikers to violence. A char-
acteristic feature of the mob was the motors packed with youths in
field-grey uniform or in civil clothes, carrying loaded rifles adorned
with a tiny red flag, constantly springing off their seats and forcing

the soldiers and officers to tear off their insignia, or doing it for them if they refused.

'They were mostly boys of from sixteen to eighteen years of age, who looked as if they were enjoying their sudden power immensely, and sat grinning on the steps of the grey motors like schoolboys out on an escapade. This, however, did not prevent their occasioning a good deal of harm in the course of the day, for of course some officers refused to obey them, which led to bloodshed and even death.'

Evelyn Blücher calculated that something like two hundred lorry-loads of young men had passed her house during the course of the demonstration. She had had all the doors of the house locked and the metal blinds over the windows pulled down, except for one ground-floor window from which she watched everything that was going on. By mid-afternoon, the street outside the house was full of people frantically shouting and gesticulating. Among the passers-by, she also noticed a lorry-load of newly released French and Russian prisoners, vigorously waving the red flag alongside their German comrades.

'We were not a little alarmed, for we knew that if the Germans began fraternising with the prisoners and liberating them, we may at any moment have a dangerous rabble of some two million Russians let loose on us, who in their underfed condition would stop short at nothing. The strangest and most disagreeable feeling of all was that nobody knew definitely what was happening and what was the meaning of it all.

'Everyone seemed to be steering for Unter den Linden and Pariser Platz, and as the afternoon wore on we heard that an attack was being made on the royal palace. The great Brandenburg Gate was soon covered with climbers who succeeded in hoisting the red flag on it, and in front of the Adlon Hotel machine guns were placed, and the mob went in forcing the officers there to tear off their badges. The revolutionists robbed the soldiers of their arms, and strutted about with them to the constant danger of the passers-by.'

At the Reichstag, just up the road, Philipp Scheidemann was well aware of the danger as the mob surged towards the parliament building. His Social Democrat colleague Friedrich Ebert had just replaced Prince Max as chancellor, pending an election after the signing of the Armistice. The transfer of power had been swift and smooth, designed to ensure a minimum of disruption in the turbulent days that were bound to follow the Kaiser's departure and the end of the war. Max was already preparing to leave Berlin that night.

But a mob coming towards the Reichstag was a different matter altogether. The big worry was that the Bolshevists would not respect a handover of power to the Social Democrats. Despite Max's press release, Germany was not yet a republic. Max had been careful to leave the door open for a regency to benefit one of the Kaiser's grandsons in due course. But the Bolshevists did not want a regency. They wanted a Bolshevist republic and they wanted it that afternoon.

Scheidemann and Ebert were having lunch in the Reichstag when word came that the Bolshevist Karl Liebknecht, a former Social Democrat now prominent in the Spartacus League, was about to declare a republic from the balcony of the Kaiser's palace at the other end of the Linden. Tens of thousands of people were waiting there to hear him. Tens of thousands were also waiting outside the Reichstag to hear Ebert and Scheidemann.

Ebert didn't want to talk to them, but Scheidemann could never resist an audience. Shoving aside his potato soup, he hurried down the corridor into the Reichstag's library. The windows looked out on to a seething mass of people waving red banners and calling out his name. It seemed to Scheidemann that they were determined to have a republic and would follow whoever gave it to them. 'The man who can bring the Bolshies from the palace to the Reichstag or the Social Democrats from the Reichstag to the palace wins the day', was how he later explained it to colleagues.

Scheidemann decided that he was the man. It was important for the Social Democrats to get in before the Bolshevists if they wanted to retain control of the revolution. Without consulting anyone, he stepped to the open window and held up his hands for silence. When the crowd had quietened down, he launched into one of the stirring off-the-cuff speeches that were his trademark. The words quickly ran away with him:

'Workers and soldiers ... the cursed war is at an end ... the people have triumphed ... Prince Max of Baden has handed over his office as chancellor to Ebert. Our friend will form a workers' government ... miracles have happened ... the old and rotten has broken down ... long live the new! Long live the German republic!'

While Scheidemann milked the applause, horrified deputies ran back into the Reichstag to say that the wretched man had just proclaimed a republic. Scheidemann later claimed that he hadn't meant it literally, but the damage was done. There was no going back now. When Scheidemann returned to his soup, feeling rather pleased with himself after his ovation, Chancellor Ebert banged the table in a rage and told him that he had had no right to declare a republic when the matter had yet to be decided. It was for the forthcoming constituent assembly to do it, if it was to be done at all, not some rabble-rousing politician acting off his own bat.

Karl Liebknecht was not to be outdone. Later that afternoon he, too, declared Germany a republic. With a red blanket serving as a flag behind him, he addressed a rapturous crowd from the balcony of the Kaiser's palace. After spending two years in prison for opposing the war, Liebknecht had been waiting a long time for this moment:

'The day of the revolution has come. We have enforced peace. Peace has been concluded in this moment. The old order has gone. The rule of the Hohenzollerns, who have resided in this palace for centuries, is over ...

'Today an incalculable mass of inspired proletarians stands in this very place to pay homage to the liberty newly gained. Party comrades, I proclaim the Free Socialist Republic of Germany, which shall include all tribes, where there are no servants, where every honest worker will receive his honest pay. The rule of capitalism, which has turned Europe into a cemetery, is broken.'

The proletarians took Liebknecht at his word. Within minutes, they had stormed the palace and were in the Kaiser's private apartments, rifling through his personal possessions. They took everything of his that they could lay their hands on – silver, plate, horses, carriages, motor cars, even the Kaiserin's dresses – and bore it away in triumph. The revolution wouldn't have been Bolshevist without some serious looting.

At supreme headquarters, Hindenburg and the other generals were wondering what to do with the Kaiser now that he had involuntarily abdicated. With soldiers setting up soviets at Spa, and revolutionaries said to be advancing from Verviers, less than ten miles away, they had no time to waste if they wanted to get him away safely. They couldn't even guarantee his security at Spa for another night.

Holland was the obvious destination for the Kaiser. Only twenty miles as the crow flies. If he cooperated, they could have him across the border in no time, safe at last from his myriad enemies.

Hindenburg, Gröner, von Hintze and a couple of others went to see the Kaiser as it was growing dark. They found him still determined to remain as king of Prussia, although he accepted that the days of empire were over. 'You no longer have a warlord,' he told Gröner stiffly, before turning away and pointedly ignoring the Württemberger. The Kaiser was never going to forgive Gröner for his plain speaking that morning.

He ranted for a long time, thumping the table, cursing Prince Max for his treachery, insisting that he was still king and intended to stay on, come what may. He kept repeating his intention to remain as king. He was hoping his generals would give him some encouragement, as they always had in the past, but this time none of them did. It was far too late for any of that. Prince Max's press release had done for the Kaiser, whether he liked it or not. The generals' priority now was to get the Kaiser to safety before the Bolshevists caught up with him.

Hindenburg was the one to tell him. The old man had played only a minor role in the day's proceedings so far, preferring to leave it to others to do what had to be done. Now, though, he told the Kaiser that the army wasn't strong enough to defeat the revolution. He said that the Kaiser would almost certainly be taken to Berlin as a prisoner and handed over to a revolutionary government if he didn't make his escape now. Hindenburg's advice to him was to accept the abdication and proceed at once to Holland while he still had the chance.

The Kaiser remained unconvinced. Not all of his generals thought he should go to Holland. After a great deal more discussion, he went off to consult his aides-de-camp, obsequious men who wouldn't give him any grief. He spent some time with them before retreating in deep gloom to his private quarters. He seemed suicidal to some observers. Bracing themselves, they half-expected to hear a single gunshot through the wall. But no gunshot came. The Kaiser wasn't about to shoot himself. In his own mind, if nobody else's, he was still king of Prussia, and kings of Prussia didn't take their own lives. It was too demeaning.

In London, it was the day of the Lord Mayor's Show, the annual procession from the Guildhall to the Royal Courts of Justice, where the new mayor customarily took the oath of allegiance to the sovereign. There had been a similar procession every year since at least 1378 and probably long before. The mayor travelled in the traditional gilded coach, built for the purpose after the incumbent of 1710 had been unseated from his horse by a drunken flower girl.

The mayor wore the traditional robes of office for the journey and was escorted by the traditional pikemen and representatives of the City's twelve great livery companies: the mercers, grocers, drapers, skinners and haberdashers, and all the rest. There were military bands in the procession, troops from all parts of the empire, flying-boats mounted on lorries and a giant sausage balloon flying above St Paul's. The troops marched ceremonially through the streets, celebrating an annual rite of passage that nothing in British history had ever prevented: not plague, not fire, and certainly not a world war. The British clung most fiercely to their traditions in time of war. It would be a victory for the enemy if they didn't.

That night, there was a second ceremony at the Guildhall. The Lord Mayor's Banquet was almost as old as the procession, a traditional feast to honour the outgoing mayor. By long-standing custom, the principal speaker was always the prime minister, delivering a keynote address on foreign affairs to an audience of City businessmen. Lloyd George had already arrived for it and was clearly in a good mood, shaking hands with everybody and winking at his friends as he mingled with the guests. The news of the Kaiser's abdication had been greeted with delight in the City. As they made their way to their tables, the guests were all excitedly wondering if Lloyd George would top it with a second, even more welcome announcement: the Armistice. Showman that he was, the prime minister would undoubtedly want to pull that rabbit out of his hat if he was able to. It would round off a perfect day.

Unfortunately for the City, Lloyd George had no Armistice to give them. He would have loved to have announced it in the Guildhall, to thunderous applause from all sides, but there was still no word from Compiègne. He confessed as much when he stood up to speak:

'As a fairly accustomed speaker, I dislike intensely letting my audience down, but if I have to do so I like to get it over quickly. I have no news for you. Owing to the rapid and temporarily inconvenient advance of the Allied troops and their relentless pursuit, the German envoys have not been able to get through and other means have had to be devised for enabling them to cross the lines.

'I may perhaps have news tomorrow, but the issues are already settled. In the spring we were being sorely pressed. Our Channel ports were threatened, and the enemy's steel was pointed at our heart. It is now autumn. Constantinople is almost within gunfire; Austria is shattered and broken; the Kaiser and the crown prince have abdicated, and a successor has not been found – a regency has been proclaimed.

'This is the greatest judgement in history. Germany has a choice today; she will have none tomorrow. She is ruined inside and outside. There is only one way to avoid destruction – immediate surrender. We must bear in mind that the German people consented to Germany's reckless wantonness – our terms will prevent a recurrence of them.

'We do no wrong if we abandon no right. We have no designs

against the German people, but we mean to secure freedom for our own people. The empire was never higher in the world's councils. We would be unwise if we forgot that we must impose justice – divine justice, which is the foundation of civilisation, must be satisfied. We do not seek a yard of real German soil – we are not going to repeat the folly of 1870.'

The speech was rapturously received. Armistice or not, the Kaiser had gone and the Germans were beaten. It was a vast improvement on the same occasion a year earlier.

In Berlin, there were sporadic outbreaks of shooting after dark as the demonstrators celebrated the departure of the Kaiser and the birth of the new republic. Rival groups fought each other outside the palace, and at eight that evening the Reichstag was invaded by several hundred shop stewards who burst into the debating chamber and decorated it with red flags before setting up a Council of People's Commissars in the name of the proletariat. The stewards' aim was to seize control from Chancellor Ebert and the Social Democrat Party and establish a Bolshevist state in their place. The stewards had no legitimate mandate, but then neither did Ebert as chancellor. Everything was up for grabs now that there wasn't a monarchy any more.

From her house by the Brandenburg Gate, Princess Blücher had heard occasional shots during the evening and also the distinctive hoot of the Kaiser's motor cars as the stolen vehicles were driven from the palace. She had hoped that the situation would quieten down after dinner, but it seemed if anything to be getting worse:

'We have just heard two shots in front of our windows in the Tiergarten. Some scared women, who tried to get into safety behind our big doors, say that two women have been wounded in the Tiergarten from rifles going off accidentally in the hands of unpractised civilians.'

A friend telephoned to advise the Blüchers against spending the night in their ground-floor apartment, so they asked the von Derenthalls, their tenants on the top floor, if they could join them upstairs instead. The servants went to sleep in the back of the house where it was a bit safer and the Blüchers crept up the stairs, hoping that their fears were exaggerated and there was nothing to worry about as they prepared for bed. But there was still shooting outside as they undressed, stray rifle shots crackling through the darkness and a general feeling of uncertainty in the air. It was not a good omen for the night that lay ahead.

In his flat in west Berlin, General Erich Ludendorff shared the Blüchers' fears about what the night might bring, but with far more reason. He was only too aware that if the mob came looking for someone to blame for the war, his name would be first on the list. The mob would show no mercy if they found him. They would drag him out at once and beat him to death in front of his wife.

Ludendorff had decided to flee in disguise. He had acquired a false beard for the purpose and a pair of dark glasses. His plan was to slip away in the dark and go to Potsdam, where his brother was an astronomer. He could stay there for a few days until the excitement had died down. If the worst came to the worst, he might even leave Germany altogether, taking the ferry to Denmark under an assumed name while his enemies hunted high and low for him. It would be an undignified end to his career, but he would rather do that than be taken prisoner by the Bolshevists. They were already calling for his arrest.

Margarethe Ludendorff wasn't at all happy about her husband running away. She thought it unworthy of him, but bit her lip and said nothing rather than interfere. She was bitterly aware that their neighbours would be delighted to see the back of her husband. They had been thrilled to share a boarding house with the Ludendorffs when the war was going well and the general's name was all over the newspapers, but they were much less enthusiastic now that he was universally reviled. They felt that his continued presence in the house was a danger to them all. If Ludendorff wanted to tiptoe down the stairs in a false beard and flee into the night before the mob arrived, his neighbours would do nothing to stop him.

*

In a house on the Kaiserallee, sixteen-year-old Marlene Dietrich sat with her diary in the attic bedroom, longing for the violence to end. Like everyone in her family, she was thoroughly sick of war and revolution. She had nothing but contempt for the Bolshevists looting the palace and running riot across Berlin. She knew exactly why they were doing it, too. They wanted to ruin her life:

'Why must I experience these terrible times? I did so want a golden youth and now it turned out like this! I am sorry about the Kaiser and all the others. They say bad things will happen tonight. The mob was after people with carriages. We had some ladies invited for tea but none of them could get through to our house. Only Countess Gersdorf did. On Kurfürstendamm, her husband had his epaulettes torn off by armed soldiers, and wherever one looks there are red flags. What does the country want? They've got what they wanted, haven't they? Oh, if I were a little bit happy, things wouldn't be so difficult to bear. Maybe soon a time will come when I will be able to tell about happiness again – only happiness.'

Marlene Dietrich loathed the war and always had done, right from the very beginning. She had been in love with her French mistress in August 1914, only to find the woman gone when she returned to school after the summer holidays. She had since transferred her affections to Countess Gersdorf ('Your feet are pink, my heart is set on fire for you! I am dying of love'), but still retained a soft spot for Mlle Breguand. She didn't see why Germany should be at war with France, or England either, for that matter. She had always refused to shout *Gott strafe England* after the national anthem, as custom demanded.

Most of the men in her family had been killed at the front. The rest had all noticed what a big girl Marlene was becoming when they returned home on leave. A male teacher at her school had noticed it too, and had been sacked as a result. Boys regularly followed her in the street or gazed up hopelessly at her window. She enjoyed the attention, but her first love was the theatre. She had played the part of a man in the school play, wearing her black sports trousers, a white lace shirt and her mother's riding coat. Marlene Dietrich was hoping to go on the stage one day, if this wretched war ever came to an end.

*

On the street, music student Kurt Weill had spent most of the day at the Reichstag, a fascinated observer as troops thronged the building and the crowds massed outside. He had seen the barracks attacked and had witnessed some heavy fighting at the Marstall by the river. Weill was all in favour of the revolution if it meant an end to the Kaiser and his court, but he distrusted Bolshevism and didn't want to see the tyranny of the aristocracy replaced by the dictatorship of the proletariat. He had listened to one of Karl Liebknecht's many speeches that day and hadn't thought much of it. Sensible government by moderate men was what Germany needed now, not workers' soviets and committees of self-appointed ideologues who had little idea of what they were doing.

There was something else as well. The political parties were using the Jews as scapegoats, accusing Jewish speculators of avoiding the fighting and making money out of the war while everyone else suffered. With both of his brothers at the front, cantor's son Weill wasn't going to stand for that. He himself was so poor that he had several times fainted from hunger in the past few months. The Jews weren't to blame for what had happened. Weill would say so, if the accusations continued. It was no good just being an observer any more. He would have to become involved in politics himself if that was what he had to do to stop everyone blaming the Jews for something that wasn't their fault.

At Spa, the Armistice details had arrived at last. Hindenburg had gone to bed early, unable to take any more, so the details had been delivered to General Gröner, who sat reading them with growing consternation as the implications sank in. On top of everything else, the Allies were demanding the surrender of 30,000 machine guns, which would leave the German army powerless to keep order at home if it became necessary. And it undoubtedly would become necessary if the situation across Germany grew any worse.

The Armistice terms were outrageous, but Gröner knew that they would have to be accepted. They were no worse than the terms

Hindenburg and Ludendorff had imposed on Russia and Romania only a few months earlier. The jackboot was on the other foot now.

Yet the terms could only be accepted if there was a stable government in Germany capable of dealing with the Allies and making good on its promises. That in turn depended on the support of the army. The question for Gröner now was whether the army should march back to Berlin to restore the monarchy, setting up an interim government to act as a regency until one of the Kaiser's grandsons came of age, or whether they should accept that Germany had become a republic and lend their support to whichever political party was best placed to run the country and keep the Bolshevists out of power.

Gröner picked up the phone. He had a few questions for Friedrich Ebert, Germany's new chancellor. Gröner wasn't completely sure where his duty lay, now that the Kaiser had released him from his oath and he no longer had a warlord to serve.

Ebert was relieved to hear from Gröner. He had not enjoyed his first few hours as chancellor. No monarchist himself, he had nevertheless done his best to keep Germany's options open for the continuation of the monarchy, only to be thwarted by Scheidemann and Liebknecht announcing separate republics on their own authority. Ebert had spent the rest of the day trying to form a new government. It had proved almost impossible, with the Bolshevists on the streets and the Reichstag full of trade unionists setting up a rival assembly of their own. Gröner's call would be very welcome if it offered a way out of the impasse.

The two men conferred over the phone. They quickly established that both wanted a rapid return to law and order and a suppression of Bolshevism. They agreed therefore that the army should march home under military discipline and transfer its allegiance to the new republic. That left just one question unanswered. Would Hindenburg want to remain in command of a republican army? It was important that Hindenburg did remain, because thousands of army officers would follow where he led.

Gröner couldn't say for sure what Hindenburg intended to do, but spoke for him anyway. He promised Ebert that the field marshal would retain command. Relieved beyond measure, Ebert put the phone down and returned to the thankless task of trying to form Germany's first republican government.

At dinner on the royal train, the Kaiser was still dithering about what he should do. He had already announced his imminent departure for Holland several times, only to change his mind minutes later and say that he was going to stay with the army instead. 'Even if only a few men remain loyal,' he had announced before dinner, 'I will fight with them to the end, and if we are all killed, well, I'm not afraid of death. I'd be deserting my wife and children if I went to Holland. No, it's impossible. I'm staying here.'

The meal itself was a funereal affair, since no one felt like talking. The Kaiser was still refusing to flee, saying that he intended to spend the night on the train, guarded by his personal troops. His aides were pressing him to make a firm decision one way or the other, in case changes needed to be made to the arrangements already in place. They thought he should proceed with the original plan and head for the border before it was too late. One of them pointed out that mutinous troops were drawing closer to Spa every minute, while others were barricading the roads back to Germany. If the Kaiser didn't go that night, he might have lost the chance by morning.

Dinner was over by ten. As the Kaiser was leaving the dining car, his aides took him aside and put it to him one last time that Holland was his only realistic option. They spoke in low voices, almost a whisper. The Kaiser said nothing, but nodded reluctantly from time to time. He understood the truth of what they were saying, even if he didn't much like it. The decision couldn't be put off any longer. Holland it would have to be.

'Very well,' he agreed. 'But not before tomorrow morning. We will leave tomorrow.'

Discussion over, the Kaiser went to his carriage to write some anguished farewell letters before snatching a few hours' rest. At the Hôtel Britannique, the military staff settled down to sleep beside their desks. They all had guns with them, in case supreme headquarters was attacked by rebels during the night.

In Moscow, Vladimir Ilyich Lenin was following the events in Germany with unconcealed delight. The reports reaching him at the Kremlin all told the same story. The revolution had begun. All the hard work put in by the Soviet cadres in Berlin was paying off at last.

Watching him exult, Lenin's wife sensed that these days of the German revolution were the happiest of his life. It seemed to her that Lenin was in seventh heaven as the reports continued to flood in through the night. He certainly had reason to be pleased. Everything in Germany was going exactly according to plan.

CHAPTER SEVEN

Sunday, 10 November 1918

I n the tenants' flat at the top of her house, Evelyn Blücher found it impossible to sleep as the fighting outside continued into the small hours of Sunday morning. Every time she was about to drift off, another gunshot woke her up again. The shooting was sporadic, but worryingly close. The Blüchers' house was right in the front line as rival factions fought it out on Berlin's streets for control of the revolution.

'Suddenly, about 2 o'clock the stillness was broken by the noise of a regular fusillade of machine guns and rifles being fired off – as it seemed – over our very heads. Trembling with fear, I rushed into the dining room accompanied by my husband, where we found Frau von Derenthall and her two little maidservants already assembled.

'There we sat crouched together in the darkness, for we dared not turn on a light, listening to the fierce fighting going on all around us from the Brandenburg Gate away over to the Reichstag, our rooms being filled with the fumes and smoke of the guns. Occasionally we crept out on to the balcony to try and see what was going on, but could only see small groups of soldiers, all armed, with red flags in their hands, standing around the Gate.'

The shooting died away after about an hour. Frau von Derenthall suggested a cup of coffee. Her husband, eighty-four years old and stone deaf, had slept peacefully through all the noise. The others sat shivering in their dressing gowns while the maids produced a weak brew of coffee made from corn. Frau von Derenthall had been meaning for almost a year to invite the Blüchers up for dinner. She had been waiting until she could find something nice to offer them. As it was, ersatz coffee in the dark would have to do.

At five in the morning, the Blüchers judged it safe to go downstairs again and return to their own apartment. They found the servants up, just as apprehensive as they were. Nobody had slept a wink all night. It seemed to Evelyn Blücher as if they were in the middle of a beehive, with swarms of bees humming angrily all around them. They had come to a point where stray rifle bullets no longer bothered them much, just so long as there wasn't machine-gun fire as well. She had the sinking feeling that there would be a lot more of both before the day was out.

At Spa, the Kaiser's chauffeur, Warner, was fast asleep when he was woken at 2 a.m. and told to get up at once. The Kaiser's car was to be made ready for a long journey. To avoid trouble with 'patrols of the revolutionary army', it was not to carry any distinguishing marks that would identify it as the Kaiser's. There would be no royal standard fluttering from the bonnet and Warner was to remove the imperial crown from the paintwork on the side. He went to work as soon as he was dressed.

While Warner was getting the car ready, the Kaiser rose early from his quarters on the royal train and was in the dining car by 4 a.m. He was still in two minds about escaping to Holland. 'I can't agree to it. What happens if they turn Bolshevist as well?' His aides assured him that Bolshevism wasn't going to happen in Holland, and if it did it would only be in a very mild form. They were adamant that Holland remained the only feasible destination for him.

It was a depressed gathering in the dining car. Many of the officers present had chosen to go to Holland with the Kaiser, accompanying him into exile on the royal train. To add to their gloom, they had just learned the terms of the Armistice, disastrous beyond their worst imaginings. They were beaten men, running away from the consequences of their own folly. They all knew it and were ashamed of it. They had played for the highest stakes and lost.

It had been announced the night before that the Kaiser wouldn't leave Spa until morning. In the event, he left at 5 a.m. without saying goodbye to Hindenburg, still fast asleep in his own quarters, or any of the others at supreme headquarters. He left on the royal train, pulling quietly out of the station while twenty-five soldiers armed with rifles, machine guns and hand grenades stood guard in the corridor along the train. He went without fanfare, stealing away in the night before anyone knew he was gone. With the revolution so close to Spa, it was probably the most sensible way to go.

Even on the train, the Kaiser wasn't safe. The line went through Liège, where the troops were said to be mutinous. They were perfectly capable of stopping the train and taking the Kaiser prisoner if they knew he was coming. For that reason, the train halted again ten minutes out of Spa at the country station of La Reide. The Kaiser and seven others got out and hurried across the platform, where the stationmaster was waiting with a lamp to guide them to the cars that were to take them the rest of the way to the border.

The plan was for the Kaiser to travel incognito by road while the revolutionaries chased after the train. Warner and the other drivers were supposed to be waiting outside the station, ready to take the Kaiser to the frontier. But there were no cars in sight when his party emerged from the station. In the heat of the moment, the drivers had been given the wrong instructions and were waiting somewhere else. There was no sign of them anywhere as the Kaiser stood forlornly in the roadway, wondering what to do next.

Fortunately for him, another car came past and was quickly commandeered. The missing vehicles were located within ten minutes and shortly afterwards were on their way to the Dutch border town of Eisden with the Kaiser and the rest of his companions on board.

It was a fraught journey. The Kaiser was in a state of high excitement all the way, yelling at the drivers to slow down, then changing his mind and telling them to speed up again in case the cars became separated in the darkness. They passed the royal train at one point and went through a German army checkpoint that was still operating under military discipline, despite the red flag flying from the bridge. The sky gradually lightened, heralding the beginning of another day.

Soon after 7 a.m., they came to a large wire fence and were relieved to learn that they had arrived safely at the border with Holland.

The border guards were militia men from the newly declared republic of Bavaria. They snooped suspiciously around the cars, one of them calling the others over to examine the paintwork where the imperial crown had been scratched off. The Kaiser kept a low profile in the back seat while his companions gripped the rifles concealed between their knees. A stand-off was averted when General von Frankenberg got out and announced that the convoy was taking him and his staff to Holland on important business. Important business to the border guards could only mean the Armistice. Delighted to assist, one of them jumped on to the running board without recognising the Kaiser and directed the convoy across the border into neutral Holland.

The Dutch were surprised to see them. They asked for the Germans' passports, only to be told that nobody had one. The Kaiser's diplomatic representative disappeared into the border post to discuss it while Dutch soldiers and civilians circled the cars curiously, wondering what this was all about. Some of them put their heads inside to have a look. The Kaiser sat tight and lit a cigarette, something he often did in times of stress. He advised his companions to do the same, telling them they had earned it.

In the distance, church bells were ringing for Sunday morning service. One of the Germans remarked that the bells were the harbingers of freedom. While they chatted nervously, Sergeant Pierre Dinckaer of the Dutch army telephoned his superiors at Maastricht to tell them he had recognised the Kaiser's car. He reported that the German emperor was at the border, seeking official permission to enter Holland.

Major Van Dyl arrived in haste and formally received the Kaiser, who surrendered his sword to him. Van Dyl escorted the Germans to Eisden railway station to wait for the royal train, which was still on its way from Spa. The Kaiser paced up and down the platform, nervously chain-smoking while the others tried to make conversation. The news of his arrival had already spread. Workers had rushed from a factory on the Belgian side of the station and were yelling at the Kaiser from a few yards away, shouting 'Vive la France!' or 'Ah, Kamerad, kaputt!' and shaking their fists at him. The whistles and catcalls shrivelled him to his soul. People were taking photographs as well, capturing the humiliation of the all highest on camera as he walked the platform like a caged animal. The Belgians had nothing but contempt for the man who had brought so much misery to their little country.

It was a relief when the royal train arrived at last, having come through Liège without any trouble. German sentries jeered as the train was uncoupled and hauled across the frontier by a Dutch engine. The Kaiser and his entourage immediately climbed aboard, glad to be on familiar territory once more. Breakfast was waiting in the dining car, but they had to keep the curtains drawn while they ate in case the crowd threw stones.

The situation remained tense until Dutch troops arrived and cleared the station, sealing it off until further notice, while the Dutch government debated what to do with the Kaiser. An emergency meeting of the Dutch Cabinet had just been convened at the Hague to discuss it. The Dutch had two equally unpalatable choices. They could admit the Kaiser to their country without further ado and grant him political asylum, or they could throw him to the wolves. It was anybody's guess which they would choose.

As the church bells sounded in Holland, so they did in France, pealing out across the fields and woods surrounding Compiègne. Few of the German Armistice commission felt like church, but Matthias Erzberger was a practising Roman Catholic and wanted to attend Mass if he could. He asked one of the attendants on the German train if it was possible, only to be told that Marshal Foch had already been to Mass at Réthondes church that morning and there wouldn't be another service that day.

This was news. They were near Réthondes. The French had repeatedly refused to tell the Germans where they were, the attendants on the train claiming that they came from a different part of

France and didn't know the area at all. But if the nearest church was at Réthondes, then the forest that the Germans could see all around must be Compiègne. They were in Compiègne forest, north of Paris. It was the first the Germans knew of it.

The knowledge brought them no advantage. The Germans were being kept in strict isolation, so divorced from the outside world that they didn't even learn of the Kaiser's abdication until some French railwaymen showed Erzberger the morning newspapers, strictly against orders, and told him the Kaiser had gone. With Prince Max gone as well and Germany in chaos, it made for a very gloomy atmosphere as the Germans sat on their train, waiting to hear from Berlin about the Armistice terms. The Allies were worried too, because Erzberger and his team appeared to be representing a regime that didn't exist any more – the very situation they had all wanted to avoid.

While the delegates waited to hear from Berlin, the Allied advance continued on the Western Front, the troops pushing forward all along the line to maintain the pressure on the Germans until the Armistice had been signed. They advanced with varying degrees of reluctance, knowing perfectly well that the war would be over soon and the fighting was about to stop. None of them wanted to be killed now, with peace just around the corner.

At Celles, north of Tournai, Captain Frank Hitchcock and his company of Leinsters were now well across the river Scheldt, moving towards the little village of Arc-Ainières. From the map, the historically minded Hitchcock saw that they were only a few miles from Fontenoy, where Catholic Irish troops like his had fought the English in 1745. They were close to Oudenarde too, where the Duke of Marlborough had seen the French off across the Scheldt in 1708.

They were on the march some time after 9 a.m. when Brigadier Bernard Freyberg came galloping up to tell them the Kaiser had gone. 'The war is over!' he announced. 'The Kaiser has abdicated!' If Freyberg was expecting a cheer from the Leinsters, he didn't get it. The Leinsters only cheered in adverse conditons like rain or shellfire. They received the news with little show of emotion, although they were glad the Kaiser had gone ('wasn't he the quare ould twister?'). Freyberg rode on to tell an English battalion and the Leinsters continued to trudge forward, advancing towards Arc-Ainières as ordered.

The villagers came out to welcome them, bringing fruit and plates of bread and butter for the men. Hitchcock had them fall out on a ridge east of the village and told them to pile their arms. As they did so, a German shell came whistling through the air and exploded three hundred yards away. Ahead of them, they could hear anti-aircraft fire as the Germans tried to shoot down one of their spotter planes.

'They do say the war is over,' remarked Private Flaherty. He found it hard to believe, as did everybody else in the Leinsters.

A few miles away, the Canadians found it hard to believe, too, as they pressed on towards Mons. The Germans there were still fighting stubbornly, hitting back with machine guns and heavy artillery as the Canadians harried them along the canal into the western outskirts of the town. They had hoped to capture Mons that day, but progress had been slower than expected. It would almost certainly be the next day now before Mons fell and the Canadians were masters of the town.

Mons was where the British and German armies had first clashed in 1914. The first British troops to be killed in the war had died there as the Germans swept through Belgium on their way to France. It had not escaped their attention that after more than four years of fighting both sides were right back where they had started.

While the Canadians inched forward, the Prince of Wales followed as closely as his equerry would allow. He and Lord Claud Hamilton had gone up as far as Frameries and Jemappes that morning, only a mile and a half from Mons. They had watched the fighting from there, as the prince recorded in a letter to his mother:

'We got a good view of the town from a slag heap, the whole country being a mass of mines!! Too thrilling and interesting for words and I found several graves of British soldiers killed in August 1914, who had been buried by Belgian civilians, who had erected crosses over the graves. As you say, what stirring times we are living through and to think that we are on the brink of an Armistice and that the war is as good as over: a Hun revolution and the Kaiser abdicated though this news hasn't reached their front-line troops yet or they wouldn't still be fighting us as they are still, holding Mons with machine guns and still shelling us!!

'I wish they would hurry up and conclude the Armistice as I feel that it's such a shame on our troops in the line who are still getting killed, though of course our casualties have been very light lately; but what rotten luck to be killed or badly wounded the last or last few days of the war!!'

The prince's view was shared by every soldier on the front line. Nobody wanted to die now, not even for king and country.

In Ostend, US intelligence officer Howard Vincent O'Brien and his companions had enjoyed a comfortable night at their hotel on the beach. They had a pleasant surprise too when the bill was presented after breakfast that morning:

'Our hotel one of most expensive on *plage*. But bill for bed and breakfast – 3fr. 50. We first of liberators. Had neither smashed furniture nor raped chambermaid and everybody appreciative.'

O'Brien hired one of the hotel's waiters to show them around Ostend after breakfast. The town was still very dangerous because the Germans had left a number of delayed-action mines behind when they withdrew. One of the mines had just killed fifty women and children, an atrocity that the Belgians weren't going to forget in a hurry. Other mines were still exploding at unpredictable intervals, particularly around the docks and other areas useful to the war effort.

From Ostend, O'Brien continued along the coast road towards Holland. He passed Zeebrugge on the way, where three British ships had been scuttled in April to block the entrance to the German naval base. O'Brien knew all about the raid from the newspapers, but seeing the place with his own eyes he couldn't help marvelling at the courage the British must have displayed to carry it out with such panache. The marines and the Royal Navy had taken seven hundred casualties in the raid, but had been happy to do it if it showed that they too were playing their part in the war, as the soldiers were on land.

O'Brien continued north and soon came to Ecluse on the Dutch frontier:

'Unforgettable picture. White painted fence, with barbed wire, formerly electrified by Germans – now full of breaks. A narrow strip of land, with another gate, and a long aisle, between tall trees, leading into Holland. Streetcar tracks. Evidently no trick getting in or out. Conversation with Belgian commanding guard, and invitation to cross border. Probably first American officers to be in neutral country without internment. Heard news of Kaiser's abdication from Dutch sentinel – told in gesture, mostly.'

It seemed unlikely that the Germans would be flooding Belgium with spies through the fence. After making further inquiries, O'Brien decided he had learned enough and headed back to France along the inland road. He found it riddled with shell holes and a long tailback of military traffic. At Oudenarde, an American division had just arrived after advancing four kilometres without seeing any Germans. O'Brien stopped at dusk to join a group of men listening to a mouth organ while guns rumbled in the distance. Then he drove on to Lille and arrived late at night hoping for a nice dinner at a good hotel, only to find that the Germans had destroyed the town's lighting plant before they left, and the waterworks as well.

East of the Meuse, Captain Harry Truman's battery of the 129th Field Artillery had been advancing steadily for the past few days and was now well beyond Verdun, supporting the US infantry as they pursued the retreating enemy. A big railway gun was pounding the Germans from a position just behind them as Truman sat writing to his fiancée:

'The Hun is yelling for peace like a stuck hog, and I hope old daddy Foch makes him yell louder yet or throttles him one. Throttling would be too easy. When you see some of the things those birds did and then hear them put up the talk they do for peace it doesn't impress you at all. A complete and thorough thrashing is all they've got coming and take my word they are getting it and getting it right.

'This has been a beautiful Sunday – the sun shining and as warm as summer ... Heinie seems to be about finished. Just to make the day interesting one of their planes came over and shot down one of our sausage balloons and came near getting shot down himself. I shot away about five hundred rounds of high-explosive shells myself. Not at the plane but at some Hun machine guns about seven miles away. I don't know if I hit them, but I have hopes as I laid the guns very carefully.

'A Hun plane dropped some bombs not far from my backyard last night and sort of shook things up. They made him run home in a hurry too. There is a big railroad gun about a kilometre behind me that shoots about every fifteen minutes and I heard one of the boys remark that "There goes another rolling kitchen over to pulverise Jerry". The projectile makes a noise like a wagon going down the road when it goes through the air, so the remark was very good.'

Truman wrote jauntily, as always in his letters home, but the reality was rather different. His nerves were stretched to breaking point, as were everyone else's in the battery. The constant bombardment was getting to them all, with German shells still dropping all around them at any time of day or night. 'The men think I am not much afraid of shells but they don't know I was too scared to run and that is pretty scared,' Truman had admitted of one barrage. Nobody under his command had been killed yet, but it was only a matter of time if the shooting didn't stop soon.

The noise of the Verdun guns was all too audible to Harry Truman and the men of his battery. A hundred miles to the east, across the Moselle river and the richly wooded slopes of Alsace, the noise had dropped to a distant murmur by the time it reached the fortress of Rastatt, a prison camp on the Rhine. The guns were loudest in the early morning, between 6 and 8 a.m., but they were a welcome sound at any time of day, proof that the Allies were coming and the war was nearly over. It couldn't end too soon for the prisoners at Rastatt, among them Second Lieutenant George Coles of the RAF.

Coles had been a prisoner of war since early September, when his bomber had been shot down near Douai by a German Fokker pilot. With a tracer bullet burning a hole in his left ankle and his own pilot unconscious in the cockpit, Coles had thought he was a goner as their aircraft plunged to earth. He had retrieved the situation by hammering his pilot over the head with his pistol, jerking him back into consciousness in time to grab the joystick and pull them out of their dive. They had crash-landed in a field behind German lines, closely followed by the Fokker pilot, who landed beside them to prevent them setting fire to their plane.

Coles and his comrade had been carried to a nearby farmhouse, where French civilians had taken care of them until a German officer arrived on horseback and laid into the French with his whip. After shaking hands with Lance Corporal Nulle, the man who had shot them down, the two British had been driven to hospital by a German soldier who had been a London taxi driver before the war. The man freely admitted that the war was lost, but, like every other German they met, blamed his country's defeat on the Royal Navy's blockade rather than military failures in the field.

Indeed, the Germans were so short of equipment that Coles had been stripped of his flying suit before he got to hospital. His helmet, puttees and sheepskin boots had been taken as well, for reuse by German pilots who had none of their own. Short of soap, rubber, cloth and every kind of metal, not to mention food and fuel, the Germans had had no compunction about taking what they needed.

Coles had been separated from his companion after a while and sent back to Germany by train. He had passed Valenciennes on the way, its gasometer in ruins from his own bombing of ten days earlier. At Aix-la-Chappelle, he had had to transfer from one railway station to another, deliberately forced to hop almost a mile over rough cobblestones while German civilians sniggered at his discomfort. At Heidelberg, he and some other British prisoners had very nearly been lynched by a vengeful mob, angered at an RAF raid the night before that had killed a number of people on a train. The RAF had been carrying the war to German soil, giving the Germans a taste of what British and French civilians had been suffering for years. The gesture had been completely lost on the people of Heidelberg.

The only bright spot of the journey had come at Darmstadt, where Coles's wound had been dressed by Anna Seehaus, a charming German girl who looked after him in the Red Cross room on the station platform. Her humanity and kindness had stood out for Coles like an oasis in a desert of German hostility. He had given her a few ounces from his precious store of Red Cross tea when she had finished and they had agreed to write to each other after the war was over.

Coles had arrived at Rastatt on 4 October. The prison camp was an old fort on an island in the middle of the Rhine. It had been built in 1870 as a defence against the French and could only be reached by a drawbridge. The prisoners were a mix of British, French, Italian and Belgian officers, all of them half-starved after a long period of captivity. Their guards were half-starved too. The remaining food from Coles's Red Cross parcel had been pilfered by a German soldier as he limped the one and a half miles from the railway station to the camp.

Life since then had not improved much for Coles. The fortress was a dismal place, run by a German commandant of the old school, a strict disciplinarian devoid of all humour or humanity. His own men loathed him just as much as the prisoners did. A captured American doctor had looked after Coles's ankle and the French had put on a pornographic sketch entitled 'Joseph and Potiphar's Wife' at the camp concert, but the only other excitement had come from Allied air raids, of which there had been several in the past few weeks.

The target was usually Karlsruhe to the north, with British planes flying directly over the camp on their way home, but Rastatt had been attacked as well, anti-aircraft guns firing blind into the mist as bombs rained down on the town. One had hit the camp, exploding only twenty yards from the prison canteen and breaking most of the fort's windows. After ten minutes of being bombed by the British, Coles had come to appreciate the anger of the Heidelberg mob as they sought to lynch the people responsible.

But there had been no bombs for the past ten days. Instead, the guns from Verdun had boomed louder and louder as the Allies maintained their advance, drawing nearer every day. The Kaiser had abdicated yesterday and the news had reached Rastatt by evening, causing great excitement among prisoners and guards alike.

At roll call that Sunday morning, Coles and the other prisoners had had a wonderful surprise when they assembled on the parade ground to answer their names. Standing right next to them, looking thoroughly sheepish in civilian clothes, were the camp commandant and his officers. They had been arrested in the night, taken prisoner by their own men and forced to surrender their swords to the revolution. The camp was now being run by a council of soldiers, presided over by a non-commissioned officer who had previously been the canteen orderly. The soldiers had removed the imperial cockades from their hats and wore the red ribbon of the new republic in their buttonholes. The people were in charge now.

Coles and his comrades couldn't resist mocking the commandant after roll call was over. 'Who won the war?' they asked him, as he was hustled off the parade ground. The commandant had been a merciless swine in his time, a Hun of the worst sort. The prisoners had no sympathy for him or his officers as they were taken to the punishment cells and locked in. Conditions in the punishment block were atrocious: lice, straw, a latrine that was a communal plank over a blocked culvert. The German officers had shown no compunction in condemning their prisoners to the cells. Now that they were locked in themselves, they were visibly trembling for their lives, worried that if their own men didn't kill them the prisoners would. It was good to see them suffer.

The Rastatt officers had got off lightly by comparison with some. In Brussels, still under German occupation, the Kaiser's abdication had triggered a similar mutiny, as German troops rebelled against their officers and made a prisoner of General von Falkenhausen, Belgium's overbearing governor general. Those officers who tried to stop them had been hanged from lamp posts, lynched by their own men as the troops took revenge on the Prussian officer class for all the indignities heaped on them over the past four years.

The troops had set all the deserters free as well and were rampaging through the Brussels streets, tearing off their cockades and making friends with Belgian civilians, declaring that they were all brothers now, fellow comrades of the proletariat. The Germans were most anxious to make friends with the Belgians, now that the war was lost. They were all for letting bygones be bygones, now that they weren't enemies any more.

It was an astonishing sight, German troops suddenly all smiles. For a few hours that Sunday, the inhabitants of Brussels were so carried away by the spectacle that they forgot their loathing of all things German and stood shoulder to shoulder with their former enemies. A large procession formed up at the Gare du Nord after lunch and headed for the Palais de Justice. It was composed of German soldiers and Belgian Bolshevists singing revolutionary songs and waving each other's flags as they marched along. The Germans tore down the Kaiser's colours and trampled on them while onlookers gaped in disbelief.

At the Palais, the new republic of Germany was announced to a roar of applause. A German soldier was haranguing the crowd when an Allied plane appeared overhead, taking evasive action as puffs of anti-aircraft fire followed it across the sky. People all over the city cheered the plane, but nobody cheered louder than the Germans at the Palais de Justice. They were delighted to see an Allied plane in the air. They had no quarrel with the Allies any more.

In fact, it had all been a big misunderstanding, the war. The Germans hadn't meant anything personal by it. Prussians might believe in the rights of conquest, Teutonic knights entitled to the spoils of war, but that was the Prussians. Other Germans weren't like that. They didn't rape chambermaids. Not them. They had only ever wanted to be friends with the Belgians.

The Germans' volte-face did not impress everybody. Miss J. H. Gifford – Gick to her friends – was the English chatelaine of a finishing school in the Boitsfort forest just outside Brussels. She had had her fill of Germans over the past four years. Unwilling to abandon her school in 1914, she had remained at her post as the Belgian army

The Germans were within sight of the Eiffel Tower when their final offensive petered out.

The Armistice came too late for this German gunner, killed at Villers Devy Dun Sassey on 4 November 1918.

Much to his frustration, Captain Charles de Gaulle was a prisoner of war in Germany when the Armistice was declared.

Harry Truman's battery fired its last round at a quarter to eleven on 11 November. Truman thought the greatest day in history was the day the United States dropped the atom bomb on Japan.

Sergeant-Major Flora Sandes, a British clergyman's daughter serving in the Serbian infantry, once fooled a prostitute into thinking she was a man.

Bitterly upset at Germany's defeat in the First World War, Herbert Sulzbach later fled the Nazis and joined the British Army in the Second.

After a scratch supper at
Homblières, the German
Armistice delegates returned
to their car for the journey
to Compiègne.

Matthias Erzberger, leader of the
German delegation, was later
assassinated for his part in the
Armistice negotiations.

Chancellor of Germany for only a few weeks, Prince Max von Baden might have saved the Kaiser's throne if his kinsman had only listened to him and taken his advice.

While his predecessor fled in dark glasses and a false beard, General Wilhelm Gröner confronted the Kaiser and told him bluntly that he had lost the support of the German Army.

Seen here at the Chancellery in Berlin, Philipp Scheidemann addressed the mob from a window of the Reichstag on 9 November and inadvertently declared Germany a republic.

Berlin's Brandenburg Gate was in the thick of the revolution on 9 November, but was later reoccupied by troops loyal to the government.

Englishwoman Princess Blücher (inset) had a grandstand view of the soldiers on the Brandenburg Gate (below) from her house nearby.

Auf dem Dache des Brandenburger Tores.
Regierungstreue Truppen sind mit Maschinen-
gewehren und Handgranaten zum Kampf gegen
die Anhänger der Spartakusgruppe ausgerüstet.

Corporal Teilhard de Chardin was so drunk on Armistice night that he couldn't unlock his door and had to sleep in a barn.

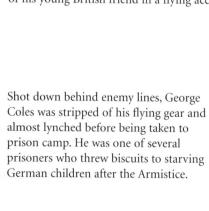

Captured by the Italians on 3 November, Ludwig Wittgenstein was haunted by the death of his young British friend in a flying accident.

Shot down behind enemy lines, George Coles was stripped of his flying gear and almost lynched before being taken to prison camp. He was one of several prisoners who threw biscuits to starving German children after the Armistice.

While Belgians jeered from behind the camera, the Kaiser (fourth from left in fur collar) waited across the Dutch border for his train to arrive at Eisden, 10 November.

Lady Susan Townley, wife of the British ambassador at the Hague, ambushed the Kaiser on Armistice day and gave him a piece of her mind.

Marshal Foch signed the Armistice for France soon after 5 a.m. on 11 November.

Exhausted but triumphant, the Canadians relaxed in Mons's main square on Armistice morning. They had fought through the night to liberate the town before the end of the war.

The Irish Guards at Maubeuge, five minutes before the Armistice.
Many felt 'flat and dispirited' after the fighting stopped.

Patricia Carver (inset) was one of the many thousands who
cheered the King at Buckingham Palace on Armistice morning.

The White House was surrounded by an expectant crowd on 7 November and again on the day of the real Armistice.

Roy Howard's premature report of the Armistice was the biggest embarrassment of his career.

Australia celebrated the false Armistice so enthusiastically that all places serving alcohol in Sydney had to be closed by two in the afternoon. The Aussies were out again in force on the real Armistice day, seen here in Sydney's Martin Place.

American troops danced through the streets of Paris on Armistice day. The US Army would have come into its own if the war had continued into 1919.

Killed at one minute to eleven as he charged a machine gun singlehanded, German–American Henry Gunther (centre) was officially the last US soldier to die in the war.

Strictly against orders, US air ace Eddie Rickenbacker was dodging bullets over the front line as eleven o'clock approached.

A Californian in the RAF, Bogart Rogers later scripted *The Eagle and the Hawk*, an aerial combat movie about the war. Starring Cary Grant and Carole Lombard, the film reflected Rogers's own disillusion with the war, which had seemed a great adventure until reality struck home.

By his own account, Ernest Hemingway was wounded 227 times during his non-combatant service on the Italian front. He had his uniform tailored to make it look more like a British Guards officer's.

Too shy to join the dancing on London's streets, Agatha Christie was hoping that her detective novel about a Belgian refugee would find a publisher soon.

John Maynard Keynes feared that the Allies would demand full reparations from Germany for all the damage done. As a leading economist, he knew it was a recipe for disaster.

Mahatma Gandhi joined the British Army during the Boer War and urged his compatriots to do the same during the Great War.

T.E. Lawrence was in London on Armistice night, desperately afraid that the Arabs would be betrayed at the forthcoming peace conference.

Marlene Dietrich was a teenager in November 1918 and Erich Maria Remarque was recovering from wounds. Each had vivid memories of the war's end in Germany.

Paris showgirl Mistinguett was very nearly executed for her attempts to secure Maurice Chevalier's release from prison camp. Both were on stage in Paris on Armistice night.

André Maurois' novel about his British comrades, *Les Silences du Colonel Bramble*, was a hit on both sides of the Channel.

General Pershing feared that the German Army would consider itself undefeated if it was allowed to go home without first laying down its arms. Chancellor Friedrich Ebert told the troops exactly that when they marched through the Brandenburg Gate on 10 December.

retreated and uhlans appeared in the woods. The uhlans had been followed by the rest of the German army marching past in a column so long that it had taken several days to pass. The smell of so many unwashed bodies had lingered along the road for days afterwards. Gick Gifford had kept out of the Germans' way as they went through her chateau. She had been horrified when she returned:

'As soon as the Germans marched off from the chateau, I turned my attention to the house and truly I got more than a shock! If seeing all these men invading the country seemed unreal, I was brought to earth quickly by the horrid disgusting realities in front of me. Never in my wildest imagination had I pictured such a scene!

'To begin with the doors had been hacked open with axes, and sheaves of corn – which they had obliged the unfortunate farmers to bring from the harvest fields – lay thick everywhere, really mercifully, or I think the dirt would have been ineradicable.

'The mattresses were lying on the floors – it looked as if the men had wiped their feet on them or worse. Everywhere lay pillows, cushions, blankets, and pell-mell on them contents of wardrobes and drawers, as well as soiled bandages, discarded socks, underclothing, remains of food and bottles – not to mention the unmentionable everywhere! ...

'They seemed to have spent the night inspecting everything. From drawers and wardrobes, jewellery and silver were taken. My letters and business papers had also been examined – no doubt for information, as I believe there is a special department for this – and all these were thrown on the floor to increase the confusion. Linen and underclothing had evidently been torn up for bandages. One could quite understand this, but one could *not* forgive the filthy manners of savages from the nation of so-called Kultur. The smell was sickening and overpowering.'

The Germans had taken pains to relieve themselves in awkward places, difficult to clean up. The chateau's staff had refused even to contemplate the job until Gick Gifford had donned her apron and taken the lead. It had been weeks before they had been able to get rid of the smell.

The Germans' treatment of British prisoners had been little better. As the war progressed, Gick Gifford had come across quite a few British prisoners, some of them with their teeth knocked out by rifle butts, others so skeletal that they had been reduced to eating leaves when they could find nothing else. 'Halt, lame and blind, tattered, ragged and all forlorn. Our brave boys. What a piteous sight they were.' Gifford had been one of the first to offer her services to nurse Edith Cavell, who was running an escape line to Holland, but it had been decided that the chateau was too far out of the way for prisoners to hide. Cavell had been shot by the Germans soon afterwards, as had many of the people who had helped her.

But the worst story of all about the Germans, the one that Gifford had always found hardest to believe, was the rumour that they had set up factories in Belgium to extract fat from the dead bodies of their soldiers. The idea seemed inconceivable and had been officially denied by the Germans, yet the rumours refused to go away. According to the chateau's gardener, a porter at Schaarbeck station had stumbled across a goods wagon full of naked corpses apparently bound for the fat factory. They had been tied together in dozens, packed so tightly that they were all standing upright when he opened the door.

The porter was probably embroidering a rumour started by the British. Gick Gifford certainly believed him, but others remained sceptical. They simply couldn't accept that the Germans would transport human beings across Europe in goods trains in order to melt them down into soap. The idea was just too far-fetched. Nobody was that depraved.

Back in Berlin, Evelyn Blücher and her husband had had a fairly quiet morning at their apartment, although they could still hear the occasional rifle shot in the street as they wondered whether it was safe to go out. Unter den Linden had been closed off to traffic and there was sporadic shooting in the Wilhelmstrasse and Friedrichstrasse nearby. The Dutch ambassador had rung to find out how they were and at midday their friend Dr Mainzer called round in person to invite them to spend the afternoon at his clinic, safely out of the line of fire. He invited them to spend the night as well, if necessary, although he didn't think it would be. He thought that the worst of the fighting was over and all would be quiet from now on. He couldn't have been more wrong:

'Dr Mainzer was describing how peaceful and orderly the crowds were round the Reichstag and in the Tiergarten, when suddenly, as if in mockery at his words, a great burst of machine-gun firing cut short his sentence. We all rushed to the windows, and looking through the cracks in the blinds, we saw people hurrying in crowds from apparently every direction at once. We all ran out into the back courtyard, where we found Prince Henckel, his brother, Count Krafft, Prince Wedel, and all their households collected. They locked and barred all the entrances, as there was danger of the mob storming them in their rush for shelter from the firing.

'The house was surrounded by dense masses of people, and, as the house porter told us, there was going to be a fight between the Brandenburg Gate and the Reichstag, presumably the Red Guard against loyal officers and soldiers. The whole street, he said, would soon be closed, and so, if we wanted to get away, we had only three minutes to do so. We therefore decided to go, and creeping out through the back entrance and crossing the back yard, we managed to get into the street some distance off by going through a little public house.

'The crowds in the street were so densely packed that we could hardly get through. Everyone was frantic with excitement; one man had been killed and some wounded quite near our house. From every crossing we saw wagons full of soldiers and sailors coming, all armed with rifles and hand grenades, and flying the red flag, whilst every soldier we met already wore the red cockade on his cap, which looked like a patch of blood over his forehead. It was not a morning for timid people.'

Forcing a way through the throng, the Blüchers stuck close to the wall for fear of stray bullets and made their way past the Brandenburg Gate to Potsdamer Platz. They found a spare cab, but were reluctant to take it in case the mob spotted them for aristocrats. Instead, Evelyn Blücher pretended to faint and Dr Mainzer shouted out that she was sick and had to be taken to a clinic. The crowd made way and the Blüchers fled to Dr Mainzer's house in the cab.

They didn't go a moment too soon. Their servants telephoned later to say that a pitched battle was being fought outside their house. Someone had mounted a pair of machine guns on the Blüchers' roof and was firing down on the crowd in the street. The crowd was firing back. The Blüchers' butler had gone up to the roof to try to appease the mob by tearing down the old imperial flag, but it would obviously be unwise for the Blüchers to return home that night. They decided to take up Dr Mainzer's invitation instead and stay with him until the fighting had stopped and the situation had returned to normal.

In Wilhelmshaven, the first president of the new republic of Oldenburg was taking a bow. Stoker First Class Bernhard Kuhnt had just been proclaimed as such, to tumultuous applause from his supporters. The imperial flag had come down over the barracks and the red flag of Bolshevism had risen in its place. Sirens were hooting across the town, ships in the harbour were sounding their bells, and the forts were firing gun salutes. Wilhelmshaven was in party mood as its people celebrated the beginning of the new era.

For seaman Richard Stumpf, it was a time of mixed emotions as he contemplated the fall of the monarchy, both in his native Bavaria and in Germany as a whole. Until recently, Stumpf had always considered himself a fervent monarchist, but the events of the past few days had turned him into a republican of sorts. He was vacillating between exultation and despair as he struggled to come to grips with the new order. He was all in favour of a proletarian revolution, but couldn't quite identify with the thousands of soldiers and sailors marching confidently through the town in the belief that all their troubles were over now that the red flag was flying. Stumpf wished he could believe it, but still had his doubts.

The celebrations continued all day and well into the evening. As it grew dark, the searchlights came on and signal rockets began to go up, thousands of them in red, white and green, lighting up the harbour while the sirens hooted and the guns started up again. Stumpf thought it was an air raid at first, or perhaps an attack by the Royal Navy. He remained at his post aboard ship and went on with his duties as the din continued:

'The hellish music had not yet ceased when a delegate from the sailors' council with a very crestfallen face ran up the gangplank and wordlessly handed me a broadsheet bearing the ominous title: *The Terms for a Ceasefire*. I read the fateful sheet with bated breath and growing amazement. What were the terms? Evacuation of the left bank of the Rhine as well as the right to an extent of forty kilometres ... 150,000 railway carriages ... 10,000 lorries ... 5,000 heavy guns ... the blockade to remain in effect ... the navy to be surrendered ... 10,000 ... 5,000 ... 30,000 ... It can't be. This is ridiculous ... It means a fight to the finish ... What a sudden change from the joy we had felt that morning! "This is what you get for your goddamned brotherhood," I shouted to the suddenly silent spectators. It was too much for me to bear and I hurried off to grieve in a lonely corner.

'The last of the rockets exploded; one siren after another turned silent; but within me the storm still raged as I was convulsed to the very core of my soul by a deep and terrible anguish. It is sheer madness to subject an industrious and undefeated nation like ours to these shameful terms. Just this morning we demonstrated our eagerness for peace by destroying our most powerful weapon. And what did we get in return? They responded by spitting in our face.'

At Beaumont, just inside the Belgian border, Lieutenant Herbert Sulzbach's feelings were broadly similar as he contemplated the Kaiser's abdication and the collapse of everything he held dear. So much had happened so fast in recent days that Sulzbach was having trouble taking it all in as his battery continued its withdrawal along the crowded roads. Morale in his unit remained high, but the same could not be said for the rear echelons they had come across. The men in the rear units seemed thoroughly defeated by all the bad news from home.

After dark, a message arrived for Sulzbach's unit from supreme headquarters at Spa. It was from Field Marshal von Hindenburg, addressed to all German troops still in the field:

'The Armistice is to be agreed with the utmost dispatch. This will end the bloody struggle. The long-awaited moment is approaching when each of us can go home to parents, wife, child and siblings. At the same time a radical change is happening in the political situation at home. The men in charge have declared that peace and order must be maintained in all circumstances. This applies especially to the army. No one is to leave his unit without permission. Everyone must obey his superiors as usual. There's no other way to ensure an orderly retreat home.

'The railways currently out of action must be brought back into service. The supreme command will not shed any new blood or support a civil war. It will cooperate with the new government authority to ensure peace and security and spare the homeland from the worst. Force is only to be used against our own people in self-defence or cases of common crime or to prevent looting.'

So that was that, then. Hindenburg had gone over to the new republic and was ordering the army to do the same.

At the German military hospital at Pasewalk, eighty miles north of Berlin, the birth of the new republic was announced to the convalescent troops by the local pastor. Addressing the walking wounded in the hall, he made a short speech telling them that the Kaiser had gone and the war was lost. They had no choice now but to throw themselves on the mercy of the victors. The pastor sobbed quietly as he spoke and so did most of his audience. To Corporal Adolf Hitler of the 16th Bavarian Reserve Infantry it seemed as if there wasn't a dry eye in the house as the elderly pastor stood in front of them, praising the Prussian monarchy in trembling tones and mourning its passing.

When the pastor moved on to the Armistice, telling the men that Germany was beaten and they must accept it whether they liked it or not, Hitler could take no more. He hadn't survived four years of fighting on the Western Front just to listen to this. Blinded by a British gas attack a few weeks earlier, Hitler was only just beginning to regain his sight, enough at least to distinguish the broad outlines of the objects around him. He was hoping to regain the rest in time. He did not feel sorry for himself, because others had suffered far worse for the Fatherland and had been proud to do it, but he did not want to listen to the pastor telling them that it had all been for nothing and they were now at the mercy of the victors. It was too much to expect:

'I could stand it no longer. It became impossible for me to sit still one minute more. Once again everything went black before my eyes; I tottered and groped my way back to the ward, threw myself on my bunk, and dug my burning head into my blanket and pillow.

'Since the day when I had stood at my mother's grave, I had not wept. When in my youth Fate seized me with merciless hardness, my defiance mounted. When in the long war years Death snatched so many a dear comrade and friend from our ranks, it would have seemed to me almost a sin to complain – after all, were they not dying for Germany? And when at length the creeping gas – in the last days of the dreadful struggle – attacked me too and began to gnaw at my eyes, and beneath the fear of going blind forever, I nearly lost heart for a moment, the voice of my conscience thundered at me: miserable wretch, are you going to cry when thousands are a hundred times worse off than you! And so I bore my lot in dull silence. But now I could not help it.'

Hitler gave way to his emotions and lay weeping on his bed, his sight apparently gone again with the trauma of defeat. He had been under psychiatric observation at Pasewalk for some time, because the doctors were unsure of the real reason for his blindness. Some of them thought that gas had nothing to do with it and he was actually a psychopath with symptoms of hysteria. They defined a psychopath as suffering from a behavioural disorder resulting in inability to form personal relationships or conform to society, often manifested by antisocial behaviour or acts of violence. They were very worried about Hitler's hysterical symptoms. They thought he might be going out of his mind.

*

153

For Maude Onions, a telegraphist in the Women's Army Auxiliary Corps, Sunday evenings always meant playing the organ at the British church in Boulogne. The church served Boulogne's small British community in peacetime, but in war it had been taken over by the army and was invariably packed for military services. The choir was made up of soldiers, nurses and WAACs, supported by a congregation in khaki which joined lustily in the singing. The soldiers had a bad habit of singing their own words, irreverent parodies of the hymns ('When this bloody war is over, Oh how happy I shall be'), but it was hard to be cross with them after everything they had been through at the front. They had to let off steam somehow.

Maude Onions had been in France since June 1917, one of a draft of female signallers sent to the port of Boulogne to relieve the men for duties further up the line. For the first three years of the war, the British army's signal office at Boulogne had been a room in the town's post office, but it had moved several times since then and had once been blown up by the Germans with the help of local agents. Maude worked as part of a team relaying messages to the units in the front line. The work was humdrum for much of the time, terse military communications that wasted few words and used acronyms wherever possible. But it was important work too, often a matter of life or death for the men at the receiving end. Maude was good at it, a safe pair of hands that could always be relied upon to do whatever had to be done.

Earlier in the year, she had been a silent witness to the German offensive of the spring, when every available soldier had hurried to the front to plug the gaps in the line and stop the Germans breaking through. Boulogne had been one of the German objectives and the town had been bombed nightly as the Germans softened it up for the attack. Many of the town's hotels had been converted into military hospitals which filled up rapidly as the casualties from the front began to mount. Maude had watched with horror as the crisis unfolded around her:

'Behind the lines we saw a little more of the realities of war, in the fortitude of the men who had been maimed for life, blinded, some of them so hideously disfigured that they died by their own hands afterwards – in the endless stream of wounded which came down day after day, night after night, with such regular ceaseless monotony that the eyes ached with the sight – the ambulances jolting over the uneven roads, so that almost every moment added to the agony of the sufferers; the incessant bombing of the base, with its nightly toll of human life, and the sordid procession of the mothers and children of France out to the open fields, to spend the night there, where the sense of security was a little stronger than in the congested area of the towns . . .

'Every available man and boy was rushed up to help to check the German advance. Men on their way for leave, often more than a year in the trenches, were turned back whilst almost in the act of stepping on board. I saw two hundred marching along to the quay, suddenly brought to halt, and instructed "Right about turn" as they were to go straight back again, and not a murmur was heard.

'At Folkestone, those of us who were returning from leave were compelled to line up and wait, while the battered and mangled bodies of the men who had saved England were carried off the boat, to be replaced by men in the fullness and vigour of strength, to be replaced in their turn by more; and so the ghastly game went on.'

But the game was almost over now and it was the Allies who had won. The Germans were on the run and Boulogne had not been bombed for a long time. The flood of casualties to the town's hospitals had been reduced to a steady stream as the fighting died down. Maude Onions was planning an early night after the service that evening because she was on the early shift at the signal office next morning. She would be at her post soon after first light, ready for another day of transmitting messages from army headquarters to the units at the front.

There had been a time when those messages had been full of grim determination as the generals struggled to contain the situation. But that time was long past. The signals were a lot more cheerful now, full of optimism and good humour as the army romped forward along a wide front, covering distances in a single day that would have been unimaginable in the past. Long might it continue!

*

As the British filed into church at Boulogne, Marshal Foch sat aboard his train at Compiègne, waiting for a response from the German Armistice delegation. It was past 6 o'clock on Sunday evening and he still hadn't heard anything. The deadline for a ceasefire was eleven next morning. If he didn't hear from the Germans soon, it would be too late to set the wheels in motion for a ceasefire and the war would have to continue regardless. By their own account, the Germans needed authorisation from the chancellor in Berlin before they could agree to the Armistice terms. Foch wondered when they were going to hear from him.

At 6.30, the marshal could wait no longer. Summoning his chief of staff, he had Weygand deliver a note to the German train:

'As the time allowed for coming to an agreement expires at 11 a.m. tomorrow, I have the honour to ask whether the German plenipotentiaries have received the acceptance by the German chancellor of the terms communicated to him, and if not, whether it would not be advisable to solicit without delay an answer from him.'

Erzberger and his team did not need reminding. They were only too aware that the hours to the deadline were ticking away. They were just as impatient as Foch to have an answer from Berlin, but there was nothing they could do to accelerate the process. The chancellor had been told the Armistice terms and would give his answer when he was ready. Until then, all anyone could do at Compiègne was twiddle their thumbs and wait.

For Chancellor Ebert, the Armistice was only one concern among many, as night fell in Berlin and the city settled down to an uneasy calm. His main priority that day had been to keep a lid on the revolution and prevent it boiling over into chaos. Ebert had largely succeeded, but the day's events had left little time to examine the Armistice terms or provide a considered response. The Armistice had been the least of his problems, with machine guns along the Linden and the wilder elements still running riot across the city.

The focus had moved to east Berlin after lunch, to a mass meeting of soldiers and workers in the arena at Busch Circus. The meeting had been called to elect a new government. All the main political leaders had attended, including Ebert for the Social Democrats and Karl Liebknecht for the Bolshevists. Support for the Bolshevists had proved to be far less enthusiastic than Liebknecht had expected. The revolution had been much more about getting rid of the Kaiser than promoting communism. After lengthy speeches and some frantic horse-trading, Ebert had won the revolutionaries' reluctant endorsement for his new government of Social Democrats.

In return, he had had to make several concessions to the far left, not least the retitling of his own job. He was supposed to be the People's Commissar from now on, rather than the Reich Chancellor. But at least he was still in charge as darkness fell and the crowds began to disperse at last, drifting peacefully back to their homes and barracks.

As for the Armistice, there was nothing Ebert's government could do about it except bite the bullet and accept the terms. A telegram had come from supreme command in Spa urging them to try for a few concessions but to sign anyway if they failed. 'REQUEST SPEEDY GOVERNMENT DECISION ALONG THESE LINES' had been the message from Hindenburg, and Ebert could only agree. There was some confusion about who actually authorised it, but at seven that evening a radio message was sent to Erzberger at Compiègne. It did not waste words:

> The German Government to the plenipotentiaries at Headquarters of the Allied High Command:
> The German Government accepts the conditions of the Armistice communicated to it on 8 November.
> Reich Chancellor, 3084.

The Germans were ready to accept the terms. The number 3084 was a prearranged code word to indicate that the message from the chancellor was genuine.

For Kaiser Wilhelm, still aboard his train at Eisden, the day had been one of unremitting gloom as he sat waiting for Holland's response to his request for asylum. A pair of officials from the German consulate at Maastricht had arrived during the morning, but they knew no more than he did about what was going to happen. At lunchtime, Wilhelm had invited the Dutch officials at the station to join him in the dining car, but the Dutchmen had declined and Wilhelm had taken it as a sign that he was to be refused asylum. He had spent the afternoon worrying that he was going to be sent back to Belgium instead.

It wasn't until nearly midnight, when a train arrived from the Hague, that Wilhelm learned his fate. The train brought the German ambassador and representatives of the Dutch government. They gave him the welcome news that he was to be granted asylum in Holland. Encouraged perhaps by King George V of England, Queen Wilhelmina and her government were prepared to give Wilhelm sanctuary from his enemies. King George had no love for Wilhelm, but he did not want to see his cousin hunted down like a dog, no matter how much Wilhelm deserved it. Blood was thicker than water.

Queen Wilhelmina had spent all day in discussions with her ministers about the Kaiser. At first, she had wanted him to be taken to her summer residence at Het Loo, until someone had pointed out that the house was too close to the Hague and difficult to protect from the inevitable demonstrations. It had needed a great deal of telephoning to find anywhere more suitable. They had eventually settled on the castle at Amerongen, a seventeenth-century mansion surrounded by a double moat. The castle belonged to Count Godard Bentinck van Aldenburg, a Dutch aristocrat whose English cousins were dukes of Portland.

Bentinck himself was not at all keen to have the Kaiser under his roof, especially when he found out how many people the Kaiser would be bringing with him. But they were both prominent in the Order of St John, a Protestant version of the Knights of Malta, and hospitality could not decently be refused among fellow Knights. Bentinck eventually agreed to accommodate the Kaiser and his entourage for three days, provided the Dutch government picked up the bill and then found somewhere else for him to stay. With half the castle closed off and the staff either conscripted into the Dutch army or sick with Spanish flu, it wouldn't be easy for the Bentinck family to accept this German cuckoo into their midst.

The castle was in Utrecht, too late to reach that evening. It was decided that the Kaiser's train should remain at Eisden for the night and start for Amerongen in the morning. After looking up Count Bentinck in the *Almanac de Gotha*, Wilhelm confided to the German ambassador that he was a broken man with nothing to look forward to except despair. The ambassador advised him to write his memoirs and tell his side of the story. Cheering up at once, Wilhelm decided to start in the morning.

Across the Atlantic, President Wilson sat in the Oval Office at the White House, waiting for new of the Armistice from Compiègne. He and his wife had been to church that morning, driving to Washington's Central Presbyterian Church in an old victoria that had been refurbished for use on gas-less Sundays. They had been the centre of attention during the service, the rest of the congregation studying their faces intently for any clue as to what was happening. But although Wilson had done his best to look wise and important, he actually knew little more than anyone else. There was certainly going to be an Armistice in Europe some time, but exactly when and where was still anybody's guess.

The Wilsons had returned to the White House for lunch and then went for a long drive in the afternoon. It was an anxious time for the president, still reeling from the Republican victories of midweek. He was worried that the Armistice would not be signed before Germany's descent into chaos. He had already sent an avalanche of telegrams to that effect, urging the French and British to secure the agreement without delay. Time was of the essence, with the Kaiser gone and a vacuum in his place.

But there was still no word of an Armistice when the Wilsons returned from their drive. Edith Wilson's mother and siblings had been invited for dinner in the White House's private rooms, but they all found it hard to settle with the Armistice hanging over them during the meal. When the news still hadn't come by ten, Edith's family decided to call it a day and return to their hotel. The Wilsons walked them to the elevator and said their goodbyes.

'I do wish you'd go right to bed,' the president's mother-in-law told him as she left. 'You look so tired.'

Wilson agreed, but knew it would be several hours yet before he got any sleep.

'I wish I could,' he replied, 'but I fear the drawer. It always circumvents me. Wait just a moment until I look.'

The drawer was the dominant feature of the president's desk in the Oval Office. All his most urgent cables were put there for his attention, an endless array of large envelopes clipped with red squares indicating that the contents were 'immediate and important'. The envelopes were the bane of Wilson's life.

He returned in a couple of minutes with four or five long cablegrams in code, which he handed to his wife. 'This is your task,' he told her. 'I have many others. There's no rest in sight for either of us yet.'

'Let me stay and help,' offered Edith's brother Randolph.

'Indeed you can help her,' Wilson agreed. 'I'll be very grateful.'

He escorted his wife's mother and sister to their car, then returned to the Oval Office to begin decoding his share of the messages. Edith Wilson and Randolph sat down at the big table in the west hall to do the same. The cables were long and detailed. It was 1 a.m. on 11 November before Edith completed the last of her batch and took it to the Oval Office for the president to read.

The German message to Compiègne accepting the Armistice terms was followed soon afterwards by a much longer message from Field Marshal von Hindenburg. The German delegation asked for time to decipher the code before meeting the Allied delegates to agree the final wording of the Armistice.

They had hardly finished decoding Hindenburg's telegram when they received another from Berlin authorising them to agree the Allies' original terms for the Armistice. To Erzberger's disgust, this telegram wasn't in code and could be read by the Allies, thus compromising the minor improvements in the terms so painfully negotiated over the past two days. It was signed by Reich Chancellor Schluss, a name unknown to the French high command or the government in Paris. The French interpreter asked Erzberger who Schluss was and whether he had replaced Ebert as chancellor. Erzberger told him that Schluss was the German for 'end of message'.

While the German delegates conferred on their train, Admiral Wemyss had a long chat with Marshal Foch after dinner. When it looked as if nothing further was going to happen that night, Wemyss decided to go to bed. He was about to undress when an ADC appeared and told him, with Marshal Foch's compliments, that it looked as if the Germans had received their final instructions and would want a meeting soon. Wemyss decided to lie down on his bed fully clothed and wait, in case Foch was right.

Midnight came and went, but there was no news from the Germans. It wasn't until just after 2 a.m. on 11 November that Wemyss got the call. The German delegation were ready to talk at last and were on their way to the railway car for the meeting. It was time to make peace.

CHAPTER EIGHT

Monday, 11 November 1918, the early hours

One by one the delegates filed into the dining car, carriage 2419D of the Wagons-Lits Company. Flanked by Weygand and Hope, Wemyss and Foch faced the four Germans across the table, taking the same seats as they had on Friday morning. They all knew, as they sat down, that none of them would leave the table again until an agreement had been reached and the Armistice signed. They knew, too, that the Allies held all the cards. There was nothing the Germans could do except swallow their pride and reach for their pens.

Erzberger opened the proceedings. His decoded telegram from Hindenburg contained nine points to be raised with the Allies. Hindenburg was concerned that the German economy would collapse if the Germans were forced to surrender all the lorries and railway carriages demanded by the Allies. They couldn't surrender all the aeroplanes demanded because they no longer had that many. Hindenburg wanted permission for part of the army to march back to Germany through a corner of Holland to save time, and he wanted the food blockade to be lifted at once to prevent starvation at home. He advised Erzberger to agree to the Armistice even if he couldn't obtain these and other concessions, but stressed that Erzberger should make 'a fiery protest' if the more important objections weren't met, accompanied if necessary by an appeal to President Wilson.

Erzberger did his best. He shared Hindenburg's worries about the collapse of the economy and starvation at home and had already made his views known to the Allies. But it was not easy to convince them of the seriousness of the situation in Germany. The Allies thought

162

Erzberger was exaggerating the problem as a negotiating tactic. Even if he wasn't, the French and British had little sympathy for German suffering. That was why the Germans felt the need to throw themselves on President Wilson's mercy if all else failed.

Nevertheless, Foch was prepared to make a few concessions, just so long as the main clauses of the Armistice remained intact. If the Germans didn't have 2,000 aeroplanes left, he would settle for 1,700. If they couldn't deliver 10,000 lorries in a fortnight, then he was prepared to accept 5,000 over a longer period of time. If they needed to keep some machine guns back to fight the Bolshevists at home, then he would accept 25,000 instead of 30,000. And since General von Lettow-Vorbeck's little army remained undefeated in Northern Rhodesia, Foch was ready to accept the evacuation of Germany's East African forces over a specified period of time, rather than their unconditional surrender.

For the navy, however, Rosie Wemyss proved much less accommodating when the Germans tried to whittle down the terms. As well as the surrender of the High Seas Fleet, Wemyss also wanted 160 of Germany's submarines. When Captain Vanselow pointed out that Germany didn't have nearly that many, Wemyss calmly crossed out the figure in the text and replaced it with the words 'all submarines'. Vanselow was bitter that the German fleet in Kiel and Wilhelmshaven should have to surrender to the British when it had never been defeated in battle. Wemyss retorted that the fleet only had to come out. He was equally sharp with Erzberger and Count Oberndorff when they complained that the Royal Navy's blockade was unfair to Germany's women and children:

'Unfair? You sank our ships indiscriminately too.'

Wemyss agreed nevertheless to refer the Germans' request for a lifting of the blockade to his government. He was prepared to 'consider supplying Germany with food, to the degree considered necessary'. Whether anything came of it of course, would be another matter.

The talking went on for hours. It wasn't until just after five in the morning – twelve minutes past, by Erzberger's watch – that agreement was finally reached. With no more outstanding matters to be resolved, the delegates were ready at last to put their names to a document that would bring four years of pointless slaughter to an end. Foch suggested that they should make the official time 5 o'clock, to be followed by a ceasefire six hours later. The others agreed and the Armistice was in place.

Erzberger immediately notified German supreme command by radio. The actual signing of the Armistice took place at twenty past five. Since it would take time to draft a fair copy, Foch suggested that the last page should be typed at once in duplicate and signed by the delegates, leaving the rest to be filled in later. He and Wemyss signed first, followed by Erzberger and Oberndorff, then Winterfeldt and Vanselow in tears. Erzberger ground his teeth as he signed, knowing full well that millions of Germans were going to hate him for what he had just done. For every German who welcomed an end to the war, others would insist that Germany remained undefeated and Erzberger had sold them down the river. In effect, he was signing his own death warrant.

Once the formalities had been completed, Erzberger read out a short statement, agreed in advance by all four Germans, to the effect that anarchy and famine were likely to ensue from the Armistice terms and that it would not be the fault of the Germans. He declared that his countrymen had held off a world of enemies for fifty months and would preserve their liberty and unity despite every kind of violence against them. 'A nation of 70 million suffers,' he announced grandly, 'but it does not die.'

'Très bien.' Foch's response was terse. He was keen to bring the meeting to an end. Among other things, this was only the second time he had stayed up all night since the beginning of the war.

There were no handshakes as the meeting broke up. The Germans went back to their own train to wait for a fair copy of the Armistice agreement before returning to Spa. Admiral Wemyss telephoned the good news to Lloyd George in Downing Street and King George V at Buckingham Palace. Foch grabbed an hour's rest and General Weygand sent a message to the army commanders in the field:

1. Hostilities will cease along the entire front on 11 November, at 11 a.m., French time.

2. Until further notice, Allied troops will not proceed beyond the line reached on this day and at this hour; keep an exact record of the line.

3. All communication with the enemy is forbidden until instructions are sent to army commanders.

At the Germans' request, it was agreed that a copy of the Armistice with accompanying maps would be flown direct to Spa with Captain Geyer. As soon as it was light, Foch and Wemyss posed for a photograph outside the railway carriage with their staff. Then the two of them drove back to Paris, leaving Weygand behind to oversee the details of the ceasefire.

They reached Paris around 9.30 and went straight to the war ministry, where they delivered the Armistice to the French premier, Clemenceau. He had heard the news at six and was delighted to see them both. Seizing Foch and Wemyss by a hand each, he greeted them effusively and offered his warmest congratulations. Wemyss disentangled himself after a while and went on to the British embassy to send a detailed telegram to the government in London.

Clemenceau had originally planned to keep the Armistice a secret – he and Lloyd George had a pact to announce it simultaneously in their respective legislatures – but had decided that it would be impossible. Instead, he was going to keep only the actual details confidential until his announcement that afternoon in the Chamber of Deputies. On the other side of the Channel, Lloyd George too was being robbed of his moment of glory. Alerted by the telephone call from Wemyss, King George V was capering around Buckingham Palace telling everyone he met that the war was over. No one had told him to keep the information under his crown. It would be a long time before Lloyd George managed to forgive Wemyss for that little oversight.

While King George capered, Maude Onions was in the British army's signal office at Boulogne, busily tapping out the official message for

165

the units in the field. Shortly after she had finished, runners began to emerge from command posts all along the line, setting out on foot and horseback, by bicycle, motor bike and car, and in one or two cases by aeroplane, to bring the news to the troops at the front. The runners carried pink flimsies, pages ripped from army signal pads bearing the news they had all been waiting for, the news they had long since decided was never going to come. The signing of the Armistice.

But although the terms had been agreed, the war was not over yet. The morning's advance was already under way in France and Belgium and would continue until 11 o'clock, redoubled if anything, to maintain the pressure on the Germans as the hours ticked away to zero. Foch had ordered the fighting to continue right up to the last minute to keep a sword at the Germans' back and prevent them seizing any advantage in the short time that remained to them. Among the thousands of troops going forward that morning, reaction was mixed as the news of the Armistice began to filter through. Some commanders immediately cancelled their operations, halting their troops where they were or else calling them back to the start line, refusing to jeopardise any more lives in pursuit of an aim already achieved. Nobody wanted to see their men killed on the last day of the war.

An astonishing number, however, were perfectly happy to go on fighting now that they had the bit between their teeth. A great many British, for example, had begun to enjoy the war now that they were winning and still had scores to settle with the Germans, accounts to be rendered for atrocities they had witnessed. They were annoyed that the war was coming to an end before they had reached German soil. They wanted to carry the war to the enemy and visit on German homes and farmsteads the same devastation that the Germans had visited on the Belgians and French. British troops understood, as their political leaders apparently did not, that the Germans would not realise they were beaten until their own towns and villages had been reduced to rubble, their own wives and children forced to abandon their homes and flee in terror.

The Americans too were keen to continue the action, for rather different reasons. They had come late to the war and had not yet fully acquitted themselves in the field. They had taken an inordinate time to deliver their troops to France and had failed to produce tanks and guns in anything like the numbers their economy warranted. Their troops still wore British helmets because they had none of their own. The Americans had fought a few battles, but on nothing like the scale of the British and French. They were conscious that they still had something to prove and only a few hours left to prove it. They would have come into their own if the war had continued into the new year. As it was, if reputations were to be forged and military careers made, it would have to be by 11 o'clock for the Americans, or not at all.

Accordingly, there was an unseemly rush to the front line that Monday morning as American officers who had not hitherto ventured anywhere near the fighting hurried forward to make sure they were in at the finish. It was important for their service records to show that they had spent command time at the front. Unfamiliar faces flooded forward for the last few hours of the war and in many cases took over the leadership, barking out orders for the attack that they themselves would not have to implement. The word from HQ was that there was to be 'absolutely no let-up in the carrying out of the original plans until 11 o'clock ... Operations previously ordered will be pressed with vigour.' Some American commanders turned a blind eye, but most were happy to pursue the war to the end, seizing the opportunity for one final crack at the enemy before hostilities ceased. Of such fire-eating were military reputations made.

Among the many Americans going forward that morning was Private Henry Gunther of the 313th Infantry Regiment, 'Baltimore's Own'. Gunther was a rifleman in Company A, still unaware that the Armistice had been signed as he fixed his bayonet at 9.30 and set off through the mist towards the tiny Lorraine village of Ville-devant-Chaumont. Company A's orders were to capture the village and then proceed to the higher ground beyond. Henry Gunther was prepared to do his share of the fighting as his regiment went into action, but without much enthusiasm. As a German-American, he had no quarrel with the enemy and had not volunteered for the war in France. He was only there because he had been drafted.

Gunther was a bank clerk in civilian life. Like many of his comrades in the 313th, he was from east Baltimore, a heavily German neighbourhood which had never shown much support for the war. The Gunthers were as patriotic as any Americans, but they still had family in the old country and were highly conscious of their heritage, considering themselves as much German as American. Gunther's girlfriend, Olga Grübl, was German-American too. They were going to be married after the war.

Not wanting to fight his own people, Gunther had waved no flags when the United States entered the war and had refused to enlist. Drafted into the 313th five months later, he had arrived in France in July 1918, serving initially as a supply sergeant responsible for distributing equipment to the men. He had disliked the work, advising a friend at home to steer well clear of the war because the conditions in France were so unpleasant. A military censor had passed Gunther's letter to his commanding officer, who had promptly reduced him to private. Humiliated, Gunther had withdrawn into himself for a while, nursing a strong grievance against the army, while the rest of the regiment adapted to the rigours of life in France.

Later, he had decided to rehabilitate himself in an attempt to win his stripes back. On their first day in the trenches, Gunther had volunteered to serve as a runner between regimental and brigade headquarters, a dangerous job which had quickly seen him wounded in the arm. Rather than take himself off to a base hospital, Gunther had chosen to remain with his company at the front. Much as he disliked the war, he disliked losing his stripes more. He would do whatever it took to get them back.

Now it was 11 November and Gunther was still a private. He had no idea how much longer the war was going to last, but it couldn't be very long now. He would have to act soon if he wanted to win promotion on the battlefield and avoid the humiliation of returning home as a private soldier. Probably he would have to do something that day, because the chance was unlikely to arise again. Gripping his rifle as he strode forward into the mist, Private Gunther of the 313th infantry regiment was determined to emerge as Sergeant Gunther again before the day was out.

The Canadians had taken Mons at last. Attacking just before midnight, they had pushed the Germans back along the canal and pressed forward into the heart of the town. The fighting had been fast and furious, but the result had never been in doubt. Before daybreak, the Germans were in full retreat and the Canadians were masters of the town. Mons's burgomaster, Victor Maistrau, was there to see them arrive:

'At five in the morning of the 11th, I saw the shadow of a man and the gleam of a bayonet advancing stealthily along that farther wall near the Café des Princes. Then another shadow, and another. They crept across the square, keeping very low, and dashed north towards the German lines.

'I knew this was liberation. Then, above the roar of artillery, I heard music, beautiful music. It was as though the Angels of Mons were playing. And then I recognised the song and the musician. Our carilloneur was playing 'O Canada' by candlelight. This was the signal. The whole population rushed into the square, singing and dancing, although the battle still sounded half a mile away.'

Corporal George Tizard was with the Canadians' 236th battalion. They reached the outskirts of Mons at 4 a.m. and moved forward cautiously past burning houses and the bodies of Germans killed in the fighting. Delirious Belgians rained kicks down on the dead Huns and rushed to greet the advancing Canadians, a number of whom were actually Americans serving in the Canadian army. Tizard was hugged and kissed, then pulled into an English-speaking home for a cup of coffee. 'I was enjoying myself smoking a good cigar and had two very nice looking girls as companions, one on each arm; everywhere you looked you saw soldiers and girls walking arm in arm.'

At seven, as it was growing light, the Canadians formed up for a march to the town square. Kilted bagpipers led the way along the Grand Boulevard while the townspeople ran alongside and cheered. The Belgians threw flowers and waved tricolours, singing 'La Brabançonne', their national anthem, while the carillon in the bell tower pealed out an inexpert rendering of 'Tipperary' across the rooftops. The Belgians had been waiting more than four years for this moment.

War correspondent Philip Gibbs was not there to record it, but he wasn't far behind. Calling at brigade headquarters on his way to Mons, he was elated to learn that hostilities were to cease at eleven. Gibbs lost no time hurrying forward to join the Canadians in the town:

'All the way to Mons there were columns of troops on the march, and their bands played ahead of them, and almost every man had a flag on his rifle, the red, white and blue of France, the red, yellow and black of Belgium. They wore flowers in their caps and in their tunics, red and white chrysanthemums given them by crowds of people who cheered them on their way, people who in many of these villages had been only one day liberated from the German yoke. Our men marched singing, with a smiling light in their eyes. They had done their job, and it was finished with the greatest victory in the world.

'The war ended for us at Mons, as it had begun there. When I went into this town this morning it seemed to me a most miraculous coincidence and a joyful one. Last night there was a fight outside the town before our men forced their way in at 10 o'clock. The Germans left many of their guns in the gardens before they ran. This morning Mons was full of English cavalry and Canadian troops, about whom there were crowds of townspeople, cheering them and embracing them.

'One old man told me of all they had suffered in Mons, but he wept only when he told me of the sufferings of our prisoners. "What shame for Germany," he said. "What shame when these things are known about your poor men starving to death. Our women tried to give them food, but were beaten for it, and fifteen days ago down there by the canal one of your English was killed because a woman gave him a bit of bread."

'Little children came up to me and described the fighting the night before, and many people narrated the first fighting in Mons in August of 1914, when the "Old Contemptibles" were there and fought their battle through the town, and then on their way of retreat outside.'

The Kaiser had been misquoted about Britain's contemptible army of 1914. He had actually said it was 'contemptibly little', as indeed it was at the beginning of the war. But the Old Contemptibles were delighted at the insult and bore the name with pride. Three men of the London Rifle Brigade who had retreated from Mons in 1914 were there again on the last day of the war, each with the ribbon of the Mons Star on his tunic. The men had come unscathed through all the battles in between and had returned after four years to liberate the town from which they had had to retreat so dramatically. All three of them were lying dead in the road, killed by a last burst of fire as the Germans themselves fled the town in the darkness and beat a hasty retreat.

East of Valenciennes, a British battalion had come to an apparently deserted village in the early morning light. Led by a corporal, a patrol went forward to check it out. They found a wounded German lieu-tenant propped against a wall. He had been hit in the thigh by a shell splinter and left for the British to look after when they arrived.

The lieutenant spoke good English. He told his captors that the Germans had pulled out two hours earlier and the village was empty. Taking him at his word, the patrol summoned the rest of the battalion from across the fields. They all formed up at the edge of the village and marched as a battalion into the village square.

They were an easy target for the machine guns that opened up from the church tower and all around the square. More than a hundred were killed or wounded before they had a chance to scatter. Enraged, the British charged the surrounding buildings and took no prisoners. The Germans all died fighting, determined to take as many British with them as they could.

The corporal in command of the original patrol made his way back through the village and found the German lieutenant, still propped against the wall. The German didn't flinch as the corporal killed him with a bayonet. Later, the corporal pushed open a barn door and found the body of a young girl. She was stark naked and she had been badly mutilated before she died. The Germans east of Valenciennes were not taking defeat with a good grace.

Further along the line, Julian Pease Fox had been up all night dealing with an ambulance full of wounded and bailing out one of his men who had been arrested by police after being found 'where he shouldn't'. As a Quaker, Fox had volunteered for the Friends Ambulance Unit at the outbreak of war rather than bear arms in the fighting. He had served on the Western Front since January 1915, driving an ambulance at Ypres under shellfire and narrowly avoiding capture by the Germans. At Champagne in 1917, he had driven so close to the French front line during a battle that the Germans had accused the French of camouflaging their tanks with Red Cross signs. The French had responded by awarding Fox the Croix de Guerre with gold star for his courage.

Fox was a Quaker on his mother's side. He had honoured her wishes by taking no part in the fighting, but as the news of the Armistice arrived he was still wondering if he had made the right decision. The Germans had committed so many atrocities during the war, against both civilians and prisoners of war, that Fox had been sorely tempted to join the army proper and play his full part in the war. On balance, he was probably glad that he hadn't, because there had been an incident earlier in 1918 that had convinced him that both sides were just as bad as each other.

The German army had been full of teenage boys by then, young lads who had only just started shaving. A group of them had been trapped in no-man's-land after an attack on the French. They had begun to cry and had got on the nerves of the French troops who had to listen to them. The French had taken them prisoner and the Germans had fallen into the hands of some North African troops. They had buggered the German boys all through the night and then shot them in the morning.

That was bad enough, but what was worse for Julian Fox was that everyone had been amused when they heard about it later:

Monday, 11 November 1918, the early hours

'We were told this story by a French officer and others and I suddenly realised afterwards that we had heard it almost as a matter of entertainment and simply hadn't been struck by the complete horror of the situation. It made me realise that war not only kills people physically but it destroys them body and soul.'

But the war was coming to an end now, so there would be no more atrocities of that kind. Fox was sitting down, exhausted after being up all night, when it crossed his mind that it might have been better if neither side had won, in the end. Victory for one side could only mean defeat for the other, and that was bound to lead to trouble sooner or later. The British would certainly have wanted a rematch if they had been on the losing side.

At La Brayelle airfield, Bogart Rogers, the Stanford boy in the RAF, was sitting with his friends at the breakfast table, waiting to fly a sortie, when news of the Armistice arrived:

Hostilities are to cease at 11 o'clock. No war flying is to be done after the receipt of this message.

It was wonderful news, of course, but Rogers couldn't quite believe that the war was over at last. It didn't seem possible that there would be no more forays into enemy territory, worrying about German fighters and anti-aircraft fire and seeing good men killed who deserved to live. Only the previous day, Rogers had escorted a squadron of bombers across the lines and had watched one of them go down, hit by a lucky burst of flak. His friend Bill Leaf had been killed a week ago; his friend Callender, 'as square and decent a man as ever lived', hadn't been dead much longer. Like thousands of others, Rogers felt guilty at having made it to the Armistice when so many of his comrades had not:

'When I think of all the fellows who aren't going home, I wonder what right I've had to live. I know that surely there has been divine protection ... People can prate until the judgement day about war being the salvation of nations, the one thing that can keep them from

173

decay, but I know that it will never be worth the sacrifice. It's all wrong.'

With the other pilots, Rogers went down to the airfield after breakfast to see the aircraft put away. The ground crew were given the day off afterwards, told to do what they liked. Most of them headed to the canteen for a beer and a sing-song. Rogers followed later and bought them all a drink. He disliked drinking so early in the day, especially when there would be more to come later. The party that night was bound to be 'wild and woolly'. It would almost certainly end up in the sergeants' mess, because that was where all the big parties ended up. A modest drinker by British standards, Rogers was glad they didn't have to celebrate peace too often.

Captain John Glubb was at Sars Poteries when the Armistice was announced, looking forward to chasing the Germans across the border into Belgium. A brigade was being formed for the purpose and Glubb was to command the Royal Engineers:

'We shall accompany the advanced guard, of course, and it should be quite exciting, if only we can overtake Brother Boche. I always have looked forward to a chance to bring my pontoons into action at a gallop and slap down a bridge under enemy fire!'

But it was not to be. Glubb was at a farmhouse, foraging hay for the horses, when he heard the news:

'As I was standing below, watching the drivers throwing the hay out of the loft window, a mounted orderly rode up and told us that the war was over. A dreadful blow! I was just beginning to enjoy it, and this will finish my dreams of the dashing column of pursuit.'

Glubb's was strictly a minority view. There weren't many people on the Western Front who were sorry to learn that the war was over.

A few miles away, Herbert Sulzbach of the German field artillery shared the gloom on his side of the line as the order came for a ceasefire at 12 o'clock, German time. Sulzbach had known it was coming, but that didn't make it any easier to bear:

'The war is over ... How we all looked forward to it, imagined it as the most marvellous moment of our lives, and now we stand here humbled, torn to pieces inside, and have surrendered – Germany to the Entente!'

Sulzbach's orders were to evacuate the area after midday and begin the long march home. Under the Armistice terms, the entire German army had to be out of Belgium and across the Rhine within fourteen days. It would be a logistical nightmare with so many different units crowding the roads. A single army group needed five ration trains a day and six hundred head of cattle to survive, and there were four such army groups around the sole railway line beyond Namur, where Sulzbach's regiment had been ordered to go.

Namur was where the war had started for Sulzbach. He had come full circle after more than fifty months at the front, as if the beginning of the war and the end were shaking hands. Bitter though he was at what had happened in between, Sulzbach couldn't repress a strong feeling of relief that he personally was going to come out of it all right:

'Every now and then I'm overcome with euphoria at going home forever, with an indescribable gratitude that in all the fights and battles, in all the years, I have never once suffered a scratch. I was at the front for four years and two months, all but fourteen days of it in the murderous west. I believe, as I have from the first day, in providence and fate. I doubt if there are many soldiers who have been at the front for fifty months and are coming home unwounded like me!'

The regiment had orders to set up a committee of shop stewards before they started for home. Each committee was to consist of one officer, one NCO and several other ranks. No one in the 63rd Field Artillery had the slightest interest in trade unions, but the orders came from above. It seemed that the Bolshevists and their sympathisers were in charge of the German army now, if only for the moment.

In Holland, the Kaiser was on his way to Amerongen. His train had left Eisden at twenty past nine that morning, heading north via Maastricht and Nijmegen towards Arnhem. The train had departed without fanfare, but everyone in Holland appeared to know that the

Kaiser was coming. Thousands were waiting at every town and village along the way to give him a hostile reception. Even in the open fields between stations they had gathered to whistle and catcall, shaking their fists as the Kaiser passed and making throat-cutting gestures at his train. For a man long accustomed to adulation, it was a deeply humiliating experience.

The Kaiser sat in the dining car with the curtains closed at first. He had been afraid this would happen. Before leaving Spa the previous day, he had said that it didn't matter where he went into exile, because wherever he went in the world he would be hated. His aides were terrified that the train would be attacked: they wondered if it wouldn't have been wiser to have travelled in the dark. They were due to reach Maarn, the nearest station to Amerongen, some time after three that afternoon. As the catcalls persisted and the garrotting gestures followed them along the line, the Kaiser and his people could only hope that they would all still be in one piece when they arrived.

In the fields beyond Verdun, the Americans were firing off their ammunition to get rid of it before 11 o'clock. A French 155 battery behind Harry Truman had begun to fire soon after first light, shooting off round after round in rapid succession as if there was no tomorrow. Truman's house shook like an earthquake every time a gun went off. His own battery was firing as well, testing a new type of shell that was said to have an increased range of 30 per cent. It was certainly reducing the village of Herméville to rubble.

Truman received official word of the Armistice around 10.30. He sent at once for Squatty Meisburger, his battery sergeant. Meisburger arrived to find Truman with a wide grin on his face:

'He was stretched out on the ground eating a blueberry pie. Where he got the blueberry pie I don't know ... His face was all smeared with blueberries. He handed me a piece of flimsy and said between bites, "Sergeant, you will take this back and read it to the members of the battery."'

Meisburger obeyed with alacrity. It was what they all wanted to hear, but there was still some ammunition to dispose of before the ceasefire. Truman's battery went back to work and fired off a total of 164 rounds that morning. They fired the last at 10.45, just fifteen minutes before the deadline.

The sound of the firing carried as far as Rastatt, the prison camp on the Rhine. It was so loud that particular day, with all the extra ammunition being fired off, that it woke Second Lieutenant George Coles long before first light. He and his fellow prisoners lay in their bunks listening quietly to the noise in the distance. They were pretty sure what it meant:

'We were awakened at 4 a.m. by the terrific roar of guns on the Verdun front. The French were obviously using up all their spare ammunition and having their final strafe in memory of Sedan. We were all up at 5 a.m. tingling with excitement and wondering what would happen next. The news we received was scrappy and contradictory as the German news service had completely broken down ... Events around us were moving so quickly that we had no time to stand still to analyse our emotions or to celebrate the victory of our arms. We, personally, were still prisoners in a hostile and sullen land – and our paramount thoughts were now bound up with release.'

Coles spent the rest of the morning 'almost in a dream', thanking God that he was still alive to see the day and conjuring up visions of his home in England, 'where khaki, prison, and war would be things of the past – dead, gone and forgotten'. It wouldn't be long now before he was released from prison camp and free to go home at last, back to his family and, best of all, his girlfriend, Connie, in Preston. It couldn't happen too soon for George Coles.

In Leipzig, Ethel Cooper, too, was longing to go home. An Australian, she had been in Leipzig when the war broke out and had been stuck there ever since, forbidden to travel anywhere else on pain of being arrested as a spy. She had made several attempts to leave Germany during the war, feigning illness at first, then persuading the Dutch embassy to intervene on her behalf, but always to no avail. The

Germans had refused to let her leave the country. She had seen and heard far too much to be allowed out.

It was music that had brought Ethel to Leipzig – that, and a love of foreign travel. She had visited Leipzig on and off for many years before the war and had made some good friends in the city, one or two of whom had had a slice from the elephant in Leipzig zoo when the Royal Navy's food blockade had begun to bite. The Germans had been perfectly civil to her during the war, although her rooms were regularly searched by the police. But Ethel was still keen to leave, if only to escape the Bolshevism that was threatening to sweep the country. She had sold the last of her furniture a couple of weeks ago and was keeping the cash in her rooms, rather than entrust it to a bank in such uncertain times. She was ready to pack a bag and take the train out of Leipzig at a moment's notice.

She had seen her first red flag on Friday, as she excitedly reported to her sister in Adelaide:

'I was on my way to lunch, and coming into one of the main streets saw a dense grey crowd coming towards me and at the head of it a great red flag. I must say I stood rooted, with my heart in my mouth. As you know, I have waited for it for weeks, but when one first sees it, it takes one's breath away. They were a few hundred soldiers, in their "field-grey", that corresponds to our khaki, but their shoulder-straps, numbers, belts and arms had vanished. I fell into the crowd and got beside a soldier in full marching outfit and heavy kit – "Have you come from 'outside'?" I said. "Nay, we were ordered out, but that is all over – this is the end," he said … I asked other questions, but he stumbled along in a sort of dream – I don't think he really saw or heard or thought anything …

'We got to the Volkshaus, the headquarters of the Social Democratic Party – then they picketed the streets, stopped the trams and took away the numbers and weapons from all soldiers and officers and police. It was absolutely orderly – an officer resisted and fired a couple of shots, but they simply disarmed him and let him go. By the evening the town was placarded with huge announcements, that the "Workmen and Soldiers' Council" had taken over the government of the town, and that the military and civil authorities had submitted to them.'

On Saturday, news had come of the Kaiser's abdication, an event greeted in Leipzig with widespread relief. It had been followed on Sunday by the publication of the Armistice terms, so stringent that Ethel had shared the general dismay at the conditions:

'I have not dared to speak to a German since, but one thing is clear to me – that everything *must* be accepted, and yet humanely speaking *can't* be fulfilled. For if the blockade is to be continued, and 150,000 wagons or trucks given up (that is one-fifth of Germany's rolling stock) while at the same time 8 million men are to be transported from all ends of Europe back to Germany, then it will be *impossible* to supply the big towns with their food.

'At the present time those big towns have, to put it mildly, none too much, and if there is a hitch the people must rise and plunder, and there will be the worst form of Russian terrorism. But I can only hope and believe that directly there is an utter capitulation, England will raise the blockade, and that the powers will arrange that the necessary food supplies come in, or are forwarded as usual.'

The day of the Armistice itself meant little to the people of Leipzig. The outside world had ceased to exist for most of them, with so much disaster at home. Ethel was wondering how much longer it would be before she could take a train out of there, to France perhaps or Holland. She had been to the police station to find out, but the station was in the hands of Red Guards who didn't know anything and suggested she come back in a few days' time. With everything so chaotic, Ethel was thinking of leaving without a permit and trusting to luck to see her safely out of Germany before the whole country collapsed into Bolshevism.

At Osnabrück, in Lower Saxony, Private Erich Maria Remarque was delighted to find himself back in his home town as the war came to an end. Technically, he was still in the German army, posted to the 1st Guards Reserve Battalion in Osnabrück for remedial training after a fifteen-month spell in hospital. In practice, however, the army was disintegrating and no one was interested in soldiering any more. Remarque was free to come and go as he pleased.

He had always been a reluctant soldier, conscripted from teacher-training college at the age of eighteen and sent to France in 1917 to join the infantry at the front. The Remarques were themselves French in origin, a family from Alsace who had been living quietly in Germany for several generations. Erich Remarque had had no illusions about the war by the time he arrived on the Western Front. He had seen and heard too many horror stories to believe the propaganda put out by the German government. He had no time for the civilians at home who pushed flags around on maps and preached the glories of war – people like the odious little teacher at Osnabrück's Roman Catholic Präparande school, who was all blood and thunder and hectored his pupils into joining up as soon as they were of age. Remarque had no time at all for people like that.

He had seen terrible things during his short time at the front: his best friend lying in the mud with his abdomen torn open, other people with their feet shot off, sprinting across the field on their stumps to avoid the shells dropping all around. Remarque had been at Passchendaele, the third battle of Ypres, when his friend Theo Troske had been hit in the leg by shrapnel. Remarque had hoisted Troske on to his shoulders and carried him all the way back to the dressing station under a hail of fire. They had almost made it when Troske died of a head wound that Remarque had failed to notice.

Remarque himself had been wounded a few days later. He had been helping another wounded man in a thunderstorm when he was hit by a British shell. Shrapnel sliced through his neck, leg and arm, lacerating his right hand so badly that he was forced to abandon his idea of becoming a professional pianist after the war. Remarque was taken out of the line at once and sent back to Germany. He had only served a few weeks at the front. He spent the next fifteen months in hospital and was not finally discharged until 31 October 1918.

He might have been released sooner if he hadn't spun out his wounds for as long as possible, exaggerating their severity in order to avoid being sent back to the line. Like thousands of soldiers in every army, Remarque had been in no hurry to return to the fighting. He had much preferred to remain safely in hospital. Even after his wounds had healed he had managed to stay in hospital for a while, making himself useful in the administration office, where his literacy was a help. He had used the time well, beginning his first novel during his convalescence and selling a few articles to literary magazines. He was thinking of becoming a writer after the war if he couldn't play the piano.

For the moment, though, Remarque was still in the army, an angry young man strutting around Osnabrück in the uniform of a lieutenant to which he was not entitled. Private Remarque had spent only June and July 1917 on the Western Front and had never been promoted. He hadn't won the Iron Cross either, although he wore it First Class on his chest.

He wore a monocle too and was accompanied everywhere by a German shepherd dog which he claimed had saved his life at the front. Erich Remarque, intelligent but lower class, was busily reinventing himself as an officer and a gentleman, a hero returning from the war. He was going to write about the war one day, when it was all over. He had decided that his few weeks at the front would make an excellent subject for a novel in due course.

At home in London's Cavendish Square, former prime minister Henry Asquith had been up all night celebrating the end of the war with his family. Someone from the War Office had rung at midnight to tell them, wrongly, that the Armistice had just been signed. Too excited to sleep, Asquith had stayed up for the rest of the night with his wife and daughter, discussing the news and speculating about the peace terms. Asquith had been prime minister for the first two years of the war, leading the country through some of the darkest days in its history. Although he had been forced to resign after the slaughter on the Somme, where his own son had been killed, he could scarcely suppress his relief that everything had turned out all right in the end.

It was just after 6 a.m. when the Asquiths learned of the War

Office's mistake. A few minutes later, an American friend rang Margot Asquith to say that the Germans had indeed signed the Armistice, at 5.30, and the war really would be over at eleven. She ran downstairs at once and ordered the staff to go out and buy as many flags as they could for the house, roof and motor car. She sent three telegrams as well, one to the king, one to his mother, Queen Alexandra, and one to General Sir John Cowans, and took them into her husband's room for him to sign.

The Asquiths had a family funeral to attend after breakfast. They skimmed through the newspapers before they left, against a background of unfamiliar noises from the street: a mix of guns going off, signal maroons being fired, loud cheers and voices singing 'The British Grenadiers' and 'God Save the King'. Looking out, Margot saw 'elderly nurses in uniform, and stray men and women clasping each other round the waist, laughing and dancing in the centre of the street'.

The funeral was at Golders Green crematorium. It was for Asquith's brother, a retired schoolmaster. Most mourners' thoughts were elsewhere as the casket disappeared through the folding doors. Some were thinking about the Armistice, others about more pertinent graves in France. The Asquiths paid their respects, then got back in the car and hurried home to central London. Margot Asquith in particular was determined not to miss any more of the fun:

'When we returned from Hampstead we could see the progress that the great news had made. Flags, big and little, of every colour and nationality were flying from roofs, balconies and windows. The men who were putting them up were waving their caps at each other from the top of high ladders, and conventional pedestrians were whistling or dancing breakdowns on the pavement; a more spontaneous outbreak of simple gaiety could hardly have been imagined ...

'We arrived at No. 20 and found that our thoughtful butler, with praiseworthy patriotism, had smothered the house in flags; even the Welsh harp could be seen fluttering greenly from the window of Henry's library.

'I was told that in a short time it would be impossible to move in the streets except upon foot, as they were already jammed with wagons, trollies, motor cars and coster-carts; and that the queues outside the shops which sold flags were of such a length as to block the passage of any passers-by. On hearing this I jumped into the motor and told our chauffeur to drive down the main streets so that I might see the crowd.

'It was a wonderful sight, and more like a foreign carnival than what we are accustomed to in this country. Heavy motor lorries were flying backwards and forwards stacked with munition workers; males and females in brilliant colours were standing on each other's shoulders yelling and waving flags or shaking tambourines at one another. Everyone was nailing up some sort of decoration, or quizzing their neighbour. No one intended to work that day, nor could they be expected to when the whole world was rejoicing.'

Lloyd George, the man who had replaced her husband as prime minister, was going to announce the terms of the Armistice in the House of Commons that afternoon. Henry Asquith would be there as well. Margot was going to watch them both from the Speaker's Gallery. Despite her exhaustion after a night without sleep, she wouldn't have missed it for anything.

At the White House, Edith Wilson, too, was exhausted after a night with very little sleep. It had been 1 a.m. when she handed the last of her decoded telegrams to her husband in the Oval Office – a message from Tiger Clemenceau in Paris about working in harmony with the United States during the peace negotiations after the Armistice. News of the signing had reached Washington a couple of hours later. The Wilsons had been told when they woke up. They had stood mute, according to Edith, 'unable to grasp the full significance of the words'. The news was already on the streets and Americans were waking up to a day of national rejoicing. The war really was over this time.

President Wilson shut himself in the Oval Office as soon as breakfast was finished. He was due to address a joint session of Congress at lunchtime, formally announcing the signing of the Armistice at Compiègne. As with Lloyd George in London and Clemenceau in

Paris, it was going to be a very important occasion for Wilson, one of the most historic days of his life. He needed the rest of the morning to work on his speech.

But the war wasn't over yet, at least not on the Western Front. Most of the German army seemed to be aware of the ceasefire at eleven, but there were still isolated units among the British and Americans who hadn't heard and didn't know. With a front of several hundred miles, both sides firing off their ammunition, and telephone wires severed in many places, it was inevitable that not everybody had learned about the Armistice. Even among those who had, it was tacitly understood – particularly among middle-ranking Americans – that the war wasn't over until eleven. A shameful number of American majors and colonels had chosen to press on regardless, rather than call their men off and risk damaging their careers. They were still sending troops into action, knowing perfectly well that the fighting would stop in a couple of hours and any further sacrifice was needless. They would rather their men died than have a permanent black mark on their promotion prospects.

The US Army's 356th Infantry Regiment was one of those that knew nothing of the Armistice as it went forward that morning. The men of the 356th had been ordered to force their way across the river Meuse on rickety pontoon bridges and then take the village of Pouilly in the fog. Second Lieutenant Francis Jordan of company H was in the thick of it as the regiment advanced. They crossed the river without mishap but hadn't gone much further when Jordan and his men came under machine-gun fire from less than twenty feet away:

'I received a minor flesh wound through the shoulder, which bullet continued on to hit my pack which was filled with cans of food. The impact tipped me over backwards, and, in falling, I threw up my hand and received a bullet at the base of my left thumb. The machine gun had been shifted quickly and killed the first sergeant immediately behind me and the sergeant immediately behind him. Our advance was stopped for the time being.'

One of Jordan's corporals crawled forward and propped his rifle across Jordan's chest to fire in the direction of the machine guns. The Germans returned fire so accurately that the wood on the corporal's rifle was splintered. The Germans were dealt with eventually and the advance continued, but it was some time before Jordan was rescued. Stretcher-bearers found him after a while and put him in an ambulance for Beaumont. His men had gone on without him and Jordan was out of the battle, left with conflicting emotions as the ambulance jolted towards the rear. He still didn't know anything about the Armistice and it wasn't until much later that he found out.

Further to the east, Brigadier General John Sherburne of the US army's 92nd division had watched a spectacular firework display the previous night as German troops fired off all their remaining flares and rockets along the Moselle river near Metz. It had been obvious from the display that the Germans were getting rid of their reserves and did not expect to do any more fighting.

All the more worrying then that two regiments of the 92nd division had been ordered forward that morning to capture the villages of Champey and Bouxières, near the river. As the officer in charge of the artillery support, Sherburne found it extraordinary that the attack was still scheduled to go ahead when everybody knew the war was going to end any minute, if it hadn't already done so.

Sherburne had rung divisional headquarters at 1.30 in the morning to find out if the attack was still set for 5 a.m. He had been told that it was. Unable to believe his ears, he had gone over the divisional commander's head to the Second Army's artillery headquarters at Toul to query the orders, pointing out that the hill dominating the two villages was strongly defended and casualties would not be light if the Americans proceeded with the attack. Everyone he spoke to agreed, and everyone was aware of the Armistice negotiations, but no one was prepared to countermand the orders. The attack was to go ahead as planned.

In the end, the 365th was allowed to stay put, but the 366th went ahead as ordered. The men of both regiments were black, most of them drafted, all of them segregated from the white troops in the same army. They had some black officers, but none higher than captain or temporary major, because blacks couldn't be promoted further than that. They were attached to the French army to prevent friction with white Americans. Nothing much was expected of them because of their colour. Their political leaders had had to lobby hard for black Americans to be allowed to fight at all.

The 366th began their advance at 5 a.m. Three hours later, Sherburne received official confirmation of the Armistice. He immediately rang divisional headquarters again, convinced that the attack would now be called off, only to be told that it was still going ahead. Nothing had changed. His guns were to continue supporting the advance.

Incredulous, Sherburne returned to his duties as the men of the 366th approached Bouxières. The Germans entrenched on La Cote hill opened up with machine guns and mustard gas as soon as they were within range. The 366th reached the edge of the village before being forced back towards the Bois de la Voivrotte. They regrouped in the wood and returned to the attack, advancing towards their objective again over the bodies of their stricken comrades. The Germans opened fire again and the 366th withdrew again.

The war had less than an hour to run as they returned to the wood for a second time and began to reorganise themselves for a third assault on the village in front of them. It wasn't until half past ten that a runner reached them with news of the Armistice. Even then, he didn't bring any orders to cancel the attack. So far as Sherburne or anyone else knew, they were all supposed to go on trying to capture Bouxières until 11 o'clock precisely.

On the British front, too, the war was far from over, not least around Mons. The British were determined to clear the town and be well beyond it before the ceasefire at eleven. They intended to put their markers down in open countryside when a halt was called and the last front line of the war was drawn up. It would be nice to have some progress to show for four years of fighting, even if it was only a few hundred yards.

Canadian infantry had taken Mons, but it was the cavalry who led the way into the countryside beyond. The 5th (Royal Irish) Lancers had been the last British regiment to leave Mons in August 1914. They were the first back again on the final day of the war, a long column of horsemen clattering purposefully through the Grande Place on their way to St-Denis to seize the high ground to the north-east. They were recognised in the Grande Place by a Belgian priest who had watched them retreating four years previously. 'We saw you going,' he yelled. 'We knew you would be back.'

It had been a frustrating war for the cavalry. Their horses had been of little use against machine guns. The Lancers had served dismounted as infantry for much of the time, doing their bit in the trenches like everyone else. They had only recently come into their own again, when the trenches had been abandoned and the war had become mobile once more, an exhilarating chase across country in pursuit of an ever-retreating enemy. It was wonderful to be back in the saddle.

The Canadians stood aside as the Lancers swept through. Once out of Mons, they wheeled into position and formed up for the advance towards St-Denis. Among them was George Ellison, a twenty-five-year-old private from Leeds. Older than most of his comrades, Ellison had a wife at home, named Hannah. There was nothing remarkable about him as he jingled along with the rest of his troop, but Ellison was destined nevertheless to make a name for himself in the short time that remained to him before the war came to an end.

On the other side of the line, Ernst Kielmeyer of the German army's 26th Reserve Field Artillery was sheltering in a Belgian school at Breuthaut when his sergeant appeared breathlessly in the doorway, bringing the news they had all been waiting for. Germany was a re-public at last and the Armistice had been signed. It was official. They could all stop fighting at 11 o'clock and go home.

The news was more than welcome to Kielmeyer. Still only twenty, he was a veteran of Passchendaele, where he had been a signalman for the artillery, crawling forward under sniper fire to repair the telephone lines between the forward observers and the gun batteries.

He had worked with a fat corporal for a while, until the corporal's bulk had attracted enemy fire. After that, he had preferred to work alone.

Kielmeyer himself had once had a couple of Tommies in his sights, two British soldiers carrying buckets alongside the Yser canal, blissfully unaware of Kielmeyer on the opposite bank. They had been unarmed as Kielmeyer took aim. He had lowered his rifle after a moment, not wanting to shoot helpless men. The Tommies might have had children at home praying for their safe return, just as the Germans did.

Kielmeyer was no Bolshevist, but he had had enough of the war and the Kaiser and all of that. He was glad it was all over, even if it did mean Germany's defeat. 'We won't have to endure another winter out here to suffer, freeze, die and join our comrades who sleep the eternal sleep far from home,' he consoled himself on Armistice morning. The Belgians were still a worry – 'how hostile they are ... trying to kill us with their eyes' – but if the Belgians didn't get them, Kielmeyer and his comrades might actually be home in time for Christmas.

Further along the line, Feldwebel Georg Bucher was counting the hours to the ceasefire. His unit had beaten off an American attack that morning, gunning them down on the wire before they got anywhere near the Germans. The Americans had transferred their attention to the neighbouring sector and were shelling it furiously, to Bucher's consternation. He couldn't understand why the Yanks were still fighting, if there was to be a ceasefire at eleven:

'We stood in the trench and watched with ashen faces and clenched hands. Why were our comrades being shelled? The enemy must have heard the news. All we could think of was how to survive the next three hours. Many of the men had got all their gear together. I saw one man lingering near the communication trench, ready to run for his life if he had to.'

Bucher was as nervous as anyone else. He was an old lag in the company, one of the very few 'front hogs' still alive from 1914. His five

188

closest friends had all been killed long ago. Bucher didn't want to join them now, this close to the end.

A boy named Walter had been wounded that morning, his leg and thigh scorched with corrosive acid from an American shell. He lay in excruciating pain in a dugout, trying to make the best of it while Bucher comforted him. Together they watched the clock as the hands moved towards half past ten. 'Only another half hour!' Walter joked to Bucher.

He joked too soon. Even as he spoke, the Americans began to bombard them again, using gas this time. A sentry staggered into their dugout to give a warning, then staggered out again. Bucher hurriedly helped Walter on with his gas mask and grabbed his own. He didn't have a moment to lose. By the light of the flickering candle, he could already see the gas in the dugout, seeping towards them in a deadly cloud of poisonous mist.

Bucher's unit was not the only one under fire. In scores of different places along the front line, soldiers were still fighting and dying as the hands moved towards 11 o'clock. Some had no idea the war was about to stop. Others did know, but didn't care. They still had ammunition to fire off, objectives to take, friends and family to avenge. Others just carried on fighting because that was what they had been ordered to do. The habit died hard in men who had never done anything else.

All along the line, they were waiting for the end to come. From the Belgian coast to Switzerland, millions of men were acutely aware that the fighting must stop soon, even if they wouldn't actually believe it until they saw it. Men from all over the world, from all sorts of different countries and backgrounds: British, German, American, French, Belgian and Portuguese; Canadian, Australian, New Zealander and South African; Maori and Afrikaner, Indian and native American, Moroccan and Algerian, Senegalese and Chinese from the labour battalions, all sorts and conditions of men, a vast cross-section of humanity, all of them waiting for the noise to stop and the shooting to end. It couldn't be much longer now.

British, French and American troops were still going forward as the hands nudged eleven. The Germans were responding when they were attacked, but were otherwise lying low, causing no trouble. Nobody wanted to be killed now, so close to the end. Nobody even wanted to think about it. Another few minutes, God willing, and it would all be over. Another few minutes and the soldiers of all sides would have made it to the finishing line. It wasn't much longer to wait.

CHAPTER NINE

Monday, 11 November 1918, 11 a.m.

For many on the front line, perhaps most, the actual moment of the Armistice was an anticlimax when it came. The troops had waited so long for something that was never going to happen that they had run out of enthusiasm by the time it actually did. They were too exhausted, too numb, to raise more than half a cheer when the moment arrived. A few threw their hats in the air and celebrated for a while. Most were just glad the wretched business was over at last.

Deneys Reitz, commanding a battalion of the Royal Scots Fusiliers, was leading his men up to the line when the moment came. As a seventeen-year-old, Reitz had fought the British during the Boer War, joining Jan Smuts's commando in hit-and-run raids against British camps and convoys in South Africa. He had once encountered a prisoner named Winston Churchill, who had claimed to be a war correspondent although he had been carrying a revolver when captured. After the war, Reitz had followed other Boers into exile rather than accept British rule. Later, Smuts had persuaded him to return and seek a compromise with the British for the good of the country. Smuts had likened Afrikaners who compromised with the British to Southerners in the United States who stood by the Union during the Civil War.

Now, Reitz was leading his Fusiliers forward after a period at the rear. They were on their way from a village near Le Quesnoy – captured so daringly by the New Zealanders a week ago – towards the old fortress town of Maubeuge, where they were to reinforce the Guards battalions along the road to Mons. They had set off at dawn, but Reitz still hadn't been told of the Armistice as they approached the fighting:

'In front and behind us were thousands of other troops going forward, and one could feel the suppressed excitement in the air, for every man realised that this was the final thrust. By 11 o'clock we were in the battle zone, British and German guns were firing, and there came the crackle of rifles and machine guns ahead.

'Suddenly, far off, we heard the faint sound of cheering borne upon the wind. It gathered volume as it rolled towards us, and then we saw our brigade major slowly making his way through the troops on the road. He carried good tidings, for around him the shouts grew deafening, and when at last he came up, he handed me a dispatch which I have carefully preserved. It contained momentous news:

> Hostilities will cease at 1100 hours today 11 Nov aaa Troops will stand fast on line reached at that hour which will be reported to Corps HQ aaa There is to be no intercourse with the enemy and no Germans are to be allowed to enter our lines, any doing so will be taken prisoners.

In contrast to the other troops along the road, the Scots Fusiliers appeared comparatively unmoved by the announcement. There were a few cheers and some backslapping, but most of the soldiers remained perfectly calm. To Reitz, though, it was a supreme moment. He saw in it the beginning of a new era for the world and for his country.

He decided to address the battalion. Forming them up in a hollow square beside the road, he set out to match the occasion with a stirring oration from his horse, but was overcome with stage fright and couldn't find the right words. He stumbled through a few halting sentences, unable to articulate the elevated thoughts going through his mind, then gave up. Instead, he led the battalion to a nearby village where they had been told to wait until they received further orders from brigade.

An old French curé came out to greet them. The man flung his arms around Reitz when he dismounted and gave him a big kiss on each cheek. The battalion sniggered, none more than Captain Hester, the quartermaster. Hester laughed too soon:

'The curé, releasing me, made a dash at him, and imprinted two more hearty smacks on his rubicund countenance. The men had been too polite to laugh at their commanding officer in trouble, but they made up for it by bursting into a roar of merriment at Hester's discomfited looks.'

It was a relief to be able to laugh again, now that they all had something to laugh about.

At Maubeuge, where the Fusiliers had been headed, Captain Oliver Lyttelton of the Grenadier Guards had been woken in the middle of the night with the news of the Armistice at eleven. After acknowledging the message from divisional HQ, he had gone back to sleep, not bothering to disturb his brigadier. He hadn't mentioned it at breakfast either, forgetting that the brigadier didn't know. It wasn't until the brigadier asked if there had been any messages from the division that Lyttelton thought to tell him the war was over.

The fighting had already ceased around Maubeuge to all intents and purposes. The Grenadiers had taken the town a couple of days ago without a struggle. There were still Germans out there somewhere, but they weren't giving any trouble. They only had one shot left in their locker, as Lyttelton discovered later that morning:

'About 10 a.m. one high-velocity shell roared into the town about five hundred yards from our house and frightened the life out of us. Then silence: silence that is, except for the clucking of chickens, the creaking of cart wheels, mooing of cows and other sounds of a country town on market day.

'We rode round the troops: everywhere the reaction was the same, flat dullness and depression. Winning in war is a most exhilarating sensation, and we had not had many days in which to savour it; we had some scores to pay off, and now they would never be paid ... We all felt flat and dispirited.'

One score in particular had never been paid off. The Grenadiers were still seething about an incident in October when they had been clearing Germans from the village of St Python. Oblivious to the danger, an eleven-year-old girl walking down the street had been deliberately shot by a German. A Grenadier had risked his own life to carry her to safety, but the child had died and the Grenadiers had not forgotten it. They would have killed every German in St Python if they had been able to lay hands on them. They had been chasing the Germans ever since but still hadn't made them pay for what they did at St Python. The debt to that little girl had not been settled and now it never would be.

At Malplaquet, five miles across the fields from Maubeuge, they had guessed the night before that the Armistice was coming because of all the shouting and cheering from the German lines. The British in the town didn't hear of it officially until early that morning, when a signaller woke Major Wilfred House and gave him the news. House was brigade major to the 57th Brigade, a staff officer who worked so hard that he sometimes went without sleep for forty hours at a stretch. He had been particularly hard pressed in recent weeks because the speed of the advance had necessitated a great deal of extra effort to keep the troops efficiently on the move.

The civilians in the town were just opening their shutters as House emerged with the news. They came rushing out to shake the British by the hand:

'I remember thinking "it's all over" and to my complete amazement "I am alive". I had always taken it for granted that I shouldn't be. We hurriedly organised a tea with rationed food for all the children in the village school; they brought bunches of flowers for the divisional and brigade commanders, and some of the villagers brought a treasured bottle of wine or Cognac or a paté which they offered us, and eggs and butter for the men. It was very moving and very simple.'

Malplaquet was an apposite place to end the war. The Duke of Marlborough and his Prussian allies had fought an epic battle with the French there in 1709. The fighting had been bloody – as bloody in its time as Verdun or the Somme – but the British and Prussians had seen the French off the field, although they had suffered too many losses to pursue them. Many of the British regiments fighting around Malplaquet in 1918 were familiar with the name, if not the details, because they carried Malplaquet as a battle honour on their colours. So did the German regiments opposing them.

Just outside Malplaquet, the 11th battalion of the Manchester Regiment had started for the front at first light, expecting to go into action later in the day. Major S. C. Marriott, their second in command, was busy at the rear as the men moved off:

'I was the last man to ride out of the village, next to Malplaquet, amidst cheers, handshakes and good wishes of the villagers, who had assembled to see us off … after marching about half a mile, I suddenly saw the CO and adjutant retreating back down the column, and then I heard terrific cheering, and saw hundreds of caps thrown into the air.

'I guessed at once what it was and my first thought was to tell those villagers, so I turned my old horse round, and galloped like blazes down the road towards our last village. I shouted the news to a gang of Royal Engineers repairing a blown-up bridge, who threw their tools, picks, shovels, hats, etc. into the air and cheered. The people in the village heard it, and as I came up I shouted "C'est fini", somebody put a French flag into my hand, and on I went as far as my billet and HQ shouting the news all round, and the people went absolutely mad.

'By this time the battalion was forming up to march back, as hostilities had ceased, and with the CO who arrived about two minutes behind me, we went to rejoin it and bring it back. And back came the men amid indescribable scenes, they were cheering, firing off signal rockets, and one chap produced a Union Jack, and the band played a lively march.

'We were accompanied by a whole squadron of planes, who swooped down, round and over us, sometimes only a couple of yards above us, looping the loop, firing signals and going completely mad, and in this fashion we marched through the village. Then came a march past and the 'Marseillaise', and the people wept and cheered alternately. We were decked with flowers and kissed … In spite of all this it will take us a long time to realise that the war, which has been present to us for so long a time, is now a thing of the past.'

In Flanders, Frank Hitchcock and his company of Leinsters had been on their way to Wodecq since early morning. There were Germans ahead, holding a bridge at Lessines, but they were being tackled by Brigadier Freyberg and a squadron of Dragoon Guards and posed no threat to the Leinsters. The Irishmen passed a battalion of the Hampshire Regiment at ten and took over the lead as the advanced guard of the brigade. They had already been told about the Armistice, so the mood was relaxed as they pressed on towards their destination:

'It was a glorious morning. The route lay over broken country; sometimes by road, more often by rough tracks through thickly wooded and hilly terrain. The men were in their usual good spirits. Many discussed the situation, some arguing that the Boches were bluffing. But optimism and pessimism centred more on the question whether or no a sequence of four rumless days would be broken. We could not realise that the war was coming to an end.

'Every now and then officers and signallers would furtively glance at their watches. At last the hands pointed to the hour, and I called out to the company the words: "Eleven o'clock!"

'Thus, the most dramatic moment passed, as we marched on in silence.

'Then some of the men began to speak of India, and of the prospects of being sent there with the 1st battalion now that the war was over. Quite a number spoke about their dead comrades, and I overheard: "If only Colonel Murphy could be with the old Battalion now!"'

It began to drizzle soon afterwards. The Leinsters were tired by the time they reached Wodecq, yet perfectly cheerful, 'as if a great weight had been lifted off our shoulders'. Hitchcock's company was billeted in a nunnery that had been a girls' school before the war. The nuns fussed over them, delighted to discover that their liberators were largely Roman Catholic. The men were put up in the schoolroom and

Hitchcock was given a room to himself with a parquet floor. What tickled the nuns most about the Leinsters was the sight of their sentries pacing up and down outside the convent's main gate. The nuns had seen men in pickelhaubes doing exactly the same thing every day since 1914. The change of headgear was more than welcome.

While the Leinsters marched to Wodecq, their brigadier was hurrying ahead to capture the bridge at Lessines before the Germans had a chance to destroy it. Bernard Freyberg had decided to secure the crossing over the river Dendre in case the Germans reneged on the Armistice terms and continued to fight after the ceasefire.

Freyberg had had a good war. Trained as a dentist in New Zealand, he had found his true calling in the profession of arms. After volunteering in 1914, he had been a pall-bearer at the poet Rupert Brooke's funeral on Skiros and had swum ashore at Gallipoli to divert the Turks' attention from the British landing by lighting flares elsewhere. Thereafter, he had gone to France, where he had won the Victoria Cross on the Somme after being wounded four times in forty-eight hours.

Lessines was his last hurrah, his last chance to hit the Germans before the deadline. There was no real need to capture the bridge, but Freyberg was determined to do it anyway because he had enjoyed the war and was sorry the fighting was coming to an end. Freyberg led the assault on the village in person, as he gleefully recounted to his friend, Winston Churchill:

'I decided to get in touch with the Boche and raid him with my cavalry and cyclists one last time. We knew he was holding the crossing over the Dendre at the village of Lessines. We started at 9.50 and galloped twenty kilometres, rushed his outpost lines at the gallop at five minutes to eleven and charged into the village only nine strong, shooting up the streets with revolvers and chasing Boches round blocks of buildings. We captured a bridgehead at two minutes to eleven and mopped up the village to the tune of four officers, 102 other ranks and several machine guns. I thought this would amuse you.'

It did not amuse the Germans, particularly after some British prisoners of war turned on their captors and attacked them. The Germans' protests were ignored and Freyberg was later awarded a second bar to his Distinguished Service Order, despite losing a few of his own men quite unnecessarily. He relished war more than most, but he was far from alone in his wish to continue the fight against the Germans. A platoon of the Middlesex Regiment found themselves within striking distance of a German position at exactly 11 o'clock and had to be restrained from attacking past the hour. No one would have known if they had, and it seemed a pity not to kill a few more Huns while they still had the chance. It wouldn't come again.

North-east of Mons, the 5th Lancers had made good progress towards St-Denis by a quarter to eleven and were sweeping everything before them in their bid to take the high ground before the ceasefire. The Germans were in headlong retreat when Private George Ellison was hit by a sniper and fell from his horse. He died at ten to eleven, almost certainly the last British fatality of the war.

He was followed soon afterwards by Private George Price of the Canadians' 28th (Saskatchewan) battalion, killed by a shot from a row of miners' houses at two minutes to eleven as his unit crossed the canal at Havre, just east of Mons. Both men were buried in the military cemetery at St Symphorien, close to the grave of Private John Parr, the first British soldier to die in 1914.

On the Lorraine front, the US army's 313th regiment had made slow progress in the mist surrounding their objective of Ville-devant-Chaumont. The 313th had taken the village eventually and were moving beyond it towards a ridge of high ground when they came under heavy fire from the Germans ahead. Henry Gunther and his friend Ernie Powell immediately dived for cover as machine-gun bullets chewed up the ground all around.

In front of them lay a roadblock defended by at least two machine guns from the Prussian 31st regiment. The gunners had watched open-mouthed as the Americans came at them out of the mist. The Prussians were counting the minutes to the Armistice, but although the news had reached the 313th's rear echelons at sixteen minutes to eleven, it still hadn't reached the men at the front. Henry Gunther knew nothing of the imminent ceasefire when he apparently decided that this was the moment to win battlefield promotion and get his stripes back before the end of the war.

It was one minute to eleven as Gunther leapt to his feet and charged the roadblock. Powell yelled at him to stop. The Germans frantically waved him back. Gunther ignored them all and continued towards the enemy, mounting a one-man attack on the German army that was terminated less than sixty seconds before the peace when a short burst from a machine gun cut him down. He was officially the last American to die in the war.

Sergeant Rudolph Forderhase, another German-American, was luckier. He was with the 356th, attacking the village of Pouilly in the fog, when an officer called him over to interrogate a couple of German prisoners captured in a machine-gun pit. The prisoners were very young, terrified that they would be killed, because it was the custom on both sides to shoot machine-gunners out of hand. The Germans had held their fire as the Americans advanced. The officer wanted Forderhase to find out why:

'I was quite surprised to see them. The captain knew I could speak a bit of German and told me to ask why they had not fired on us. They informed me that all fighting was to end at 11 o'clock that morning and they saw no reason to sacrifice their lives, or ours, needlessly. Neither the captain, nor I, knew whether to believe them or not.'

The prisoners were sent to the rear and the 356th continued their advance. They soon came under sniper fire and Forderhase forgot about anything except the bullets whizzing over his head:

'We were somewhat concerned about this when suddenly the sniper's firing ceased – everything became perfectly quiet. I then remembered what the two German prisoners had said earlier that morning. I took a look at the cheap wristwatch that I had been wearing. It had stopped at 11 o'clock and I never did get it to run again.'

*

Eddie Rickenbacker, the US air ace, was flying over the front line at eleven. Strictly against orders, he had flown up through the fog to enjoy a last sight of the war from the air. He arrived just as the final shots were being exchanged:

'Reaching the village of Pont-à-Mousson on the Moselle river, I flew at about a hundred feet along the front, over no-man's-land, passing to the left of Metz, and then over the village of Fontoy. I crossed the line about two minutes before the hour of eleven, and the troops on both sides – Germans and Americans – could be seen very clearly.

'There were some shots fired at me, but at the appointed hour all shooting ceased, and then slowly and cautiously, soldiers came out of the German and American trenches, throwing their rifles and helmets high into the air. They met in no-man's-land and began fraternising just as a group of schoolkids would after a football game – happy in the realisation that they would not be killed in this terrible conflict. It was fantastic to them, and to me, to know that the war was over.'

Others were watching from the ground:

'A quite startling thing occurred. The skyline of the crest ahead of them grew suddenly populous with dancing soldiers and down the slope, all the way to the barbed wire, straight for the Americans, came the German troops. They came with outstretched hands, ear-to-ear grins and souvenirs to swap for cigarettes ... They came to tell how glad they were the fight had stopped, how glad they were the Kaiser had departed for parts unknown, how fine it was to know that they would have a republic at last in Germany.'

The fraternisation was the exception rather than the rule. It may have occurred in places, but it was not a replay of Christmas 1914. Too much had happened since then. The British and French in particular had nothing to say to the Germans any more. A more typical response was recorded by Webb Miller, a United Press correspondent who had arranged to fly to the front for the Armistice with another member of Rickenbacker's squadron, only to be told that there was too much fog and he wouldn't see anything. Instead, Miller had driven up through Verdun, dodging a heavy barrage from the Germans as he covered the last half mile on foot along a muddy communication trench. He reached the front at a quarter to eleven to discover that none of the Americans in his sector knew anything about an Armistice. They were interested to hear about it, though:

'As the hour of eleven approached, the men kept their eyes on their wristwatches. From the direction of Verdun the fog-muffled rumble of the cannonade gradually died away. In our sector somewhere to the left there had been occasional rat-tat-tat-tats from machine guns. Now they ceased.

'Eleven o'clock! The war ended!

'It would make a better story if I could tell of men cheering, yelling, laughing and weeping with joy, throwing their tin hats in the air, embracing one another, dancing with delight. But they didn't. Nothing happened. The war just ended …

'The men stood talking in groups. The captain let me talk on the telephone to the outposts. No drama there, either. They said they couldn't see anything in the fog or hear anything. Further up the line it was the same. The army's reason for existence had suddenly ceased. The men didn't know what to do next.

'Here I was covering the greatest story in the world and nothing was happening. This was the end of the greatest war in the history of the world, the war that killed 8½ million men, the war that affected in some way every man, woman and child on earth. And here in the front line there was less excitement, less emotion and less delirious joy than you'd find in a lively crap game.'

On the German side, the gas fired by the Americans at Georg Bucher's unit had blown away in the wind, but Bucher and his young friend Walter were taking no chances as the war came to an end. They still had their masks on, just in case. They were in their dugout, terrified with so little time to go that they might not live to see the peace:

'The minutes seemed an eternity. I raised my head and listened, though I could feel far more distinctly than my ears could tell me that the shellfire was decreasing like rain gradually easing off. The din became less and less violent, though punctuated by an occasional crash close at hand. Then it ceased – ceased altogether over our sector though we could still hear it in the distance.

'I took off the youngster's gas mask and silently held my wrist-watch before his eyes. Then I pressed my helmet firmly on my head, pulled out my pistol, grabbed the bag of grenades and leaped out into the trench.

'Every man who could hold a rifle or throw a grenade was standing ready. Were the enemy going to attack us? We were taking no chances: but as we stood there waiting, hope and determination to live flashed in every eye.

'The company commander, with his usual smile and shock-troop air, made his way arrogantly along the trench, making sure that every man had his rifle and grenades ready. There were still ten minutes to go. He gave me an order; I nodded. Then he moved on and we stood there waiting and hoping. The minutes went slowly by. Then there was a great silence. We stood motionless, gazing at the shell smoke which drifted sluggishly across no-man's-land.

'Those minutes seemed to last for ever. I glanced at my watch – I felt that my staring eyes were glued to it. The hour had come. I turned round: "Armistice!"

'Then I went back to the youngster. I couldn't bear to go on staring at no-man's-land and at the faces of the men. We had lived through an experience which no one would ever understand who had not shared in it.

'"Armistice, Walter! It's all over!"'

On the Meuse near Damvilliers, Captain Lebreton of the French army's 415th regiment spent the last half hour of the war looking for a bugler to sound the ceasefire at eleven. There wasn't much call for bugles at the front, but Private Octave Delaluque of the 11th company was said to have one with him. Delaluque was sent for and crawled forward under machine-gun fire. He hadn't played the ceasefire since 1911, so Lebreton whistled it to him to remind him how it went. Delaluque searched for his mouthpiece and found it in his pouch, clogged with tobacco.

Monday, 11 November 1918, 11 a.m.

The last German shells were screaming overhead as he cleared the mouthpiece and put the bugle to his lips. At precisely 11 o'clock he began to play: 'Garde à vous' first, and then the ceasefire. It came with unofficial words ('T'as tiré comme un cochon. T'auras pas de permission.' 'You've been shooting like a pig. No leave for you.') Delaluque followed it with 'Au Drapeau' ('To the Flag'), and every Frenchman within earshot began to sing the 'Marseillaise'. The Germans responded with a bugle call from their own trenches and that was the end of the war for them.

For the South Africans, the end came at Grandrieu, just inside the Belgian border. The men of the 1st regiment were looking at their watches when a German opened up with a machine gun at two minutes to eleven. He fired off a whole belt before the deadline. Then he stood up, removed his helmet and bowed to his former enemies. The South Africans could only watch in astonishment as he turned his back on them and walked off unhurriedly towards the rear. Elsewhere, whole platoons of Germans did the same, taking off their helmets and bowing to the foe at 11 o'clock as if they had all just been having tea together instead of a war.

General Pershing was in his HQ at Chaumont when the clock struck the hour. He had known about the Armistice since six, but he still couldn't rid himself of the feeling that the Allies should have insisted on Germany's unconditional surrender rather than just a cessation of hostilities. 'I suppose our campaigns are ended,' he told an aide as he studied the wall map in his office, 'but what an enormous difference a few more days would have made.'

Ten days was all it needed. Ten more days and they could have captured the whole German army, humiliating the Huns and making it clear to them beyond any shadow of a doubt that they had lost the war. Instead, the Germans would march home in good order, claiming that they had never been defeated. Pershing was afraid that it might all have to be done again some day if the Germans didn't know they were beaten.

Plenty of people agreed with him, not least former president Theodore Roosevelt, who had lost a son in the war. Unconditional surrender was the only language the Germans understood. Roosevelt was a dying man, but he had been campaigning hard at home for unconditional surrender. Anything less was folly.

The Americans hadn't taken Sedan either, which they had been longing to do before the war's end. Marshal Foch had pulled rank, insisting that Sedan was for the French to recapture when the time came. Instead of marching into the city in a blaze of glory, General MacArthur and his men had been taken out of the line and were spending the last day of the war in reserve at Buzancy. It was a frustrating way to end the campaign.

But this was no time to carp. Eyes on the clock, Pershing and his staff all began whooping at once when the hands reached eleven. Then they spilled out of the office and headed for the centre of Chaumont, only to meet the townspeople coming the other way. There was singing and dancing in the street, tears, laughter, cheering. Pershing's staff were planning a big party for that night, before the general left for Paris. There was going to be more dancing and champagne by the bucketful. The champagne was to be kept on ice in a German helmet that the owner didn't need any more.

In Paris, Marshal Foch had gone home after delivering the Armistice to Clemenceau, perfectly satisfied with the terms he had negotiated. The German army was to leave France and Belgium immediately and was to remain beyond the Rhine for the future. The war aims had been achieved at Compiègne 'without any further sacrifice of life'. Foch would certainly have liked to see the German army surrender unconditionally, but with more than 1,300,000 Frenchmen already dead, he had few misgivings about not prolonging the war any further.

He lived in the Avenue de Saxe on the Left Bank. The weekly street market was in progress as he arrived. Foch's car was parked outside his house, but it did not remain unrecognised for long. Foch was besieged by a delighted crowd, forced eventually to make a run for it and seek sanctuary at army headquarters. The whole of Paris wanted to shower him with flowers and sing the 'Marseillaise' at him. It was that kind of day in Paris.

The signing of the Armistice became official at 11 o'clock, when two cannon were fired from the Quai d'Orsay and the bells of Notre Dame began to toll. They were followed by more cannon and the bells of all the other churches. The streets filled rapidly with an ebullient, ecstatic crowd as shops and factories closed and everyone came out to celebrate. Schools had a holiday and hundreds of thousands of people converged on the Champs-Elysées, the Place de la Concorde, the Tuileries and the area all around.

The shops had long sold out of flags, so every flag not nailed down was cheerfully stolen and waved aloft as the people of Paris thronged the boulevards and danced triumphantly on top of cars and lorries heading for the centre. They climbed trees as well and shinned up the barrels of the big German guns that had been put on display in the Place de la Concorde, guns that had all too recently been pointing towards Paris. They took hold of the smaller guns as well and wheeled them round the streets; they even wheeled a German aircraft or two which had also been captured and put on display.

Alison Strathy, a Canadian in the American Red Cross, was part of the crowd as the celebrations began:

'I was standing on the corner of the Place de l'Opéra by myself – there was almost a silence – the significance of what it meant was overwhelming – PEACE. Then here and there excited little groups gathered – then a mob came down the Avenue de l'Opéra – it developed into a procession. At its head marched Latin quarter students (large black ties) carrying the flags of the Allied countries. They were followed by soldiers, sailors, midinettes, members of the Red Cross, the YMCA, civilians and soldiers. As they marched they were joined on every side. In front of the Opéra the procession seemed to hesitate for a moment, then with one accord they broke into "La Marseillaise". It was like a match to a bonfire, now we were a seething crowd celebrating VICTORY! VICTORY! VICTORY!

'I joined in and found myself arm in arm with poilus I had never seen before. I forget where we went, we toured the streets and sang and sang and the procession kept growing longer and longer. Finally, we ended up at the Place de la Concorde and stopped before the statue to the "City of Lille". The statue was draped with flags and loaded with laurel leaves – it had been liberated from German hands by the British. The statue to the "City of Strasbourg" was similarly decorated, as it had been recaptured by the Americans.'

Marie Curie was part of the crowd too. She had been in her laboratory at the Radium Institute when the guns began to sound. She had gone out at once to buy some flags, but hadn't been able to find any anywhere. Instead, she had bought materials in red, white and blue and hastily stitched some makeshift flags together with the help of the institute's charwoman. She had hung them from the institute's windows before jumping into a radiology car with the janitor and her assistant, Marthe Klein, and heading off to join the fun.

The janitor drove. The radiology car was a battered old Renault, one of many that had served as mobile X-ray units during the war. Marie Curie's team had driven them to the front for use at the military hospitals. She had personally procured and equipped eighteen cars during the war and had set up almost two hundred permanent radiology posts in addition. She had been a familiar figure at the front with a Red Cross armband over her civilian clothes.

The streets were already crowded as they set out. By the time they reached the Place de la Concorde, they could hardly move at all. A dozen complete strangers jumped on to the car and clung on for the rest of the morning. Madame Curie raised no objection. A severe figure as a rule, she was just happy the war was over at last, not least because she would be hearing from her family in Poland again now that there was no more fighting. She hadn't heard from them since the Germans marched in at the beginning of the war.

The war had begun badly for the Poles. There had been widespread rape as the Germans pushed through on their way to fight the Russians. The Poles had no love for their Russian masters, but they had no love for the Germans either, even though some had ended up fighting for Germany as the lesser of the two evils. Poland had been occupied by the German army for most of the war and the Poles had not enjoyed it one bit.

But the Germans were gone now and the Russians had not come back. Poland was to be a sovereign state again for the first time since the eighteenth century. The Ukrainians were disputing it, but the Ukrainians did not amount to much. Poland was free and Marie Curie could see her family again. She could also get on with her real work now that there was no more need for X-ray cars. Marie Curie was never a particularly happy woman, but she was a lot less gloomy than usual as she drove through the streets of Paris past a cheering, prancing crowd which was only just beginning to warm up as more and more people came hurrying in from the rest of France to join the celebrations.

In the English Channel, the crew of HMS *Amazon* knew nothing of the Armistice as they patrolled the waters between Dungeness and Beachy Head. Ahead of them, they could see a French fishing boat decorated from stem to stern with flags. The French cheered and waved their caps as the Royal Navy approached. An officer hailed them by megaphone, asking why they were there and what they were celebrating. The French told him the war was over. The officer didn't believe a word of it and ordered them back to harbour.

Later, the *Amazon* received a signal to cease hostilities. She returned to Dover, where the church bells were ringing and all the ships' sirens were hooting across the water. Another signal announced that all shore leave had been cancelled for all forces until further notice. Ship's cook W. G. Evans was bitterly disappointed, but recognised the wisdom of the order. The sailors would have gone berserk if they had been allowed ashore.

At Folkestone, Lieutenant Dickie Dixon of the Royal Garrison Artillery was looking forward to a spot of home leave as his ship arrived from France. They had been at war when he left France, but they were at peace when he arrived in England. Dixon knew nothing about the Armistice until he heard the sirens and cheering in Folkestone and guessed what had happened. The fighting had stopped while he was in mid-Channel:

'No more slaughter, no more maiming, no more mud and blood and no more killing and disembowelling of horses and mules – which was what I found most difficult to bear. No more of those hopeless dawns with the rain chilling the spirits, no more crouching in inadequate dugouts scooped out of trench walls, no more dodging of snipers' bullets, no more of that terrible shellfire. No more shovelling up of bits of men's bodies and dumping them into sandbags; no more cries of "Stretcher-bear-ERS!", and no more of those beastly gas masks and the odious smell of pear drops which was deadly to the lungs, and no more writing of those dreadfully difficult letters to the next of kin of the dead … The whole vast business of the war was finished. It was all over.'

Stunned to think that they might actually have a future, Dixon and his friend Captain Brown took the train to London. They waved bottles of beer at the people beside the line, who waved back. It was raining when they reached the capital early in the afternoon, but nobody minded. Dixon parted company with Brown at Charing Cross and went off to send messages to his girlfriend and his parents to tell them he had arrived safely:

'I emerged into the Strand to find that thoroughfare packed with a seething mass of excited citizens shouting and cheering and waving flags and bottles and hats – literally thousands of folk, civilians, soldiers, sailors, WAACs and WAAFs, nurses, every kind you can think of, all welcoming the end of hostilities and cheering the king and queen! For as I got into the Strand, I saw driving slowly along in the midst of that wildly cheering mob, King George and Queen Mary in a stately open victoria drawn by a couple of horses.

'Thinking of the last time I had seen King George V at that chateau prior to the big offensive which drove Jerry out of France, I plunged into the crowd, intent on getting across the road to the other side, where there was a post office. I managed it in the end, and sent off a couple of telegrams; one to Babs, telling her I was arriving at her home that evening, and one to my mother and father in Southport,

Lancashire, informing them that I was home on leave and would be with them some time tomorrow.'

Dixon acted without thinking. The last thing his parents wanted was a telegram from London. Like every family with a soldier at the front, the Dixons had come to loathe and detest telegrams from London: curt little missives from the War Office regretting to inform them that the fine young man they had given to the nation had been killed and the government would not be returning the pieces. The Dixons didn't want a telegram like that. Not today of all days. The last thing they wanted was a telegram from London.

The telegram was delivered to the Hesketh Park Hydro in Southport, where the Dixons were living. It was quite some time before Mrs Dixon could bring herself to open it.

The streets of London had begun to fill soon after first light as people gathered to wait for news of the Armistice. Nothing official had been said, but everyone knew that this was the day. Crowds had begun to gather outside Buckingham Palace and other public buildings, waiting for the formal announcement, the words they were all longing to hear. More people arrived every minute, determined not to miss the moment when it came. The crowds at Downing Street were rewarded at length when the door to No. 10 opened and the prime minister came out. Harold Nicolson, a young diplomat at the Foreign Office across the road, was fetching a map when he happened to look out of the window:

'A group of people stood in the roadway and there were some half a dozen policemen. It was 10.55 a.m. Suddenly the front door opened. Mr Lloyd George, his white hair fluttering in the wind, appeared upon the doorstep. He waved his arms outwards. I opened the window hurriedly. He was shouting the same sentence over and over again. I caught his words. "At 11 o'clock this morning the war will be over."

'The crowd surged towards him. Plump and smiling he made dismissive gestures and then retreated behind the great front door. People were running along Downing Street and in a few minutes the whole street was blocked. There was no cheering. The crowd over-flowed dumbly into the Horse Guards Parade. They surged around the wall of the Downing Street garden. From my post of vantage I observed Lloyd George emerge into that garden, nervous and enthusiastic. He went towards the garden door and then withdrew. Two secretaries who were with him urged him on. He opened the door. He stepped out into the Parade. He waved his hands for a moment of gesticulation and then again retreated. The crowd rushed towards him and patted feverishly at his back.'

At the same time, maroons began to go off around the city, signal rockets to announce the peace. The maroons had been used as air-raid warnings during the war. A few people assumed that another German attack was on the way, as did some of the Parisians who heard the guns on the Quai d'Orsay. The majority realised at once that the maroons were an invitation to abandon work for the day and run yelling into the street. They needed no further urging.

Everyone headed for Buckingham Palace. In thousands at first, then in tens of thousands, the population of London dropped whatever they were doing and swirled up the Mall towards the Palace. They wanted the king. He was the embodiment of the British people. They wanted to see him and cheer him like he had never been cheered before, up on the balcony at the front of the palace.

King George was waiting for them. His wife and daughter were there too, ready to do their bit. King George had stood shoulder to shoulder with his people during the war. The Kaiser's son had waved German troops off to the front in his tennis flannels, but George had worn military uniform throughout the war and had never once been to the theatre because he thought it wrong to do so while his subjects were fighting and dying. George had been with the British people every step of the way during the past four years. They knew it and appreciated it and loved him for it. He was their king.

He made his first appearance on the balcony as the old guard was marching off from the morning's changing of the guard ceremony. The crowd erupted at the sight of him. George's cousin, Nicholas of Russia, had lost his throne during the war and had been murdered by the Bolshevists. His cousin Wilhelm had lost his throne as well and was even now escaping to Holland. But George V still had his throne. He stepped out on to the balcony and the largest crowd he had ever seen roared out their wholehearted endorsement.

Nineteen-year-old Patricia Carver was one of them. She went to the palace with her parents and told her schoolgirl cousin about it later:

'This morning at 10.22 I was in the room where the tape machine is (we are simply glued to it always) when I saw news come through "Armistice signed" – so of course we knew there would be great joy, and that people would go at once to Buckingham Palace, so off we all went, Ma and Pa and Little Peg.

'At 11 o'clock when hostilities ceased, maroons were fired and the crowd was simply great but most awfully well behaved in front of the palace, boys climbed all over the monuments, the police tried to keep them down but of course no use, they sat on the heads of the figures and everywhere!! Well the king (God bless him) came out with the queen and Duke of Connaught & Princess Mary in VAD uniform and the crowd cheered like mad and we all sang 'God Save the King': then they went in and the crowd got thicker and thicker, we had a very good place on the steps of the monument, you should have seen the taxis each one with *at least* fourteen people on it, outside and inside & on the bonnet! Oh I did wish you'd been with us, well the crowd yelled and yelled "WE WANT KING GEORGE" about every moment, *too* thrilling for words. We had seen the Duke of C. go off somewhere earlier on in the morning and now he came back right down the steps with Princess Pat (Pa got doff with both of 'em!!) We were absolutely next to 'em, Princess P. simply grinned at him and the duke returned his salute! Then they went on to the palace and the massed band of the Guards came and the king came out again and we all sang "Keep the home fires burning", "Tipperary", the Doxology, all the Allies' anthems & a few others, at the end of each we cheered and yelled, "We want a speech", and at last the king spoke. I was very nearly at the palace gate with Ma and I could just hear what he said … Oh if only you'd been there with us.'

The king's speech was brief and to the point. 'With you I rejoice and thank God for the victories which the Allied arms have won, bringing hostilities to an end and peace within sight.' His sentiments were noble, but they were drowned out by all the noise. Hardly anyone could hear him.

Esmée Mascall's mother had found a seat in a taxi in the scrum below. She was one of those who couldn't hear, but she did have a wonderful view of the crowd, as she later reported to her daughter:

'I can't tell you *what* the sight was! Never have I wanted the gift of a ready writer so much before. Lorries crammed with men and women all with flags – people crammed on the top of taxis and inside too. Large govt motors with hospital nurses, WAACs and WRENs and soldiers, and the *mass* of all kinds on their feet. There we all waited. Presently there was a great to-do, for mounted policemen pushed the crowd in front of them to let the bands through for the Quadrangle. I just imagined what it would have been if we had been caught there, for though it was a good-natured crowd everybody was swept in front of the bobbies on their horses.

'Directly the bands got into position they struck up "God Save the King" – and he and the queen, Princess Mary, the Duke of Connaught and Princess Patricia appeared on the balcony. I think Queen Alexandra was there too but am not quite sure. The roar as they appeared was one roll and everyone sang with the bands. Then the king said something – but of course we couldn't hear – and then the band played "All people that on earth" and everyone sang again. Then the band struck up "Home Sweet Home" and it was this that touched the crowd really. It was solemnly sung, almost with a sob, and darling, I felt it a moment never to be forgotten. One could imagine what a moment it was for the king and queen.

'After that the English reserve gave way and they sang "For he's a jolly good fellow!" Then "Tipperary" was played and after that the different anthems – and then again everyone sang with the bands "Now thank we all our God". After that, the national anthem was played again and the cheers roared and roared, and the royal family went in...'

Monday, 11 November 1918, 11 a.m.

Arthur Conan Doyle, still mourning the death of his soldier son, was in the crowd as they sang and cheered:

'A slim young girl had got elevated on to some high vehicle and was leading and conducting the singing as if she was some angel in tweeds just dropped from a cloud. In the dense crowd I saw an open motor stop with four middle-aged men, one of them a hard-faced civilian, the others officers. I saw this civilian hack at the neck of a whisky bottle and drink it raw. I wish the crowd had lynched him. It was the moment for prayer, and this beast was a blot on the landscape…'

Winston Churchill, the minister of munitions, was in his office at the Hotel Metropole as Big Ben struck the hour. Commandeered for the war effort, the hotel looked up Northumberland Avenue towards Trafalgar Square. Churchill was at the window, wondering what to do with 3 million redundant munitions workers, when Big Ben began to sound:

'And then suddenly the first stroke of the chime. I looked again at the broad street beneath me. It was deserted. From the portals of one of the large hotels absorbed by government departments darted the slight figure of a girl clerk, distractedly gesticulating while another stroke resounded. Then from all sides men and women came scurrying into the street. Streams of people poured out of all the buildings. The bells of London began to clash. Northumberland Avenue was now crowded with people in hundreds, nay, thousands, rushing hither and thither in a frantic manner, shouting and screaming with joy.

'I could see that Trafalgar Square was already swarming. Around me in our very headquarters, in the Hotel Metropole, disorder had broken out. Doors banged. Feet clattered down corridors. Everyone rose from the desk and cast aside pen and paper. All bounds were broken. The tumult grew. It grew like a gale, but from all sides simultaneously. The street was now a seething mass of humanity. Flags appeared as if by magic. Streams of men and women flowed from the Embankment. They mingled with torrents pouring down the Strand on their way to acclaim the king. Almost before the last stroke of the clock had died away, the strict, war-straitened, regulated streets of London had become a triumphant pandemonium. At any rate it was clear that no more work would be done that day.'

Churchill's wife arrived to join him. They decided to go and congratulate Lloyd George. Twenty people swarmed all over their car as they inched along Whitehall towards Downing Street. Churchill couldn't help remembering that he and his wife had driven the other way along Whitehall on the afternoon of Britain's ultimatum to Germany in August 1914. The same crowd that was cheering now had cheered then too, but with no idea of what was about to happen to them.

Churchill was proud of the British people who had borne so much since 1914, who had never once wavered or lost faith in their country. He was uncomfortably aware, though, that they had been badly let down by some of the decisions taken by the country's leaders during the war. He himself had carried the blame for the fiasco in the Dardanelles. He was glad that the happy faces in front of him appeared ready to forgive and forget all the disasters and disappointments, now that it had all come right in the end.

At Millbank, just beyond the Houses of Parliament, nurse Vera Brittain was on the day shift at Queen Alexandra's Hospital when the maroons went off. She was washing dressing bowls in an annexe outside her hut and had just begun to dry them when the other VAD nurse on her ward came running into the annexe:

'Brittain! Brittain! Did you hear the maroons? It's over – it's all over. Do let's come out and see what's happening.'

Mechanically, without enthusiasm, Brittain followed her into the street. She had long since lost all interest in the war. All the young men she had ever cared about – her fiancé, her brother, their closest friends – had been killed long ago. It was hard to get excited about the end of the war when there was no one left to share it with.

A taxi was turning in from the Embankment as they appeared. It knocked over a little old lady who had been distracted by the commotion. Even as Vera Brittain ran to her side, she could see that nothing could be done for the lady. Her dying face reminded Vera of her brother's friend Geoffrey Thurlow, whose eyes had remained firmly fixed on his orderly as his life ebbed away in France. Thurlow's body had vanished by the time they came back to bury it.

Thirteen-year-old Olive Wells was at Streatham secondary school in south London when the maroons sounded:

'We came to school this morning hardly realising what a great day this was going to be.

'Miss Bassett told us that the Armistice was signed – we had received the news about 5 o'clock a.m. We cheered until we were hoarse!

'At 11 o'clock a.m. the guns were fired, the church bells were rung, the sirens were blown. We did not think of air raids as we would have done any other day.

'We went out into the road and cheered. The Union Jack was sent up the staff and there it fluttered in the breeze.

'Our homework was excused for the week.

'It was not a bright day but very damp.

'The guns are booming while I am writing this.'

Virginia Woolf was at home in Richmond, writing to her sister in the country, who was expecting an illegitimate baby:

'The guns have been going off for half an hour, and the sirens whistling; so I suppose we are at peace, and I can't help being glad that your precious imp will be born into a moderately reasonable world. I see we're not going to be allowed any quiet all day, as people seem to be whistling and giving catcalls and stirring up the dogs to bark, though it's all done in such an intermittent kind of way that it's not in the least impressive – only unsettling. Besides it's very grey and smoky – oh dear, now drunken soldiers are beginning to cheer.

'How am I to write my last chapter with all this shindy, and Nelly and Lottie bursting in to ask – here is Nelly with four different flags which she is putting in all the front rooms. Lottie says we ought to do something, and I see she is going to burst into tears. She insists upon polishing the door knocker, and shouting out across the road to the old fireman who lives opposite. O God! What a noise they make – and I, on the whole though rather emotional (would you be, I wonder?) feel also immensely melancholy; yes, you're well out of it, because every taxi is now hooting, and the schoolchildren I know will form up round the flag in a moment. There is certainly an atmosphere of the deathbed too. At this moment a harmonium is playing a hymn, and a large Union Jack has been hoisted on to a pole ... We've now had marriage bells, one hymn, "God Save the King" twice over, about a dozen separate cheers, and the old gentleman opposite has climbed to the top of a tree with an immense Union Jack.'

Bertrand Russell was in the Tottenham Court Road, watching a man and a woman kissing in the middle of the street. They didn't know each other, but they kissed anyway as they passed, two complete strangers going in opposite directions. The Tottenham Court Road had been full of sights like that since 11 o'clock. Everyone had rushed out of their shops and offices at once and commandeered the buses in the road, demanding to be driven around the town. Russell was happy for them and wished he could feel part of the crowd as they celebrated the end of the fighting. Instead, he felt completely solitary, a ghost from another planet.

It had not been a good war for Russell. A philosophy don at Cambridge, he had seen his colleague Wittgenstein go off to fight for Austria in 1914, but had not felt able to support the British war effort. He had been a pacifist from the start, vehemently opposed to the idea of conscription, actively campaigning against its introduction at the beginning of 1916. He had lost his job at Cambridge as a result, after being shunned by the other dons on high table. He had been attacked by women wielding clubs studded with nails and forbidden to go anywhere near the sea in case he signalled to German submarines. After writing an inflammatory article in a magazine he had ended up being sentenced to six months in prison for sedition. He had only just got out.

Monday, 11 November 1918, 11 a.m.

Ironically, Russell was perfectly patriotic and delighted that Britain had won the war, even though he didn't approve of it. He just wished that he could feel part of the crowd who had gone so unthinkingly to war in 1914 and appeared to have learned nothing since, except to snatch at their pleasures more recklessly than before. As he watched his none-too-bright countrymen cavorting along the pavement, Russell could feel nothing in common with them at all. He had suffered for his pacifism during the war, but in truth Russell was very far from being a pacifist. He could think of plenty of wars in history that had been amply justified in their time. Unfortunately, this wasn't one of them.

Agatha Christie was not a pacifist either, but she shared Russell's wonder at the sight of Londoners letting their hair down. She was at a bookkeeping class when her teacher rushed in to announce that there would be no more lessons that day:

'I went out in the streets quite dazed. There I came upon one of the most curious sights I had ever seen – indeed I still remember it, almost, I think, with a sense of fear. Everywhere there were women dancing in the street. English women are not given to dancing in public: it is a reaction more suitable to Paris and the French. But there they were, laughing, shouting, shuffling, leaping even, in a sort of wild orgy of pleasure: an almost brutal enjoyment. It was frightening. One felt that if there had been any Germans around the women would have advanced upon them and torn them to pieces. Some of them I suppose were drunk, but all of them looked it. They reeled, lurched and shouted.'

Agatha Christie didn't join them. Shy and retiring, she was hoping to be a writer some day. She had written a detective novel in her spare time and sent it off to a publisher. The novel featured a Belgian detective inspired by Sherlock Holmes. Agatha knew about Belgians because there were a lot of them living as refugees near her home. The first publisher she tried had rejected the novel out of hand. Undeterred, she had sent it to another and was still waiting for a reply. Perhaps she would hear soon, now that the war was over.

*

From the windows of Alexandra Palace, with a magnificent view across north London, Rudolf Sauter and his fellow internees heard the guns at eleven and immediately ran outside, laughing and chattering as they made their way to the compound where they took their exercise. After years of being cooped up as enemy aliens, they would be free again soon, able to go where they wanted and do exactly as they liked. They could hardly wait.

The men all had German names – Müller, Fischel, Habermann, Kesselburg – but most had lived in England for many years before the war and some all their lives. They were Germans in name, but quite a few of them couldn't even speak the language. They had thought of themselves as British until their friends and neighbours turned on them after the Zeppelin raids and they were taken away by the authorities, banged up in prison for the duration.

Sauter was a case in point. His Austrian-born father was an artist, long resident in the United Kingdom. His mother was as British as they come, a sister of the novelist John Galsworthy. His wife was British too. Sauter had been educated at Harrow and had made the pilgrimage to Lord's every summer to watch the Eton and Harrow match with his Old Harrovian uncle. But none of that had counted for anything when the war came. Sauter's father had been taken away first, and then Sauter himself. Their bitterness at their treatment was indescribable.

Sauter's father was determined to leave England for good as soon as he was released. He didn't want to make his home in England any more, after what had happened. Sauter himself was in two minds as to what to do. So were many of his fellow inmates, as he reported to his wife on Armistice day:

'These men here chose England for their home. Most of them now feel how impossible it will be to live here afterwards. Most have suffered much through their enforced captivity amongst unnatural surroundings; they have been parted from their families, their businesses have, in many cases, disappeared as in a quicksand and now they are about to be thrown out into a world already made poor enough by war ...

Monday, 11 November 1918, 11 a.m.

'Of course there are many who will try and stay here, either through love of this country or on account of their families or again for business reasons, or because Germany is to them a strange land whose language even they do not know, have not learnt in all their four years of internment. How many of these, whom this life has narrowed and embittered, can see in Armistice – the end of organised murder – the beginning of the pipes of spring?'

What Sauter feared most of all were the consequences of the peace. He had read the Armistice terms that morning with a sinking heart. The Allies were effectively reducing the Germans to slavery. As the bells sounded across London and his fellow inmates crammed excitedly into the compound, Sauter could not help wondering what the consequences would be if the Allies persisted with such a draconian settlement. Their intransigence would almost certainly lead to 'another war, the child of this very day, like a ghost, haunting the future'. Rudolf Sauter could see it coming.

As the bells rang out across London, so they did across the rest of the country as well. In cities, towns and villages all over the land the church bells pealed and the guns went off as the people of Britain celebrated the return of peace. Ernest Cooper, town clerk of Southwold on the Suffolk coast, was at work when he heard the news:

'I went to the office and at eleven was rung up by the county adjutant who told me that the Armistice had been signed and that guns were firing and bells ringing at Ipswich. I did not take it in at first and could hear him shouting "War is over" at the other end. I hurried down to the mayor and found he had just received the news and in a few minutes a car came in from the Covehithe air station full of mad officers, cheering, waving flags and blowing trumpets. Flags soon came out, the bells began to ring and a few of us adjourned to the mayor's house and cracked some bottles of fizz – an impromptu meeting was called and the mayor read the official telegram from the Swan balcony, some soldiers came up on a wagon with the Kaiser in effigy, which they tied to the town pump and burnt amidst cheers.'

Southwold had done its bit in the war. It had been bombed by

219

Zeppelins and had maintained a strict blackout every night in case it was bombarded from the sea, as other east-coast towns had been. As the adjutant of the local volunteer force, Cooper had played an active part in its defence. As captain of the fire brigade, he had been out night after night on fire-watch duties. He found it hard to believe that there would be no more of that and they could all sleep safely in their beds from now on. They could even leave the lights on if they wanted to and open the curtains. It seemed too good to be true.

In Liverpool, Miss McGuire shared very similar feelings, as she told her sister in Massachusetts:

'I think we have all gone mad. Such a day! It seems too good to be true. Of course in a way we thought the Armistice would be signed but now that the deed is done we can hardly realise that the war is over. I was dressed ready to go to the Red Cross today but the news came just before I started from the house and all the sirens commenced hooting so of course I could not sit working all day. I went into town instead and Aunt Tilly followed later. I wish you could have seen Liverpool. All shops and offices closed immediately and the streets were thronged with people. You could walk on their heads.

'Soldiers in gangs, munition girls, American Red Cross nurses, all sorts and conditions. We met the Misses Harrington and after meeting Aunt Tilly thought we would try to get some tea and watch the streets from a window. We went to Boots Café but all the waitresses had gone so went to King's. We waited some time but no one came to attend to us – they said the waitresses had taken French leave and gone …

'You never saw anything like the streets. Flags were flying, drums going, etc. One man was playing the drums with wine bottles. The medical students marched past in their overalls. We heard one of the Yanks make a speech from the American Centre in Lord Street. We were too late to hear the speeches from the Town Hall.'

Retired clergyman E. H. Moberly was in Southampton with his wife. They had an appointment, but had to abandon it in the crush:

'Every tram was full to suffocation, and hundreds of children taking joy rides on the top with flags. So we settled to walk down to the junction, and go that way, to see what was going on ... We forced our way down to near the clock tower, the crowd thickening all the way. Soon the American naval band came tramping down, playing "Hail, hail, the Yanks are here", followed by a hundred US soldiers and then by nearly a thousand sailors from Eastleigh, all singing – no officers, just their own show. Plenty of girls and women marching arm in arm with them in the ranks, singing, laughing and *yelling*. Sometimes there were as many as eight sailors abreast. I never heard such a noise, and never has such a crowd been seen in Southampton.'

At Windsor, the mayor had put on his official tricorn hat and was being driven up to the castle on a big red fire engine. He was accompanied by the band of the Coldstream Guards and a military escort. They all halted at the statue of Queen Victoria beside the castle gate. The mayor got down and made an inaudible speech to a crowd of townspeople and Eton boys far too excited to listen.

The Eton boys had bought up every Union Jack in Eton High Street before coming across the river. They wore the flags on their top hats as they capered about. Well over a thousand Old Etonians had been killed in the war, including quite a few older brothers – a disaster that had transformed the aristocracy for ever. The band played the 'Marseillaise' and other Allied anthems after the mayor had finished talking. Then they all sang 'God Save the King' and cheered.

In Cambridge, the bells of the university church had remained mute at 11 o'clock. They were the traditional harbinger of good news in the town, but they had been silenced for the duration of the war in case a passing Zeppelin heard them and used the sound to pinpoint its location. The mechanism for ringing the bells had been damaged, so the news was announced instead by the raising of the Union Jack above the Guildhall.

A gang of undergraduates rampaged through the town as the streets began to fill. They burned an effigy of the Kaiser and attacked a pacifist bookshop on King's Parade, throwing all its copies of the *Cambridge Magazine* into the street. The *Cambridge Magazine* had long claimed to speak for the ten thousand Cambridge men on active service when it argued for a compromise peace instead of continued slaughter. Its claim was far too presumptuous for the undergraduates. They smashed the shop's windows and trampled the magazines into the mud, just to show what they thought of a compromise peace now that they had total victory instead.

In Aldershot, home of the British army, a salute of 101 guns was fired, so loud that the sound carried as far as Farnborough Hill, where the widow of Napoleon III lived. Ninety-two years old, the Empress Eugénie had learned of the Armistice early that morning but had waited to hear from King George before believing it. He had rung just before eleven and she had gone to share the news with the wounded officers in her hospital. She had converted a wing of her house into a hospital for the war and continued to fund it out of her own pocket. The officers did their best to sit at attention as the empress walked down the line of beds, silently shaking hands with each occupant in turn while the guns boomed in the distance.

The wheel had turned full circle for Eugénie. The German triumph at Sedan in 1870 had caused her husband to lose his throne and flee abroad. Now the Kaiser was doing the same. Alsace and Lorraine would return to France and honour would be restored after a wait of almost half a century. Eyes full of tears, the Empress Eugénie quietly thanked God for letting her live to see the day.

As in France and Britain, so too in much of the rest of the world. Everywhere from Gibraltar, Malta and colonial Africa to India, Japan, Australia, New Zealand, Canada and the United States, millions of excited people dropped whatever they were doing when they learned of the Armistice and hurried out to celebrate the end of the fighting. It was the first truly global event the world had ever known.

In Canada and the United States, it was not yet light when the news arrived. In India it was late afternoon and in Australia early evening. In New Zealand, it was the next morning; in Japan, the day after. But wherever and whenever the news came, the reaction was almost invariably the same: the end of work for the day and a street party that carried on far into the night. From the church bells of Auckland to the engine whistles of the Canadian Pacific railway and the factory hooters of Chicago and New York, the world was celebrating the end of a truly disastrous war. It was the party to end all parties.

But the fighting hadn't completely stopped yet. In Northern Rhodesia, General von Lettow-Vorbeck had heard nothing about the Armistice as he bicycled to Kasama to confer with one of his forward commanders about a raid they were planning on the British depot at Chambezi. It wasn't until 13 November, when a British motorcyclist was captured, that the Germans learned that the war was over. Even then, they found it impossible to believe that Germany had lost.

On the Western Front too, the fighting had still not stopped altogether. At Erquelinnes, just across the Belgian border from Maubeuge, British cavalrymen killed a German machine-gunner at 11.15 who wouldn't stop firing, perhaps because his watch was wrong. Elsewhere, a British battery commander was killed at one minute past the hour, prompting his companions to continue shelling the German lines for another hour. At Inor, on the river Meuse, Lieutenant Thoma of the 19th Uhlans set off for the American lines well after eleven to ask if they needed help with billeting their troops now that the war was over. The Americans gunned him down at once, an error on their part which left the uhlans reeling with disgust. Badly wounded, Thoma apparently finished the job by shooting himself in the head.

At Stenay, a few miles to the south, the Americans were still firing at four that afternoon, blasting away at nothing under the impression that some noisy engineering work they could hear was an enemy attack. Isolated units were still in action in various places, mines were still exploding, ammunition dumps going up. Booby traps left by the

Germans continued to detonate for days and weeks to come. The war might be over, but there was still plenty of dying to be done. The Western Front saw something like 10,944 casualties on 11 November, including 2,738 dead. It was almost as many as D-Day.

CHAPTER TEN

Monday, 11 November 1918, afternoon

For most people at the front, the prevailing mood was one of distinct anticlimax as 11 o'clock passed and the firing died away all along the line. For as long as anyone could remember, there had always been firing somewhere within earshot, but now there wasn't any more. The quiet seemed unnatural after all the noise, almost a contradiction in terms. It took a great deal of getting used to.

Brigadier Richard Foot, an artilleryman supporting the Guards battalions at Maubeuge, had fired off the last of his surplus ammunition before 7 a.m. and then went to visit a couple of wounded soldiers at an advanced operating station. He spoke for millions as he returned later to his unit:

'It was a strange feeling to ride back to the battery in the quiet that followed 11 o'clock. One had got used to the background noise of shellfire, which could often be heard as far away as the south coast of England. Near the front, it seemed a continuous orchestration of deep and echoing sound, punctuated by the sharper rat-tat-tat of rifle or machine-gun fire. The landscape was different too; no observation balloons to be seen, no plumes of smoke from shell bursts or burning buildings, no aeroplanes glinting in the sky. After three and a half years of front-line service, broken only by short spells of leave or hospital, peace seemed a very strange and new experience.'

Just outside Perquise, some German officers came forward in the silence to show the Royal Welch Fusiliers where the road was mined. They were followed by a hunchback with an accordion who played the 'Marseillaise' in triumph as the Fusiliers marched into his village.

The refugees were already beginning to return, wending their way home again now that there was no more shooting. Army chaplain Harry Blackburne watched some of them near Mons:

'The roads filled with civilians hurrying back to their homes which they had been forced to leave by the Germans, all of them struggling along the muddy roads, pushing their handcarts and barrows. It is like it was during the retreat from Mons: old women, pinched and ill, absolutely deadbeat. Our lorries pick up as many as they can, and our soldiers push along the wheelbarrows for the older ones who can hardly walk. More often than not, on arrival at their homes they find no home – it has been battered to pieces by shellfire: "It doesn't matter," they say, "we have tasted liberty."'

In Mons itself, the inhabitants were determined to have a party for their liberators, even though many of the Canadians were so exhausted that they lay fast asleep in the street. The Canadians weren't due to make their official entry into the town until half past three, when they would march in with bands playing and colours flying, but the party had already begun and the inhabitants weren't about to stop now. The reprisals were beginning too. The Belgians wanted to get at the Germans captured in the fighting and take their revenge for four years of occupation. It needed all the Canadians' tact to stop the Belgians falling on their German prisoners and tearing them limb from limb.

Not far from Mons, men of the Royal Marine Light Infantry were lying in a line along a railway bank as the fighting came to an end. A battalion of the Manchester Regiment had lined up along the same bank during the retreat from Mons in 1914. After the shooting stopped, marine Hubert Trotman and a few others got up and strolled down to the wood in the nearby valley. They stumbled across some skeletons from 1914, men of the Manchesters still lying there from the beginning of the war. 'Lying there with their boots on, very still, no helmets, no rusty rifles or equipment, just their boots.' The sight was one that the marines never forgot.

Everywhere, there was a feeling of disbelief that the war was actually over, a sense that it was all just a dream that wasn't really happening.

US Private Arthur Jensen was one of many who said, 'Don't worry, it'll soon start up again', when the firing stopped at eleven. British rifleman Aubrey Smith at Erquennes echoed his sentiments:

'To think there would be no more shells, no more bombs, no more gas, no more cold nights to be spent on picket through fear of lighting a fire. Of all the incredible announcements that had ever been made to us, this left us the most staggered. It must be only a dream! Surely we should hear the distant sound of guns in a minute or so, which would prove we had been deluded! We strained our ears for distant gunfire … Silence! Only the sound of church bells in other villages proclaiming the event …

'Twice during the afternoon our hearts sank to our feet at the sound of a distant report like the firing of a big gun, but word came along presently that it was either blasting or else the exploding of some German mines under the roads! Everyone, troops and civilians, had knocked off work for the day, and we were welcomed into the cottages, where the good folk made cups of coffee out of the scanty supplies they had, and told us many tales of suffering and hardships. We palled up with a peasant and his family in a small cottage near our field, and we listened to stories which were a replica of those we had heard during the past week.'

All along the line, French and Belgian civilians produced food that they had been hiding for this special day. The Germans had been through their houses so often that they had very little left beyond a bottle or two of wine buried in the garden and a few choice items that they had somehow managed to conceal. They happily produced what they had and thrust it on the soldiers, not realising that the troops on the Allied side were perfectly well fed and had no need of anything to eat. It had been so long since civilians behind the German lines had eaten properly that they had forgotten what it was like to have a full stomach. Food was their greatest gift, the most valuable present they had to offer to their liberators. They gave it willingly, delighted to do what they could to mark the occasion. At Maubeuge, one elderly Frenchman was so pleased at the day's events that he dressed up in his old uniform from the Franco–Prussian war in celebration.

Among the Americans, Harry Truman had been as glad as anyone to see an end to the war. Like everyone else, however, he found it distinctly unsettling when the guns ceased to roar at eleven:

'It was so quiet it made me feel as if I'd been suddenly deprived of my ability to hear. The men at the guns, the captain, the lieutenants, the sergeants and corporals looked at each other for some time and then a great cheer arose all along the line. We could hear the men in the infantry a thousand metres in front raising holy hell. The French battery behind our position were dancing, shouting and waving bottles of wine ...'

Truman's men promptly joined in, drinking all the red wine they could find and more cognac than they could hold. The sun came out at midday and the party continued throughout the afternoon into the evening. Rockets were fired and Very lights soared as the men of the 129th Field Artillery celebrated the release from tension. Above them, Lieutenant Broaddus of battery F watched unhappily from his balloon. He had been sent up earlier to direct the last of the artillery fire. The war had stopped while he was up there and everyone had forgotten about him in their excitement. It was two hours before they remembered him again and hauled him down.

Elsewhere, Americans wandered out into no-man's-land, looking for souvenirs to take home now that the fighting was done. There was a market for souvenirs behind the lines, a brisk trade among base soldiers who had not themselves been anywhere near the action. Pistols, helmets, bayonets, anything good would fetch a price. Sometimes the souvenir hunters strayed close to the Germans in the trenches opposite. Feldwebel Georg Bucher and his fellow lice-ridden scarecrows had emerged cautiously from their holes in the early afternoon, scarcely able to believe that their heads wouldn't be blown off as soon as they raised them above the parapet. They watched warily as the men they had machine-gunned that morning, who had dropped gas on them in return, now hunted for trophies a few yards away:

'We were squatting with incredulous eyes in front of the parapet. The Americans were wandering around in no-man's-land, but there wasn't much they could find, for the shellfire had played havoc there. Some of them came within twenty yards of us. How angrily and contemptuously they looked at us! They didn't seem pleased that we still had hand grenades hanging from our belts and rifles in our hands ...

'Some of us tried to make friends with the enemy, but to no avail. The Americans were too bitter from the events of the previous day, which wasn't surprising. They had attacked three times and been beaten back with heavy losses.

'It was indeed a strange sensation to be sitting openly in front of the trench. The reality was hard to believe; we were conscious of a vague fear that it might all turn out to be a dream.'

It was no dream. The war really was over and the fighting really had stopped. Whoever was in charge of the nightmare had finally come to their senses, and not a moment too soon.

Lieutenant Colonel George Patton wrote a poem to commemorate the occasion. He was at Langres on Armistice morning, recovering from a wound in his side. A legend later arose that Patton had been one of those American officers who hurried to the front when the ceasefire was announced in order to be in at the kill. He was said to have bribed a hospital orderly and commandeered a taxi to drive him up to Verdun. In fact, he remained well behind the lines, lamenting the coming of peace:

> We can but hope that ere we drown
> 'Neath treacle floods of grace,
> The tuneless horns of mighty Mars
> Once more shall rouse the Race.
> When such times come, Oh! God of War
> Grant that we pass midst strife,
> Knowing once more the whitehot joy
> Of taking human life.

Patton had seen only five days of action during the war. He later got his wish for more killing.

＊

At Cambrai, the British army commanders were meeting to discuss the arrangements for the next few days before the march to Germany. Eleven o'clock had passed with barely a ripple at British headquarters as Field Marshal Sir Douglas Haig and his generals planned a programme of events to keep the men out of mischief. They posed for the newsreels afterwards, Sir Julian Byng and others doing their best to make Sir Herbert Plumer laugh on camera. Then Haig went back to his command train for a celebratory lunch with Prince Fushimi of Japan, who was going to present him with a Japanese decoration before making a tour of the battlefields.

Haig was walking tall as he returned to his train. The victory over the Germans was a British victory as much as anyone's. British and imperial troops had borne the brunt of the war since the French mutinies of 1917. In the past few months, they had taken almost as many prisoners and captured almost as many guns as the French, American and Belgian armies combined. But if the war had been won by force of arms, Haig was less certain about the peace. He had grave misgivings about the Armistice conditions and had said as much in a letter to his wife:

'I am afraid the Allied statesmen mean to exact humiliating terms from Germany. I think this is a mistake, because it is merely laying up trouble for the future, and may encourage the wish for revenge.'

Haig distrusted Lloyd George in particular, an antipathy that was fully reciprocated. Faced with an unprecedented war in which none of the commanders had been able to see the whole battlefield, Haig had chosen to lead his armies from well behind the line, issuing directives from the comfort of a well-appointed chateau far from the heat of battle. There were sound reasons for keeping his headquarters out of the line of fire, but Lloyd George had been a vociferous critic nevertheless, and so had others as the casualties mounted. Lieutenant Colonel Harold Alexander, commanding a battalion of the Irish Guards, and divisional chief of staff Bernard Montgomery had both promised themselves that if ever they became generals they would lead from the front, thoroughly familiarising themselves with the conditions before sending men into battle. Haig was perfectly aware of the conditions, but had failed to make himself sufficiently visible to the men who had to do the fighting. Cynics among his countrymen regarded him as Scotland's finest-ever general, because his strategy for the war had killed more English than all the other generals combined.

If he had any regrets, he did not voice them as he greeted Prince Fushimi at the train. Marquis Inouye of the Japanese peerage was with him, and Prince Arthur of Connaught. The Japanese had done well out of the war. After joining their British allies against Germany, they had sensibly kept their distance from the Western Front, concentrating instead on seizing the Marianas and Marshall Islands from the Germans and capturing the Chinese port of Tsingtao. They had occupied the Russian port of Vladivostok as well, when the Russians had been in no position to stop them. They were hoping to hold on to their gains when the map of the world was redrawn at the forthcoming peace conference.

Haig accepted the decoration and led his guests in to lunch. The Prince of Wales arrived afterwards for a meeting with Fushimi. He arrived reluctantly, because he would much rather have been with the Canadians at Mons. He had advanced with the Canadians for the whole of the last month and now, as he complained to his mother, he was going to miss the grand finale:

'I'm very sick not to have been there but I was ordered to meet Prince Fushimi at advanced GHQ at 2.00 p.m. where he lunched with the C-in-C on board the train!! I was inwardly furious as think how interesting to have entered Mons the same day as the first troops entered it; but "orders is orders" and I had a short chat with the Japanese prince who certainly talks very good English and then Arthur was with him and they go to Paris tonight. But I had a very interesting half-hour talk with the C-in-C who showed me plans and maps for the march into and occupation of Germany as well as Foch's terms for the Armistice which I hadn't seen before!!'

The Prince of Wales wondered how the Kaiser was feeling that day, forced to abdicate his throne and flee in disgrace to Holland.

'Far worse than any man has ever felt before I should think and hope too.' The Kaiser thoroughly deserved everything that had happened to him, in the Prince of Wales's opinion.

In Brussels, the city was still in chaos as the war came to an end. The Germans were still fighting each other, pulling officers off trams and lynching them if they caught them wearing their badges of rank. At the Gare du Nord, some German officers had turned machine guns on their own men, killing a couple of civilians in the process. The officers were chased into a hotel on the Place Rogier and bombarded into submission while the Belgians remained indoors and watched from the safety of their windows. The previous day's camaraderie between Belgian and German Bolshevists had evaporated during the night. The Belgians wanted nothing more to do with the Germans. They were perfectly happy for them to go on killing each other, just so long as no Belgians were hurt in the process. The more Germans who died the better.

The streets were sullen and deserted on Armistice day except for gangs of drunken soldiers rampaging along the boulevards, looting every shop in sight and breaking into banks and private houses. They took what they wanted from the Belgians, but they also robbed their own people, forcing their way into Prince Rupprecht of Bavaria's villa and pitching his furniture into the street, while the general took refuge with the Spanish ambassador. Rupprecht's possessions were auctioned on the spot and piled on to carts and wagons for the long haul back to Germany. Columns of troops had been passing through Brussels for days, heading for home with their booty. Their one aim now was to get safely out of Belgium and back across the German border with as much loot as they could carry.

Gick Gifford, the English schoolteacher, was there to watch the Germans go: 'What a dishevelled, ragged, hungry-looking mob they were, waving the red flag, their wagons even being decorated with this flag of revolution! In fact, desperate-looking men, and one dared hardly lift an eye as they passed. Such a contrast to that magnificent invincible-looking host of 1914. What a Nemesis!

'Many were dragging carts, not to mention cows, foals – in fact anything they had been able to lay their hands on.'

As an Englishwoman, Gifford naturally had more sympathy for the livestock than the human beings:

'The horses we saw being led were the most pitiful objects and in a terrible condition, nothing but a rattle of bones and a mass of open sores and wounds. Poor, poor dumb animals! It made one sick to think of their mute sufferings.'

The Belgians complained to the new German soldiers' council in Brussels about all the looting. They were solemnly assured that the revolutionary government in Berlin would make full reparation in due course. The Belgians decided to believe it when they saw it.

The Armistice had little immediate impact in Brussels. In Berlin too, it passed almost unnoticed in a city still preoccupied with its own problems. The situation had calmed down a little from the previous two days, but it had yet to return to normal. There were still armed men everywhere and repeated outbursts of machine-gun fire as rival factions continued to shoot at each other, hoping to provoke a bloody response. The crowds were no longer as big as they had been and the mood was less ugly, but it would be a while yet before it was safe to go out on the streets again.

Princess Blücher and her husband were still at Dr Mainzer's house on the Winterfeldstrasse, where they had taken refuge when their own was attacked. Despite the continued shooting, Prince Blücher decided to risk a return to their own house to assess the damage and start restoring it to order. Evelyn Blücher didn't go with him. Instead, she went with Frau Mainzer to visit their friends and congratulate them on having survived the last forty-eight hours. In visits over the next two days, she found everyone horrified at the terms of the Armistice, particularly the refusal to lift the naval blockade until the peace treaty had been signed. The Germans were already half-starved and dropping like flies from Spanish flu. A continuation of the blockade could only mean a slow death from exhaustion for many more of them:

'As one Englishwoman said to me, the idea of continuing to exist and work on the minimum of food still possible under the circumstances was so dreadful that she thought it would be the most sensible thing to go with her child and try to get shot in one of the numerous street fights; whilst another lady whose husband is at the front, and from whom she has heard nothing for a long time, is contemplating turning on the gas on herself and her two small children, and putting an end to the horrors of living.'

The food shortage in Germany had been dismissed as a secondary issue by the Allies at Compiègne, perhaps even a negotiating ploy. It seemed real enough to Evelyn Blücher and all the other hungry women in Berlin.

In Paris, the party was now well under way as the city continued to celebrate. The Champs Elysées was a seething mass of people by early afternoon, so many of them that the road itself had all but disappeared from view. The Place de la Concorde was equally crowded, full of people in their Sunday best, laying flags and wreaths on the 'City of Strasbourg', the allegorical statue that had witnessed the guillotining of Louis XVI during the French Revolution. Strasbourg was the capital of Alsace, restored to France for the first time in almost half a century. Its recapture had avenged a widely resented stain on the national honour.

Music, singing, dancing. Flags and coloured streamers, rousing choruses of 'La Madelon de la Victoire', a popular song about a barmaid. War widows in black dancing with one-armed, one-legged soldiers released from hospital for the day. A young man climbing up to a balcony to kiss a giggling group of midinettes. A doctor on the corner of the rue de Rivoli distributing flowers from a stall. With so many Frenchmen killed or maimed, novelist Marcel Proust was shocked at the abandon of his fellow Parisians in their hour of triumph. 'We are weeping for so many dead that gaiety like this is not the form of celebration one would prefer,' he complained to a friend. But he was wrong. The French had worked hard for their victory. They needed to let off steam for a few days, before they returned to sober reality.

Norah Broadey, a French Red Cross worker at the American hospital at Neuilly, was one of the revellers in the crowd:

'Everybody is in the streets and boulevards and *no work* is the order of the day. The streets are absolute *vistas* of Allied flags, and everywhere people are singing, marching in processions and waving flags. Everyone fraternises! And everywhere you hear over and over again the national anthems of the Allies and the war songs. The sound of "Tipperary" sung by a little group brought a great lump into my throat. I couldn't help remembering the gallant men who sailed from England to the sound of it, and never returned.

'Great scenes of animation going on in the Place de l'Opéra, and a British colonial demonstration which made us feel very happy. A French aviator did stunts close over our heads – he flew quite low along the rue de la Paix and then rose over our heads and the Opéra, amid great cheering. Men were standing up on the roofs and one man was dancing up there and playing around with a chimney pot. The band played the "Marseillaise", "God Save the King", and other national anthems.'

At the British embassy, the ambassador, Lord Derby, was mobbed as he set off for the Palais Bourbon to hear Clemenceau announce the Armistice terms. The band of the Royal Horse Guards played the national anthem while Decima Moore, who ran the British leave centre in Paris, waved a Union Jack from the top of a taxi and shouted 'Rule, Britannia!' Derby struggled through the crowd and made his way to the Palais. Everyone else was going there too. Arriving eventually, Derby headed for the Chamber of Deputies, where Clemenceau was to make the announcement.

It was an emotional moment for the French premier. As a young man, Clemenceau had been one of more than a hundred deputies who had signed the official motion deploring France's defeat in the Franco-Prussian war and the annexation of Alsace-Lorraine. Now, forty-seven years later, the only survivor of the original signatories, he was able to announce Alsace-Lorraine's return. He had been kissed by several hundred women since morning and embraced by his old political enemy Raymond Poincaré, France's diminutive president.

He was cheered to the rafters as he stood up in front of the deputies to read out the terms of the Armistice. Every clause was greeted with a roar of approval as the implications sank in. The Germans hadn't just been defeated in the war. They had been abjectly humiliated. It was France's turn to triumph and Clemenceau paid due tribute:

'In the name of the French people, I honour our magnificent dead, who have brought us this great victory … France has been liberated by the power of her armies … Thanks to them, France, yesterday the soldier of God, today the soldier of humanity, will always be the soldier of ideals.'

No mention of France's allies. British and imperial troops had died in industrial quantities on soil not their own, but they and the Americans might have played no part in the victory for all the tribute Clemenceau paid to them. Lord Derby left the chamber afterwards 'looking less exuberantly cheerful than is his wont', according to a French friend. He felt better later, when an American stood up in the Café de Paris and drank to the health of England, 'who really won the war'. That was much more what Lord Derby wanted to hear.

Across the Atlantic, the party had begun before dawn as the New World woke up to a ceasefire that had already been signed and sealed in the Old. Guns had been fired at 5 a.m. from the citadel at Halifax, Nova Scotia, followed soon afterwards by church bells and dancing in the streets. There was an ecstatic victory parade in Montreal and a massed band playing 'Maple Leaf Forever' on Parliament Hill in Ottawa. In Toronto, the crowds were so enthusiastic that they over-turned a delivery wagon and pushed it through the front window of a shoe shop before looting the contents.

In New York, the Statue of Liberty had been lit up before dawn for the first time since the United States had entered the war. At Grand Central Station, eight hundred newly drafted men from the Bronx were mightily relieved to learn of the Armistice as they stood wait-ing for the train that was taking them away to the army. Along Fifth Avenue, hundreds of thousands of New Yorkers joined an excited crowd parading up across Forty-second Street towards Broadway, headed by circus elephants and accompanied by every kind of person imaginable:

'Fashionable ladies jingling cowbells; street urchins yelling and dancing; stenographers in red, white and blue paper caps; sailors grinning under the floppy picture-hats of the girls and girls flaunting sailors' hats. There were autos bursting with vociferous passengers, one-horse carts, farm-wagons full of giggling girls, lifeboats mounted on trucks, sightseeing buses boiling with people.'

In San Francisco, a huge bonfire blazed on Telegraph Hill. In Minnesota, bells rang and whistles blew at the Wahpeton Indian School. In Mississipi, the pupils of Tupelo High School fought a sham battle with roman candles and firecrackers. And in Gettysburg, Pennsylvania, Lieutenant Colonel Dwight Eisenhower cursed inwardly, furious that the war had finished before he had had a chance to get any front-line experience. He had been due to sail for France on 18 November. Now he would have to remain forever silent at West Point reunions, left out of it while his classmates reminisced about the war, patronising him because he had never heard a shot fired in anger.

Eisenhower had seen those recruiting posters, 'What did you do in the war, Daddy?', where an embarrassed father sat in his chair while the real men marched off to fight. He wondered what he would tell his own son when the time came. Irritatingly, he would have gone to France long ago if it hadn't been for his exceptional talents as an organiser. The army had sent him to Gettysburg instead to train men in tank warfare on the old Civil War battlefield. Eisenhower had seen thousands of others off to war without ever going himself.

In Michigan, Captain Winn Johnstone Wilson of the Royal Sussex Regiment had been woken at five that morning by the Armistice celebrations. 'Amazed at the American who can enthuse in cold blood at such an hour', he had left Bay City after breakfast and caught the train to Cheboygan, at the top of Lake Huron, where he had a speaking engagement to explain the war to the locals. Badly wounded on the Western Front, Johnstone Wilson had survived against all expectations, but had been declared unfit for further active service. He had been sent to the United States instead, as part of Britain's military mission to promote the war effort and help Americans understand just what it was they were fighting for.

Johnstone Wilson had found it uphill work. He liked Americans and greatly admired their democracy, but he found their ignorance of the outside world horrifying. Many were strongly anti-British, and not simply because they preferred the Germans. Johnstone Wilson resented, too, the widespread assumption that the Americans had won the war on their own, as if no one else had done any fighting:

'They have not even a glimmering of this war, Chateau-Thierry being to them the *only* battle. The ignorance of the intelligent American is astounding, by which I mean his knowledge of anything outside business. They have kept their eyes on the markets and America and think to solve the problems of Europe with such knowledge. Anti-English is still prevalent and was more than pro-German ... When they are not working or organising they are eating ...'

Johnstone Wilson was worried that the Armistice had come too early for safe-keeping. He had been in Washington for the false Armistice on 7 November, one of a party of glum Britishers reluctant to celebrate while everyone around them went wild. He had felt then, and felt still, that the German army should have been properly defeated before an Armistice was declared:

'I am still uncertain now that it is all over whether it is not a great pity that it came before the Allies broke the German army. It is also distinctly bad for thought over here and quite difficult to convince the casual uneducated American that he hasn't won the war alone.'

Johnstone Wilson disliked and distrusted all the unreflective patriotism he had come across in America. Flag-waving apart, though, he found the people of the United States a pretty decent bunch: 'I should love them if they were not so self-satisfied with America.'

In Burrton, Kansas, a posse was on its way to an outlying farm to grab John Schrag and bring him into town. The men wanted him to join the Armistice celebrations to show that he wasn't a 'slacker'.

Schrag was a Mennonite, a God-fearing man of Swiss-German descent. Along with the rest of the Mennonite community, he had refused to support the war from the start, resisting pressure to buy the war bonds that were the local test of loyalty. It was against the Mennonite creed to support violence in any shape or form.

His sons refused to say where he was when the men arrived. They ransacked the property, hauled Schrag out of his hiding place and daubed the farm buildings with the yellow stripes of cowardice before dragging him back to town. Bonfires were burning around the main square as a hostile mob surrounded Schrag, insisting that he must lead the victory parade around Burrton and buy war bonds or face the consequences. He offered to give $200 to the Red Cross or the Salvation Army instead, but the mob wasn't having it. Either he supported the war or he was a traitor.

An American flag was shoved into his hand. Schrag refused to take it. The flag fell to the ground and someone in the crowd yelled that Schrag had stepped on an American flag. Farmer Charles Gordon watched what happened next:

'I never saw so much yelling and a' cursing and slapped him. And buffeted him and beat him and kicked him. He never offered any resistance whatsoever. One of the fellows went to a hardware store and got a gallon of yellow paint. Pulled the lid off and poured it over his face. He had a long beard, kind of a short heavy-set man, had a nice beard, and that ran down all over his eyes, his face and his beard and his clothes ...

'He never offered no resistance whatsoever and they, one man, went to the hardware store again and he got a rope and put it around his neck and marched him down close to the city gaol, a little calaboose there. Had a tree there and they were going to hang him to this tree.'

The deputy sheriff stepped in, holding the mob back at gunpoint and arresting Schrag to save his life. He was put on a raised platform in the gaol so that people could jeer at him through the window. That night, while everyone else celebrated the Armistice, he was taken to another town for his own safety and charged with desecrating the

American flag. On Long Island, at the same time, Sergeant Irving Berlin was wondering what to do with a song he had written that had proved too solemn for his army show *Yip, Yip, Yaphank*. The song was 'God Bless America'.

In Washington, President Wilson had arrived on Capitol Hill to address a joint session of Congress. The House wasn't full, because many of the senators and representatives were still making their way back to Washington after the election campaign, but the galleries were crammed with diplomats and the atmosphere was electric as Wilson prepared to announce the Armistice terms. Roman Dumowski, president of the Polish National Committee, was there to watch; so was Tomáš Masaryk, head of the Czecho-Slovak National Council. It was a new beginning for the small countries of Europe, now that the old empires were falling apart.

Everyone cheered as Wilson appeared. He was looking tired and spoke huskily, as if he had a cold. He shook hands with the Speaker and vice president and then addressed Congress for thirty minutes, outlining the Armistice terms clause by clause, before concluding with a few observations about the peace:

'It is not now possible to assume the consequences of this great consummation. We know only that this tragical war, whose consuming flames swept from one nation to another until all the world was on fire, is at an end and that it was the privilege of our own people to enter it at its most critical juncture in such fashion and in such force as to contribute in a way of which we are all deeply proud to the great result.

'We know, too, that the object of the war is attained: the object upon which all free men had set their hearts; and attained with a sweeping completeness which even now we do not realise. Armed imperialism such as the men conceived who were but yesterday the masters of Germany is at an end, its illicit ambitions engulfed in black disaster. Who will now seek to revive it?'

Wilson was cheered again when he had finished, given a rousing ovation by politicians from both parties. He and his guests drove back to the White House afterwards for a late lunch and were applauded along the way. Wilson emerged again at 4 o'clock to review a parade of war workers from the steps of the Executive Office. Then he walked down to the White House gates, looking happier than anyone could remember, to watch the growing party on Pennsylvania Avenue. The whole city had come out to celebrate the end of the fighting. Whatever doubts people had had about the war had been dispelled now that it was all over and the United States had won. The entire nation was rejoicing at the outcome.

As Americans celebrated across the land, the last of their war dead who had made the victory possible were lying still unburied on the battlefields of France. A few days after the Armistice, Private Arthur Jensen came across a mix of dead Germans and Americans on the Meuse heights near Brandeville:

'In some places the men had been killed by bullets; but in others they were blown to pieces by shells; an arm here with the hand gone, and a leg there with the genitals hanging to it, or a solitary head which seemed to accuse civilisation with its silence! In one place I found a stomach lost in the grass, while wound around the limbs of a nearby tree were the intestines.'

Further on, Jensen came across four dead Germans, known as Dutchmen in American slang, lying together in a heap:

'Their stinking flesh had turned green and presented a spectacle so gruesome that I could see, smell, and taste them all at once! Sickening as it was, I suppose history will say this battle was a glorious victory for American arms, which it is, without a doubt. Yet if those poor abandoned human carcasses could talk, they'd probably say:

> We are the dividends of war;
> We're what you came to Europe for.
> Our cause is lost; we died in vain,
> And now we're rotting in the rain!

'But I hadn't seen anything yet. A little farther on was an American soldier stamping a dead German's face into a pulp. I suppose the

Germans had killed one of his buddies; because, as he stamped, he ground his teeth and mumbled, "You dirty Dutch son-of-a-bitch!"'

In London, British Zionist Chaim Weizmann had a long-standing lunch engagement with Lloyd George at No. 10. Telephoning beforehand to see if it was still on, Weizmann was surprised to learn that it was, and that he and the prime minister would be lunching alone.

There was no chance of any transport, so Weizmann walked all the way to Downing Street from his home in Addison Road. He started at midday, but found it heavy going through the dense crowds:

'By about 1.30 (the hour of my appointment), I was in Green Park, just outside the little iron gate that leads into Downing Street. So were a great many other people. The gate was closely guarded by several policemen. Timidly I approached one of those on our side with a request to be let through, which was of course promptly refused. "But," said I, "I have an appointment with the prime minister for lunch." The policeman looked at me. "So several other people have already informed me," he remarked dryly. I then produced a visiting card, and asked if he would show it to his colleague on the inside of the gate, who might then inquire from the porter at Number Ten whether I was telling the truth. After some hesitation he agreed to do this, and in a few minutes returned all smiles to let me through.

'I found the prime minister reading the Psalms; he was moved to the depths of his soul and was, indeed, near to tears. The first thing he said to me was: "We have just sent off seven trains full of bread and other essential food, to be distributed by Plumer in Cologne."'

The trains were apparently a myth. Weizmann briefed the prime minister over lunch about the possibility of a homeland for the Jewish people in Palestine following the Turkish surrender, but it was obvious that Lloyd George's mind was elsewhere. Weizmann didn't want to take up any more of his time than he could help. He watched afterwards as Lloyd George set off from No. 10 to announce the Armistice terms to the House of Commons. A cheering crowd fell on the prime minister as soon as he stepped out of the door and carried him off on their shoulders out of Weizmann's sight.

At the Commons, Lloyd George received another ovation when he entered the chamber with Henry Asquith. After prayers, he read out the Armistice terms to an attentive House. Conservative MP Stanley Baldwin felt closer to tears than exultation as he weighed the cost of the victory: 'My brain is reeling at it all. I find three impressions strongest: thankfulness that the slaughter is stopped, the thought of the millions of dead, and the vision of Europe in ruins.' Watching from the Speaker's Gallery, Margot Asquith could not help feeling sorry for the Germans as the severity of the terms became apparent:

'I pressed my forehead into my hands and a wave of emotion moved across my heart. To the average individual the terms that we had listened to were what had been expected; but I could only conjecture with compassion what they must mean to a proud race who, until 1914, had everything that industry and science could achieve, and had maintained a conflict for four years, in which they expected not only to beat France, but half Europe; and not for the first time I felt I was in a position to obey the high command that tells us to extend mercy with judgement.'

But there was no mercy for the Germans. The mood across Europe was unforgiving after everything they had done. When he had read out the terms, Lloyd George called an end to the House's proceedings for the day:

'This is no time for words. Our hearts are too full of a gratitude to which no tongue can give adequate expression. I will, therefore, move: "That this House do immediately adjourn, until this time tomorrow, and that we proceed, as a House of Commons, to St Margaret's, to give humble and reverent thanks for the deliverance of the world from its great peril".'

Henry Asquith seconded the motion. Both Houses of Parliament trooped across the road to St Margaret's, the little church beside Westminster Abbey where Sir Walter Raleigh lay buried. The Archbishop of Canterbury conducted the service. The congregation sang 'O God our help in ages past'. Then they got down on their knees and prayed to the Almighty that nothing like the past four years would ever happen again.

*

While the Commons were at prayer, King George and Queen Mary were driving through the streets with their daughter, showing themselves to the people in their open carriage. In slanting rain, they drove along the Strand to the Mansion House in the City, then back to Buckingham Palace via Piccadilly. As the king remembered it, 'there was a vast crowd, most good humoured, in some places it was hardly possible to get along'. Londoners of all kinds threw themselves at the carriage, wanting to say hello to their sovereign. The police tried to hold them back, but George wouldn't have it, insisting that even the poorest of the poor should be allowed to cling to his carriage if they wished. They had all been in this war together.

American poet Ezra Pound was in an open-topped bus in Piccadilly when the king's carriage came past, only a few feet away. 'Poor devil was looking happy, I should think, for the first time in his life,' Pound reported to a friend. The king was certainly enjoying himself on what was for him 'a wonderful day, the greatest in the history of this country'. People viewing him up close saw that his beard was grey and his face exhausted, but he was a happy man nevertheless. He had laboured as long as anyone to bring the war to a successful conclusion.

Queen Mary was pleased too. 'This has repaid us for much hard work and many moments of keen and bitter anxiety,' she wrote to one of her children. The royals had lost friends and family in the fighting, just like everyone else. They had endured a brief period of republicanism when the war had been going particularly badly. They had shared the worst of it with their subjects and now they were enjoying the fruits.

They went out on the balcony again when they got back to the palace. The crowds were as large as ever, showing no sign of dispersing. If anything, they were growing larger as people continued to flood in from other parts of London and surrounding areas. Everyone wanted to be there to enjoy the occasion. It would take more than a little rain to stop the people of England celebrating the end of the war.

*

Not all of them were having fun. Vera Brittain could think only of the dead as she watched the crowds from the top deck of a bus in Piccadilly. Duff Cooper, arriving from Norfolk with Lady Diana Manners, felt much the same. Fifteen-year-old Malcolm Muggeridge, on a bus from Woolwich to Croydon with a friend, was far too priggish to join the party, although he secretly wanted to:

'From the open upper deck we watched the crowds singing, shouting, dancing, embracing, vomiting, climbing on to the tops of taxis, grabbing one another and making off to the parks. It was, to me, an eerie and disturbing, rather than a joyful, scene – those flushed animal faces, dishevelled women, hoarse voices ... was this what freedom meant?'

At home in Hertfordshire, George Bernard Shaw was glad the war was over but wanted no part of the celebrations in his village. 'Every promising young man I know has been blown to bits,' he had lamented earlier in the war. Shaw couldn't bring himself to rejoice now, with so many dead and gone forever. At Bateman's, in Sussex, Rudyard Kipling couldn't rejoice either. He had lost his only son at Loos in 1915 and the body had never been found. No amount of flag-waving would bring his son back, or even reveal his last resting place.

In his diary, Henry Rider Haggard was delighted that the war was won but felt deeply uneasy about the forthcoming peace:

'The Germans will neither forgive nor forget; neither money nor comfort will tell with them henceforth. They have been beaten by England and they will live and die to smash England – she will never have a more deadly enemy than the new Germany. My dread is that in future years the easy-going, self-centred English will forget that just across the sea there is a mighty, cold-hearted and remorseless people waiting to strike her through the heart. For strike they will one day, or so I believe.'

At Shrewsbury, the Owen family were just glad that the war was over, without worrying about the future. Tom and Susan Owen had sent three sons to the war and had lived for years with the gnawing fear that one or another might not come back. Wilfred, their eldest boy, was with the Manchester Regiment in France. Harold was at sea with the Royal Navy. Colin was in the Royal Flying Corps. The Owens' fears were over now that the bands were playing and the bells were ringing for peace. Their sons would be home soon, back where they belonged.

The bells were still pealing at midday when the Owens heard a ring at their front door. There was a telegram for them, from London.

While the Owens reeled, a German spy in Liverpool was wrestling with very different emotions as he watched the English singing and dancing in the church square outside his window. Julius Silber had spent the entire war as a postal censor, in theory reading the mail leaving the country and deleting anything of value to the enemy, in practice passing it all on to the Germans. As a spy on this terrible day, Silber needed to get out there with everyone else and join in the celebrations to avoid blowing his cover. As a patriotic German, though, his stomach revolted at the prospect.

Born in Silesia, Silber had left Germany in his teens and had spent much of his adult life knocking around the British Empire. He had worked as an interpreter and censor in British concentration camps during the South African war, moving on later to India, where thousands of Boer prisoners had been transferred. From there he had ended up in America, where he had been in 1914 when Great Britain declared war on Germany. Wondering how best to serve his country in the war, Silber had decided to go to England as a spy.

He had no passport, so he told the British he was French-Canadian when he arrived. After a less than thorough vetting procedure – no one even queried his German name – Silber had been taken on as a censor again, working in London first, then Liverpool. The blackboard in the censors' office had a list of names to look out for in the post, people under surveillance as suspected German agents. Silber had got a warning to them by sending the list to his contact in an envelope marked 'Opened by the Censor'.

In Liverpool, he had joined the Civil Service Club, playing bridge with various officers who chatted freely about the war. As the casualties mounted, Silber himself had been registered for military service and had lived in dread of being called up. Without a birth certificate or any proper documents, he would have been unmasked at once. He had tried to delay the inevitable by faking symptoms at medical boards, but the inevitable could not be delayed forever. At his wits' end, he had decided to flee the country instead, only to get lost in the fog as he tried to board a neutral cargo ship near the mouth of the river Dee.

His latest medical board was scheduled for 12 November. Perhaps it would be cancelled now that the war was over. But even if it was, Silber's job wasn't over yet. He was still a German spy. The penalty for what he had done was still death. As he went home early through the ecstatic crowds, Silber decided that he would have to attend the celebratory dinner at the club that night, to keep up appearances. Tomorrow he would attend the medical board if they still wanted him, and then he would return to his job, because the mail still had to be censored until a peace treaty had been signed. He might still be able to help the Fatherland if he discovered anything interesting in the mail that Germany's negotiators could use at the peace conference.

While Silber went home, the bells were ringing out from Lincoln cathedral, high on its hill above the town. The people of Lincoln had fought hard in the war, but they were as happy as any at the return of peace. They came from an ancient town, home to one of the four surviving copies of Magna Carta. Steeped in the age-old traditions of liberty and justice, the yeomen of Lincoln had been horrified at Germany's march into Belgium, a large and powerful country pushing its way into a small, defenceless one. They had been outraged when Belgians who resisted had been put up against a wall and shot. They had flocked to the colours to fight the Germans, to guarantee the rights of small nations to be masters of their own destiny without any bullying from their neighbours. That was why the war had been fought, if it had been fought about anything at all.

From his cell in Lincoln gaol, Eamon de Valera heard the bells and was delighted to learn of the ceasefire. With luck it would mean that he and his fellow Sinn Feiners would be released in time to fight the general election that Lloyd George had called for December. De Valera was already the Member of Parliament for East Clare, although he had refused to take his seat. If his assessment was correct, Sinn Fein would win the vast majority of the Irish seats at the election, leaving the British government no choice but to acknowledge Irish independence at the peace conference following the war.

First, though, the candidates had to be let out of prison to fight their campaigns. After the failure of the 1916 rising in Dublin, and the execution by firing squad of the ringleaders, de Valera and his fellow Irish republicans had made such a nuisance of themselves that seventy-three of them had been arrested in May on trumped-up charges of plotting with the Germans against the government. No one had believed a word of it – certainly not the British officer who had asked for their autographs on the way to gaol – but they had been locked up anyway, interned without trial until such time as wartime regulations no longer applied. They could only assume that they would be released soon, now that there was no longer any legitimate excuse for keeping them under lock and key.

Even if they weren't released, de Valera was determined not to remain in gaol much longer. He intended to escape if the British still refused to let him go. His plan involved making a wax impression of the chaplain's gate key and getting friends on the outside to send him a file baked into a cake. It was a bizarre idea, baking a file into a cake, but de Valera was willing to try anything to get out of Lincoln gaol.

Across the Irish Sea, the man responsible for de Valera's incarceration was busy sending off telegrams to the victors of the war, congratulating the commanders on their triumph and assuring them of the Irish people's heartfelt gratitude for all they had done. As Britain's viceroy in Dublin, Field Marshal Lord French had sent one telegram to Marshal Foch, another to Admiral Sir David Beatty, and a third to Field Marshal Sir Douglas Haig, the man who had replaced him as

British commander-in-chief on the Western Front after French had been sacked at the end of 1915.

The war had not gone well for French. Already a field marshal at the beginning, he had led the British army to France in August 1914, but it had rapidly become apparent that he wasn't up to the job, either intellectually or physically. He had been quietly relieved of his command as soon as it was practicable, given a title and later bundled off to Ireland in the hope that his own Irish blood might somehow commend him to the natives.

His sex life had suffered as a consequence. French had a large appetite for women and had indulged it freely during the first years of the war. Women are attracted to powerful men. French had had the power to post their sons and husbands away from the front. A constant stream of wives and mothers had accordingly found their way into his bed, lying back and thinking of England while this dreadful little man grunted and slobbered all over them. Their menfolk had been gratified in due course, if a little puzzled, to find themselves pulled out of the line and posted safely out of harm's way. Everyone had had to make sacrifices in this war.

But French's powers of appointment had been curtailed once he had lost his job on the Western Front. Women had proved a lot less willing to feel his breath on them, especially if they were taller than he was, as they always were. The Irish didn't like him either. French had held out the promise of home rule for Ireland if the Irish would only agree to conscription in return, but the Irish had refused to agree to any such thing if it meant their young men being killed for nothing in a British war. They would rather have complete independence on their own terms.

There was Ulster too, another of French's problems. De Valera and his Sinn Feiners might sweep the elections everywhere else, but the men of the north wanted no truck with republicanism. They hadn't fought like demons on the Somme just to become a republic. Home rule was Rome rule, so far as the Protestants of Ulster were concerned. They wouldn't countenance it for a moment.

*

Back in France, Maude Onions had been too busy in Boulogne's signal office to do anything except glance at the clock as eleven struck and war turned to peace. The moment came and went with hardly a murmur in the office and was initially ignored by the French in the town as well. The only people who took any immediate notice of it were the Australian troops convalescing in the cliff-top camp overlooking the harbour. They were quite drunk by mid-morning as they lurched downhill into Boulogne and headed for the rue de Saint Pol, where the girls lived who kept red lights in their windows.

The Australians had fought magnificently during the past few months. Along with the Canadians, they had led the break-out from Amiens in August, a day assessed by Ludendorff as the blackest in the history of the German army. They had done the lion's share of the fighting in the weeks that followed. Bigger than the British, much better paid, they had pursued the Germans with courage and dash, pressing forward where the exhausted British had been more cautious and wary. In Sir John Monash the Australians had been blessed with an outstanding general who led by inspiration and knew exactly what he was doing. They wondered why Monash wasn't in command of all the British troops, since he appeared to be the best leader they had. They hoped it wasn't because Monash was Jewish.

But the Australians had a wild side as well. They were a byword for indiscipline in the army. They had torn Cairo apart in 1915 and still committed a significantly higher proportion of serious crime than other Allied troops. Even as the Australians lunged towards the rue de Saint Pol, Sir Douglas Haig was telling his generals at Cambrai that 'very often the best soldiers are the most difficult to deal with in periods of quiet'. It was certainly true of the Australians.

Eric Hiscock, a British private recovering from shrapnel wounds, was with the Australians as they lurched down the hill. He had made friends in the camp with a huge rancher from the outback who took him by the arm and led him firmly towards their destination:

'We went into the red light area. Men and women, they seemed to be of all nationalities, with British and Australians predominating, were jostling in the street, where, from the brothel windows, women and girls looked out with something short of pleasure.'

Hiscock had never been to a brothel, but plenty of the Australians had. With Antipodean directness, one of them said what many of them were thinking:

'"Come on, boys, let's fuck 'em free", yelled a husky great sergeant, waving his khaki sombrero with an ostrich feather in it, and he made a dash for one of the doors, which quickly doused its red glim. Others followed him, and through the open windows I could hear screams of the women, and hoarse cries of the tipsy men. Panic-filled tarts appeared at the windows shorn of their chemises, and were immediately pulled back from view to the accompaniment of even more strident cries. Then, out of one of the windows, was thrown a burning mattress, to be followed at most of the other windows by other pieces of past pleasure, all burning furiously. The Australians were purging their erstwhile pleasure-dromes with any amount of vicious energy, and I, for an innocent one, couldn't help but feel sorry for the tarts.

'The gendarmes arrived, reluctantly, I thought, and within another minute or two the red-capped army police rolled up on their Triumph motorbikes, but there was a half-hearted feeling about it all and I saw no arrests made. The burning beds were doused with hoses brought into action by the gendarmes, and by noon the rue de Saint Pol was quiet, but, I imagine, back in business. As some hardbitten Aussie said, as we staggered back to camp: "That was a fucking good end to hostilities", and maybe only a pacifist would have failed to agree with him.'

Elsewhere in Boulogne, the peace arrived with more decorum. The initial silence was replaced by a cacophony of sound as church bells rang and every siren in the harbour began to hoot simultaneously. The flags were all out by early afternoon as the crowds thronged the streets around the quays, watching the British soldiers going home on leave. Miss T. F. Almack was among them, a British VAD nurse still waiting for her own leave pass but happy for the soldiers who had got theirs and were on their way back to Blighty:

'After lunch I walked along the sea front and watched the leave boat go out – every boat in the port blew its siren for at least two hours and every boat was heavy with flags. The men on the leave boat were shouting and waving flags, answered by the crowds who had gathered on the quay. It was a wonderful sight but one could not keep one's thoughts from turning to the hundreds of men who would not go back and to the homes in England which would never again be thrilled by the arrival of the leave train.'

Maude Onions felt the same way. She had gone down to the quay at the end of her shift, but it seemed to her that no one felt much like rejoicing with so many dead to mourn:

'On the stroke of three, every siren and hooter was let loose, every church bell clanged out – a deafening roar. But not a sound, not a movement, came from the hundreds of human beings who thronged the streets. The stricken soul of France seemed to have lost even the desire to rejoice.

'A deafening noise, the flags of the Blighty boat ran up, and for the first time for four weary years she sailed without an escort. Some of us tried to cheer, but voice failed. Then suddenly through the noise and din, the sobbing of a woman, a few yards away – "*Finis – finis – incroyable …*"

'Almost unconsciously, I found myself in the little military cemetery behind the congested streets of the town, where our men were buried three deep, for land was dear in France, and where the graves had been so beautifully kept by the loving hands of a khaki girl. I could not distinguish the names, for the mist of tears.'

Maude was about to walk away when she tripped over a broken piece of wood, buried so deep that it was almost invisible. The wood was all that remained of a cross marking the untended grave of a German soldier. Cautiously, afraid that someone might see her, Maude stooped down and placed some flowers on the grave. The soldier might be an unspeakable Hun in Boulogne, but he was somebody's loving son back in Germany.

While Maude wept, Emperor Karl I of Austria was leaving Vienna's Schönbrunn Palace for the last time. Accompanied by his wife, he had said a short prayer in the chapel before bidding farewell to his retainers in the Hall of Ceremonies. From there, he had made his way down the broad staircase to the convoy of cars waiting in the fading light to take the royal family to Eckartsau, their private shooting lodge in lower Austria.

It was an emotional moment for the thirty-one-year-old emperor. Later beatified by the Catholic Church, he had always been a peace-loving man, a complete antithesis to the Kaiser. He had inherited the throne from his great-uncle in 1916, and with it a situation emphatically not of his making. Karl had entered into secret negotiations for a separate peace with the French in 1917, greatly annoying the Germans when they found out, since it was their alliance with Austria that had brought them into the war in the first place. The negotiations had come to nothing and Karl had been floundering ever since.

His prime minister and minister of the interior had been to see him that morning with a document for him to sign. They had wanted him to sign at once without wasting any further time studying it. The document required the emperor to relinquish all participation in affairs of state and recognise in advance any form of constitution chosen by the new Austrian assembly. It wasn't quite an abdication, but it effectively spelled the end of six and a half centuries of Habsburg rule.

Reluctant to put his name to the document without due consideration, Karl had fled from room to room through the palace, hotly pursued by the ministers. 'If you won't even let me read it, how do you expect me to sign it?' he had demanded. The ministers had relented eventually and allowed him a chance to leaf through it. Retiring to the Porcelain Room with his wife and an aide, Karl had mulled it over and come to the conclusion that the document would avert the looming crisis in Austria, while also leaving the door open for a monarchy in the future. He had signed grudgingly and the ministers had gone away, leaving the emperor to depart in peace for Eckartsau with his family.

The empress was by his side as they left Schönbrunn with their children:

'Along the sides of the arcades, drawn up in two ranks, were our cadets from the military academies, sixteen- and seventeen-year-olds with tears in their eyes, but still perfectly turned out and guarding us to the end. They had really lived up to the motto the Empress Maria Theresa had given them: "Loyal Forever".

'It was dark by now, and a misty autumn night. We got into the vehicles ... We did not risk driving out of the main gate in front of the palace. Instead we continued parallel with the main building along the broad gravel path that leads to the eastern side gate. We slipped out of this and left the capital by a special route. Late that night – without any trouble or incidents – we arrived at Eckartsau.'

It was Karl's uncle who had been shot at Sarajevo. The assassination of Archduke Franz Ferdinand by the Serbian nationalist Gavrilo Princip had been the trigger for the war. Princip would never have done it if he hadn't been dying of tuberculosis, with nothing to lose. A butterfly flaps its wings and there's an earthquake in Peru. An angry young Serb gets bad news from his doctor and thrones tumble all over Europe.

The Kaiser reached Maarn at 3.20. It was only a country station, but hundreds of sightseers were waiting for him in the rain. They were being held back by police while his host, Count Godard Bentinck, stood on the platform with the governor of Utrecht.

The Kaiser was still in uniform as he emerged from the train, but he had removed his decorations. Bentinck introduced him to the governor as 'Wilhelm of Hohenzollern'. The crowd watched in angry silence as the Kaiser took leave of his retinue and accompanied Bentinck to the car that was to take them to Amerongen. Watching too was Lady Susan Townley, wife of the British ambassador to Holland. She had driven over from the Hague in Gladys, her two-seater, to confront the Kaiser and give him a piece of her mind.

She had travelled incognita, intending to lose herself in the crowd, but despite her veil had been recognised by General Onnen, a Dutch friend who was part of the official delegation. He had found her a place to stand where she would have a good view of the Kaiser as he

254

departed for Amerongen. Susan Townley took full advantage of it:

'It was a pouring wet day, and everybody seemed in a very bad temper. The approach to the station from the direction of Amerongen was by a long and very narrow lane, which was completely blocked by the vehicles of the onlookers. I wondered how room could possibly be made for the emperor's car to drive away, as there appeared to be no other exit. The whole reception was extremely badly stage-managed.

'But this fact gave me the five minutes' opportunity I had of seeing the Kaiser at very close quarters; his car, as I had anticipated, was unable to leave until many others had been shifted, and he was forced to wait, seated beside Count Godard, exposed to the curious stare of all present, at what I suppose must have been the most unpleasant moment of his life. He looked very white, white-haired and white-faced, when he stepped out of the train and walked past me to the motor car, talking to Count Godard. But his gait was firm, and his nonchalance, whether natural or assumed, perfect.'

Most undiplomatically, Susan Townley hurled herself at the Kaiser as he headed for the car. She had to be prised off the bonnet and forcibly restrained until a path had been cleared and the vehicle was able to get away. A few Dutch boys cheered from the branches of a tree as the Kaiser left, but they were drowned out by the boos and hisses from everyone else as the adults made it clear what they thought of the war. Chastened, the Kaiser had little to say for himself during the seven-mile journey to Amerongen.

It was getting dark by the time they arrived. The Kaiser perked up a little as the car crossed the inner moat and pulled up outside the main door of the castle. Thirty years too late, his English blood began to assert itself as he went indoors with Bentinck, safe at last after his journey. 'Now,' he told the Count, 'give me a cup of real good English tea.'

CHAPTER ELEVEN

Monday, 11 November 1918, evening

While the Kaiser went in to his tea, Ivone Kirkpatrick was in Rotterdam, preparing to go to Maastricht to reconnoitre the German border. The British secret service was worried that the revolution in Germany would spread to Holland if it wasn't nipped in the bud. As head of the service's Rotterdam operation, Kirkpatrick's job was to make sure that it was.

Kirkpatrick was a subaltern in the Royal Inniskilling Fusiliers. Badly wounded at Gallipoli, he had been invalided home before being sent to Rotterdam to handle Britain's spying operations across the Dutch border into Belgium and France. For the past year, he had been running a network of some three thousand agents who kept him supplied with a constant stream of information from behind German lines. The Germans had built an electrified fence along the border to keep the information from getting out. Kirkpatrick's agents had circumvented it in a variety of ways, everything from carrier pigeons and invisible ink to bribing the guards with soap, butter and shoes. There had been shoot-outs occasionally and German agents quietly liquidated, but the information had continued to get through. The border leaked like a sieve.

The worry now was the Bolshevism spilling over into Holland. Many Dutch regiments had already been infected and Kirkpatrick himself had seen a trainload of troops waving red flags, just like their German counterparts. The people of Holland were not celebrating the Armistice with the same enthusiasm as the French and Belgians. They were too afraid of a revolution for that.

Kirkpatrick was ready for the worst as he set out for Maastricht on Armistice night. His plan was to drive from there next morning to the Dutch frontier opposite Aix-la-Chapelle. Aix was in Bolshevist hands, full of German troops sporting the red cockade. The Dutch army had an observation post on a hill overlooking the Aix railway line, from where they had illicitly reported German troop movements to the British since the beginning of the war. It was as good a place as any to spy out the land, in case Kirkpatrick and his team needed to set up shop in Germany in the next few days, to stop the Bolshevists from running amok.

While Kirkpatrick headed for Maastricht, Brigadier Hubert Rees and his fellow prisoners of war at Bad Colberg had only just heard about the Armistice. Cooped up in a former sanatorium right in the heart of Germany, they were always the last to hear about anything significant. It was welcome news, all the same, if it meant that they would be out of there soon, on their way back to England.

Rees had been captured in May near Beaurieux. The following day he had been taken to meet the Kaiser, who was touring the Aisne battlefield with Hindenburg. Rees hadn't believed it at first, until he saw the royal party on top of a hill:

'When we approached, the Kaiser was apparently having lunch but stepped forward on to a bank and told me to come and speak to him. He asked me numerous questions with regard to my personal history and having discovered I was a Welshman said, "Then you are a kinsman of Lloyd George." He asked no questions which I could not answer without giving away information and made no indirect attempts to secure information of this character either. Presently, he said, "Your country and mine ought not to be fighting against each other, we ought to be fighting together against a third. I had no idea that you would fight me. I was very friendly with your royal family, with whom I am related. That, of course, has now all changed and this war drags on with its terrible misery and bloodshed for which I am not responsible."'

The Kaiser had continued in similar vein, discussing France's hatred of Germany and asking if the English wanted peace. He had seen some English prisoners captured at the same time as Rees and they had been very young. Rees had expressed the hope that the youngsters had fought well before being taken prisoner.

'The English always fight well,' the Kaiser had answered, nodding to Rees to indicate that the interview was over.

Now the Kaiser was gone and Hubert Rees would be free again soon. News of the ceasefire reached Bad Colberg on Armistice night, but it wasn't until the next morning that the camp interpreter stood up and told the prisoners what they all wanted to hear: 'We hope soon that we can you to Blighty send.'

Rees hardly wait could.

At Rastatt, the cookhouse had been busy all afternoon as the prisoners dug into their precious supplies of food for a celebration Armistice dinner. During roll call that evening, the camp commandant and the other German officers were forced to parade again, in the uniform of private soldiers this time. News sheets were distributed with details of the Armistice terms and the Kaiser's flight to Holland. Ludendorff had fled too, according to the sheets, vanished without trace. George Coles was glad to hear it, delighted that the Armistice terms were so severe. He reckoned the Germans had got what they deserved. 'Extermination is the only cure for such a fiendish race as the Huns.'

Coles went to bed on Armistice night 'tired out with joy and excitement'. He found himself in a whole new world next morning:

'About 10 o'clock a German town band paraded outside our camp playing the "Marseillaise" and the "Red Flag". The crowd addressed us as "comrades" and invited us outside to celebrate with them the dawn of the new era. Had we complied we would have been as mice amongst the cats. The temper of the German mobs changed hourly. Knowing this we received orders to sleep in our clothes with our boots on – ready to march, fight or flee as the occasion prompted. Our prison bars now became our security.

'During the day a few of us threw some Red Cross biscuits through the barred windows into a passing thoroughfare. Before ten minutes had elapsed the streets were crowded with starving children crying for biscuits. The colonel – the senior British officer – gave us ten boxes of camp biscuits which were scrambled for below.'

At Kleinblittersdorf, there was no celebration dinner for Private Tom Bickerton and his fellow prisoners on Armistice night. They were so weak from hunger that they had been reduced to eating potato peelings, sugar beet, 'any rubbish we could get hold of', to stay alive. Stricken with dysentery as a result, they were covered in lice and sores, so undernourished that many had died of malnutrition. Whatever had happened to the food from the Red Cross, Bickerton and his mates had seen little of it in their camp.

Bickerton had been a prisoner since March, captured during the Germans' spring offensive. His life had been saved by a friendly German who pulled him into a shell hole to protect them both from British fire. Other Germans had clubbed the British prisoners with rifle butts and stolen their rations as they were taken to the rear. Bickerton had found the Germans a mixed bag ever since. Some had been utter bastards, goose-stepping, throwing their weight around, threatening the prisoners with their weapons. Others had been perfectly decent, sharing what little meat they had, privately confiding to Bickerton that the Kaiser was on his way out and the war was coming to an end. They had been people much like himself, civilians in uniform, with no more interest in war than he had.

Henrik Simon had been one such German, Ida Brodac another. Bickerton had met Ida in the timber yard at Littenweiler where he had been put to work. He was a nice-looking boy and Ida had taken a fancy to him. She had smuggled food in for him and written him a letter that would have got her into a lot of trouble if it had been found. He would be seeing her still if he hadn't suddenly been moved to Kleinblittersdorf.

The rumour now was that the prisoners were to be marched to the front line during the next few days and handed over to the French for repatriation. Not everyone believed it. Some people reckoned the war was still on and the Germans were planning to march them up to the front in order to use them as human shields when they arrived. Whatever the truth, Tom Bickerton was determined to keep up his spirits and come out of it all right. He had arranged to remain in touch with Ida after the war, and Henrik too. He wanted to be alive to keep that promise.

In Serbia, the Armistice meant very little to Isabel Emslie Hutton, a Scottish doctor at the British-run hospital in Vranja. With six hundred people to look after, she had been too busy all day to think about the Armistice and certainly had no time to celebrate. 'We heard it was Armistice day,' she later remembered, 'but nobody seemed happy about it, and we hardly seemed to realise what it meant.' As in Germany, food was a far more immediate concern than the coming of peace:

'On the afternoon of this Armistice Day a great convoy of Bulgar prisoners was waiting for treatment at the outpatients' entrance when Jean Lindsay, one of our orderlies, crossed the yard with a large bowl of scraps for some scraggy chickens we had acquired. Suddenly the Bulgarians pounced upon her, knocking her this way and that; they were like hungry wolves and looked scarcely human, fighting, wounding each other, snarling, hissing, swearing and devouring what they could. Then, as they spied the refuse pail in a corner, they overturned it and grovelled on the ground, devouring the potato skins, bones and garbage it contained. What a gruesome sight it was, and this on a day when all should have been happiness and relief!'

The good news was that the generator was installed at last. It had arrived on a lorry a few days earlier and was now up and running. To everyone's delight, the hospital didn't have to be lit by candles any more. It was a blaze of electricity on Armistice night:

'The whole building had been wired up by Rose West and her assistant, and our Lister engine gave us electric light – a circumstance that gave us far more delight than the Armistice.'

In Egypt, British VAD nurse Kit Dodsworth had gone to bed early on Armistice night, knocked out by a combination of overwork and the aftermath of Spanish flu. She had taken the day off from her hospital in Alexandria and turned in about eight. She would never have known anything of the Armistice if her friend hadn't come in later to tell her about it:

'At 11 o'clock I was rudely awakened by Eve shaking me vigorously. I hadn't seen her all day. She'd been on duty and then went off celebrating in the evening and now she was yelling in my ear, "You must wake up! The Armistice is signed and I have got engaged!"

'I sat up and leapt out of bed and hugged her. I put on my dressing gown and we went out on to a flat roof overlooking the main street. There was the most extraordinary cosmopolitan procession that one could imagine. Every little crowd that passed was singing its own national songs. There were French, Greek, Italian, Belgian and, intermingled with them all, the Britishers. We all sang and shouted ourselves hoarse. What a night it was! I don't know what time we eventually got to bed and to sleep. We were very happy and elated and altogether it was a happy time, because I was engaged too. Exactly a week later I married my officer at the consulate in Cairo.'

At Lod, in Palestine, the British had known about the Armistice since four, but it wasn't until after dark that they really began to celebrate. The fighting with the Turks had stopped in October and the troops were already on their way home, heading back from Syria towards Egypt and the boat to Blighty. They took the news of the Armistice in their stride, as a soldier from the 179th Machine Gun Corps recalled:

'At first everyone received the news quietly, but after dark rockets and Very lights began to go up in all directions, and the boys began to catch something of the excitement of the great hour. Even up at distant Ramallah in the hills we could see the lights going up. At Lod station every engine turned its whistle on for about half an hour, artillery fired, as well as smaller arms; bonfires were lit; and the singing, cheering and other hilarious noises lasted till long past the accustomed hour of retirement. We may well rejoice, for we shall never live to see such a great day again.'

The Indian troops were rejoicing too, all the Sikhs, Kashmiris and

Punjabis who had answered the British call to arms. The campaign had gone well in Palestine. The Turks had been comprehensively routed and the people were their own masters now, although for how long was still uncertain. Colonel T. E. Lawrence had promised the Arabs an independent state if they rose against their Turkish rulers. Foreign secretary Arthur Balfour had promised the Jews a homeland. The British and French governments had agreed to divide the land between themselves as a colonial mandate. The only certainty in the muddled politics of the Middle East was that the British were not to be trusted. For T. E. Lawrence, in London on Armistice night, it was a shameful betrayal of everything he and the Arabs had fought for.

In India, news of the Armistice didn't reach the Delhi cantonments until evening. Major Arthur Hamilton was at dinner with the other officers of the 16th Cavalry when they heard. Rather than have the party in their own mess, which was bound to be destroyed in the process, they decided to go and rough up the 93rd's mess instead. On the way, they bumped into the officers of the 93rd, who had had the same idea and were coming towards the 16th. So they joined forces and with a band at their head made for the 72nd's mess:

'Then all of us marched up to the Duke of Cornwall's Light Infantry barracks and raised the roof off, eventually leaving there about 2 a.m. by which time the officers', sergeants' and corporals' messes were dry.'

In Gujarat, Mahatma Gandhi was in bed with dysentery, so ill after a visit to the Sabamarti ashram near Ahmedabad that he could barely speak or read. An active supporter of the war, he had worn himself out after a long recruiting campaign to raise more troops for the army. As a former sergeant in the Boer War, he had even thought of volunteering again himself to set a good example. His disciples were puzzled that a peace-loving man should support a British war, but for Gandhi the issue was simple. If the Indians wanted to be equal partners with the British in the empire, then they must do their bit to defend it. And they had, well over a million of them, in Africa, the Middle East and all along the Western Front.

In Australia, the official cablegram announcing the Armistice reached Adelaide's post office in the early evening, cheered on by a raucous crowd that had been waiting for it. In Melbourne, the bells rang out and fireworks exploded in the street, unsettling soldiers invalided home with shell shock. A tramcar was derailed and pushed through an office window. In Sydney, the crowd gathered in Martin Place, singing and dancing late into the night. Effigies of the Kaiser were hanged or burned all over the city as the Aussies celebrated the end of a war that had hit them as hard as anyone. Almost two-thirds of the Australian troops overseas had become battle casualties of one kind or another. It was the highest proportion of any force in the British Empire.

In South Africa, Sub Lieutenant Harold Owen of HMS *Astraea* had spent the afternoon in deep gloom, walking by himself along the cliffs outside Cape Town. There had been champagne in the captain's cabin that morning, followed by shore leave, but Owen couldn't share the general excitement at the end of the war. With so many dead, he didn't see it as any reason for a party. He was worried among other things about his brother Wilfred. He couldn't rid himself of the feeling that something had happened to Wilfred, something awful that he didn't know about yet.

Walking back into Cape Town as it grew dark, he decided to cable his parents to find out if they knew anything. Cape Town was celebrating and the streets were thronged as Owen fought his way through to the post office. Reaching for a telegram pad, he began to scribble a note to his father:

'I had actually written out the cable when I hesitated. I remembered too well the dread fear that telegrams inspired in England – the sight of a red bicycle within a hundred yards of your own house could make your heart jump and miss a beat ... at home, perhaps secure in the knowledge of Wilfred's safety, might not a cable from Africa mean only one thing … slowly I tore up my telegram and threw it in the waste-paper basket … It *must* be all right. After all I had had no cable from home and the war *was* over …'

Owen had arranged to meet another officer from the ship for dinner. Adderley Street was choked with people as he made his way to the hotel. The mob was mostly good-humoured, but a few Boers were taunting men in British uniform. There had been an insurrection at the beginning of the war, Boer rebels attempting to overthrow the British while their attention was elsewhere. The rebels had been defeated, but they would have shed no tears if the British had been defeated in turn by the Germans.

From their table on the upstairs veranda, Owen and his friend had a good view of the party in the street:

'Here and there we could see fracas were breaking out more and more frequently. In the distance what looked like a party of English sailors was being set upon, their caps being torn off their heads and lanyards and silks wrenched from their necks; whether the actions were hostile or souvenir hunting it was difficult to decide. In any case there was nothing we could do about it. Groups of women and girls in the grip of mass hysteria were making flauntingly sordid exhibitions of themselves. Maudlin songs and shouts of drunken laughter broke through the undertone of throbbing sound that pulsated with steady rhythm from the packed streets.'

Feeling more depressed than ever, Owen followed his friend into the street after dinner:

'As we tried to struggle through the crowds we were jammed to a standstill by the people in front of us; peering over and between them we could see a gang of street roughs and very drunk individuals stripping Union Flags from parked cars and windows and throwing them on the road to be trampled on. Resentment flared immediately from other sectors who at once retaliated with equal violence …

'I could not get Wilfred out of my mind and wondering about him perhaps sharpened my sensitivity so that revulsion was all I could experience – revulsion for the mawkish patriotic songs, the drunkenness which was becoming more evident everywhere, men

lying senseless in the gutters, young women and some girls drinking out of bottles in the streets, empty bottles being thrown down
to splinter on the roadways. I must get out of it all; with a force that
in itself must have been provocative I charged and elbowed my way
through the crowds. Before I got clear I was set upon by a gang of
girls and young women crazed with a mixture of alcohol and hysteria
– souvenir hunting – obviously pro-British, much too pro-British
for my comfort, but somehow I managed to escape from their too
demonstrative attentions. My last unpleasant memory of this horrid
Armistice night was the sight of a very young girl spreadeagled over
the bonnet of a stationary car being violently and disgustingly sick.'

Across the Atlantic, Lieutenant Arch Whitehouse shared Owen's
feelings as he watched the celebrations in Newark, New Jersey. Home
on leave from the RAF, Whitehouse had discovered that men in
uniform could not legally be served liquor, not even aerial gunners
with sixteen enemy aircraft and six kite balloons to their credit. That
hadn't stopped anyone else, though:

'Mobs and gangs roared through the street, dragging stuffed
effigies of the Kaiser and Little Willie. Flivvers rattled along the high-
ways, daubed with the crudest vulgarities of triumph … A few men in
khaki or blue were to be seen amid the howling mobs, but most of the
frenzied commotion seemed to be promoted by bedraggled women,
screeching girls and middle-aged gaffers who were stupidly drunk.'

British-born Whitehouse had worked for the Edison Storage
Battery Company in West Orange before joining up. Thomas Edison
himself was so dismayed by the Armistice celebrations that he broke
the rule of a lifetime and made a public recording of his voice to mark
the occasion, pleading with Americans not to be chauvinistic about
the victory. The perception that the war hadn't really started until
the United States joined in, that no one else had done any serious
fighting, was wide of the mark. American troops had run away from
the Germans more than once and their generals had proved just as
inept as anyone else's. The inventor of the phonograph put in a plea
for a sense of perspective:

'This is Edison speaking. Our boys made good in France. The word "American" has a new meaning in Europe ... I hope that while we do reverence to the memory of our brave boys, we shall not forget their brothers in arms who wore the uniforms of our allies.'

Americans happily heeded his call. Fifth Avenue in New York had been renamed The Avenue of the Allies for the day and the flags of Britain, France and Italy hung from the lamp posts, alongside effigies of the Kaiser. At the Metropolitan Opera that night, Enrico Caruso and a swelling chorus sang the Allies' national anthems between the acts of Saint-Saëns's *Samson and Delilah*. At the Garrick Theatre, a new play by French prime minister Georges Clemenceau was premiered. It was dire, but the audience cheered anyway before filing out at the end to join the party on Thirty-fifth Street.

Manhattan was lit up for the first time in a long while, the street lights back on now that there was no possibility of attack. A New York official had announced the move at noon, calling on every office and household to do the same, lighting up the sky that night as never before:

'Let us give the Kaiser a wake so bright and gorgeous that for the moment the memory of all the fires his armies started and all the guns his armies fired will be smothered and obscured.'

New Yorkers responded to the call, switching on all their lights at home and starting bonfires in the street as well. They sang 'Tipperary', 'Over There', 'Pack up your Troubles', all the wartime favourites as they danced in the firelight. In Chicago, up to a million people crowded into the Loop and did the same, a woman in a soldier's hat directing the traffic at State Street and Monroe while the police indulgently looked the other way. All over America the people partied, while in Michigan, Henry Ford told his factory managers to stop making tanks and start retooling for peace. Tractors were where the money was now, particularly for those who got there first. It was time to beat the swords into ploughshares.

Back in Europe, Kapitanleutnant Martin Niemöller and the crew of U-67 had no idea the war was over. They were at periscope depth, trying to sneak through the straits of Gibraltar under cover of darkness. The straits were no place for a German to be with the Royal Navy still smarting from the loss of HMS *Britannia*, sunk by Niemöller's friend Heinrich Kukat two days earlier. To add to his problems, Niemöller was having to do all the piloting himself because his navigation officer was sick with Spanish flu, as were several others in the crew.

There were too many patrol boats about for Niemöller's liking. At 10 p.m. he spotted a pair of torpedo boats carrying lights and wondered for one crazy moment if the war might be over. But they were followed by other vessels still in darkness, so Niemöller took no chances as he inched U-67 past the Rock of Gibraltar and out into the Atlantic. All being well, the submarine would be safely back at Kiel within a couple of weeks. After that, if there was no imperial navy any more, Martin Niemöller was thinking of becoming a Lutheran pastor.

In Italy, ambulance driver Ernest Hemingway was writing to his parents from the American Red Cross headquarters in Milan. The celebrations there had begun on 10 November, when Benito Mussolini – a sergeant himself until invalided out – had harangued a crowd of Italian soldiers in a Milan café, claiming that Italy had won the war for the Allies. Resplendent in a British-style officer's tunic that he had had specially made, Hemingway was recovering from shrapnel wounds sustained four months earlier on the river Piave. Bored with driving ambulances behind the lines, he had volunteered to man a canteen instead for the Italian soldiers at the front. He had bicycled up to a trench near Fossalta, bringing chocolate and cigarettes for the men. A shell had exploded after dark, badly wounding him in the legs. Hemingway had just had time to carry another man to safety before losing consciousness.

He had been in and out of hospital ever since, slowly recovering with the help of nurse Agnes von Kurowsky. He had just met Eric Dorman-Smith, a British officer and gentleman of a type Hemingway had not come across before and much admired. Dorman-Smith was regaling him with tales of the retreat from Mons which Hemingway thought he might use in a short story one day, if his writing ever progressed beyond the journalism he had been doing at home.

On Armistice night, though, his only writing was for his parents in Chicago:

'Well its all over! And I guess everybody is pretty joyous. I would have liked to see the celebration in the States but the Italian army showed the wonderful stuff it is made of in that last offensive. They are great troops and I love them.

'I have about a month and a half more mechanical treatments on my leg ... I did come very close to the big adventure in this last offensive and personally I feel like everybody else about the end of the war. Gee but it was great though to end it with such a victory!'

By his own count, Hemingway had been wounded 227 times during his non-combatant service in Italy. The figure would have been greeted with scepticism on the Western Front.

In Belgium, war correspondent Philip Gibbs was still trying to get used to the silence of peace. On his way back from Mons, he could even hear the leaves rustling, it was so quiet:

'There was no light of gunfire in the sky, no sudden stabs of flame through the darkness, no long spreading flow above the black trees, where for four years of nights human beings were being smashed to death. The fires of hell had been put out. It was silent all along the front with the beautiful silence of the nights of peace ...

'Other sounds rose from the towns and fields in the yellowing twilight, and in the deepening shadow-world of the day of Armistice. They were the sounds of human joy. Men were singing somewhere on the roads, and their voices rang out gladly. Bands were playing, as all day on the way to Mons I had heard their music ahead of the marching columns ...

'Motor cars streaked through the Belgian streets, dodging the traffic, and now and then when night fell rockets were fired from them, and there were gusts of laughter from young officers shooting off Very pistols into the darkness to celebrate the end of hostilities by this symbol of rising stars, which did not soar so high as their spirits. From dark towns like Tournai and Lille these rockets rose and burned a little while with white light.

'Our aviators flew like bats in the dusk, skimming the treetops and gables, doing Puck-like gambols above the tawny sunset, looping and spiralling and falling in steep dives which looked like death for them until they flattened out and rose again, and they, too, these boys who have been reprieved from the menace which was close to them on every flight, fired flares and rockets which dropped down to the crowds of French and Flemish people waving to them from below.'

In France, artillery officer George Mallory had gone to visit Geoffrey Keynes, an old rock-climbing chum from before the war. They had a grandstand view of the fireworks from Keynes's surgical unit near Cambrai, as Keynes later recalled:

'Together we witnessed that extraordinary scene, when the whole front in France seemed to be occupied by maniacs, letting off flares, Very lights, and every other form of demonstration they could lay their hands on. Engines whistled and hooted. Discipline had temporarily vanished. We all thought we had seen the last of war.'

Watching from St Roch nearby, Private Arthur Wrench shared Keynes's worries about the breakdown of fire discipline as everything was fired off indiscriminately:

'It is pandemonium and I am sure we must all be mad. From one extreme to the other. Even as I used to think that some day we would wake up and find the war was over so now I hope we will all sober up and come back to our senses. The bonfire is blazing again out in the courtyard and boxes of German star shells and signal flares are being piled on to feed it. They are bursting and flying all over the shop, as if they too were revelling in a new-found freedom. It is certainly dangerous and someone is liable to get hurt.'

Wrench hoped that people would remember the dead after the party was over and that 11 November would not be forgotten in years to come. Mallory spent the rest of the evening with his younger brother, Trafford Leigh-Mallory, at the officers' club in Cambrai. Trafford had begun the war in the infantry but was now a squadron commander in the RAF. The big question for him, as the war came to an end, was whether he had any future in the RAF now that the Germans had been beaten or whether, like everyone else, he should join the rush for civilian life instead.

In Rouen, the bridges across the river had been transformed for the night, festooned with hundreds of coloured lights which twinkled happily at their own reflections in the water. An Australian band was playing outside the theatre and from somewhere nearby came the sound of bagpipes. Elizabeth Johnston, a Scots-born WAAC driver, watched as her countrymen answered the call:

'Jocks mobilised without a moment's delay and fell in behind the piper. They swarmed around and after him, keeping step to "Hielan' Laddie". And in behind the Jocks, French soldiers in their picturesque blue uniform, wounded Belgians, Aussies in hospital suits, fell into step. Americans, Portuguese and Chinese swelled the procession, and crowding behind them came swarthy South African Scottish in Atholl tartan, stalwart Canadian Highlanders and Indians. One thought of the Pied Piper, enticing the children through the streets of Hamelin. But up the rue Grand Pont, grown-up children from the ends of the earth pranced and danced to the skirl of the bagpipes.

'French civilians joined in the procession and armed the soldiers up the street. Little children crowded in between the ranks, or were hoisted shoulder high … The children beamed and shrieked with delight as, hand in hand with giant New Zealanders and Tommies, they skipped and danced their way into rue Jeanne d'Arc and thence to the Hôtel de Ville. Here the historic procession halted and, in the shadow of the magnificent equestrian statue of Napoleon, Jocks and French girls, Aussies and Tommies, danced and capered to the piping.'

Pennsylvanian Quaker Owen Stephens of the American Friends' Reconstruction Unit witnessed similar scenes in Troyes:

'We ate an early supper and joined the city. Humanity was by now wild. Thousands thronged the narrow streets and concentrated in the Place des Boucheries and about the Hôtel de Ville. Masses and mobs of people moved and shoved in all directions. The air was filled with yells, shrieks, songs. Old women sold from push-carts flags and tricoloured ribbons; everybody carried flags and tricoloured ribbons ...

'A Tommy carrying a French flag lurched in a drunken walk up rue Émile Zola; a laughing, shouting crowd followed; a snare drum rasping from its midst ... Mac was wearing a small American flag; a group of girls rubbed by us and one snatched the flag ... A few hotels were ablaze with lights, although, following the custom of four years, people did not show lights from their homes. Walking along one of the deserted alleys, a Frenchman was roaring the socialist hymn: "L'Internationale".'

At Lille, the celebrations had been muted all day and dwindled away to nothing after nightfall. The electricity still wasn't back on and the city lay in darkness. A factory had blown up that afternoon, booby-trapped by the Germans before they left. The explosion had narrowly missed some men from the Machine Gun Corps who were moving out as it detonated. Alick McGrigor, General Birdwood's ADC, had driven all the way back to St Omer that day in search of champagne for a celebration dinner. He had managed to find some, but it was a 'cheery' dinner rather than a wildly exciting one. They had had the king of the Belgians to dinner the night before, dropping in impromptu after an unscheduled visit to Tournai.

For Sister Catherine Macfie, at a casualty clearing station on the outskirts of the town, the Armistice brought no respite from all the young men dying on her ward. Some were dying of wounds, but an awful lot more from Spanish flu. All over the world, the young were dying of flu and there was little she or anyone else could do about it:

'We couldn't send them down the line because they were too ill to move, and we had ever so many deaths. We were kept very busy and it was a most depressing time – worse, in a way, when all the good news was coming through. The boys were coming in with colds and a headache and they were dead within two or three days. Great big handsome fellows, just came in and died. There was no rejoicing in Lille the night of the Armistice. There was no rejoicing.'

At Wimereux, just up the coast from Boulogne, VAD nurse Peggy Marten couldn't rejoice either:

'Armistice Day was the most appalling day I've ever lived through. We had a big convoy of flu cases and sister was very busy, so she asked me to go along to represent the ward at a little ceremony they were going to have, a little thanksgiving service in the open air by the flagstaff with the "Last Post" and a silence after it.

'As I was walking to the flagstaff I saw two parents being escorted to the mortuary. They must have been sent for to come and see their wounded boy and got there too late, and now they were being taken to see his body. I thought, "Here we are at the end of the war – but we're not at the end of the grief."

'In the evening my three chums and I had a little session in our hut after supper. One of the girls had been down in the town and brought back a bottle of wine and some biscuits and we were having a little party, just the four of us, drinking each others' health.'

In the cathedral city of Abbeville, Second Lieutenant André Maurois of the French army had dinner as usual with his British colleagues at the headquarters of Lieutenant General Sir John Asser. Maurois was attached to the headquarters as part of the French mission to the British army. For the past two years, he had been working alongside an Old Etonian allegedly descended from Hereward the Wake, another who was held to be an authority on strategy because he had once won a cup for pig-sticking, and a young artillery officer who gave voice to hunting cries whenever Maurois was on the telephone. They were all men for whom the German bombing of innocent civilians was a crime almost as heinous as shooting a fox or catching trout with a worm. Out of this unlikely material Maurois had fashioned a novel about the British that he had banged out on the headquarters type-writer in his spare time. Entitled *Les Silences du Colonel Bramble*, the book had been an immediate best-seller on publication, enchanting

French and British alike with its portrait of the British as a taciturn but agreeable mass of contradictions. Everyone from Clemenceau to Field Marshal Haig had read the book and enjoyed it.

Now the British were showing their appreciation. Maurois's colleagues had a surprise for him on Armistice night after the plates had been cleared away:

'At the end of dinner they rose, forced me to remain seated and sang with great seriousness: "For he's a jolly good fellow, and so say all of us ..." Then they presented me with a beautiful silver platter on which they had had their signatures engraved. I was deeply touched. Their affection, as I well knew, was sincere; for my part I had learned to esteem and love them.'

Near the Place de la Concorde in Paris, Canadian nurse Alison Strathy had teamed up with her friends Bea and Dr and Mrs Ladd. Mrs Ladd was a sculptress, currently making face masks for mutilated soldiers. The armies provided ready-to-wear masks for soldiers whose faces had been disfigured, but Mrs Ladd offered a bespoke service, designing personalised masks from old photographs. It was worth it, for once-handsome men, if it meant that little children no longer ran shrieking from them in terror.

The four of them headed across to the Latin quarter for dinner. They sat with a blind French NCO in a restaurant while everyone made toasts and speeches. Then the soldier stood up and sang a patriotic song in gratitude for the recapture of Lille. It was for Lille that he had given his sight. Alison and the others kissed him goodbye after dinner and left him to return to hospital while they rejoined the crowds:

'A lorry was going uptown in charge of some doughboys, so we climbed in – or on, I sat in front with four lads. When we got to the Place de la Concorde a couple of Tommies – London Scottish – attached a whiz-bang (a small gun) to the rear and sat on this till they fell off!

'When we reached the boulevards there are streams of taxis and camions touring the streets and everyone who can, climbs aboard

– soldiers, girl on their laps, anyone, anywhere. We toured around Paris but when they started to pack the roof, my party hauled me off, they said it was getting too risky and too rough. I said goodbye regretfully. We made our way then to the Opera House. There, on an illuminated balcony, members of the Opera were singing – "La Marseillaise", "Madelon", "Tipperary" – and again the crowds were joining in the chorus. Searchlights played all over. There were more processions and the people were dancing in and out amongst the guns, everyone gay and light-hearted, and "La Marseillaise" still ringing down the street. Finally, back to our hotel, where we parted from our hosts, the Ladds.'

It was the "Madelon" that everyone loved, the song about a barmaid filling her glass and drinking the health of the French poilus who had won the war. On stage at the Casino de Paris, singer Maurice Chevalier departed from his script for the night and gave the audience what they wanted to hear:

> Madelon, emplis ton verre!
> Et chante avec les poilus!
> Nous avons gagné la guerre!

The song brought the house down. Chevalier had been a poilu himself until the Germans ended his war with a bullet in the chest. It was still there, since his captors hadn't been able to extract it. Imprisoned near Magdeburg, he had learned English from a British prisoner and had an affair with a French one, while Mistinguett, his music-hall girlfriend from Paris, was frantic with worry about him. A star of stage and screen, she had made herself agreeable to King Alfonso of Spain in an attempt to have Chevalier repatriated. She had set out for Germany via Switzerland to see Chevalier, only to be arrested as a spy and sentenced to death by firing squad. Strings had been pulled, Chevalier had been released, and so had Mistinguett, apparently in an exchange of hostages. She too was on stage that night, showing her famous legs in *Phi-Phi* at the Théâtre des Bouffés Parisiens.

But their affair had cooled. Chevalier's boyfriend had been released with him and was still close. There was also the matter of the pink knickers Mistinguett had discovered on Chevalier's bedroom floor, and the girl she had caught him with in his dressing room in the middle of the night. With only a coat over her nightdress, Mistinguett had gone after him with a meat cleaver, seeking appropriate revenge. The gendarmes had been called, Chevalier had remained intact, but their amour had never been quite the same again, although they still worked together occasionally. The show had to go on.

While Chevalier sang and Mistinguett danced, Georges Clemenceau had gone home quietly and was sitting in his study in the dark, with the phone off the hook. His sister Sophie found him there and cooked him something to eat. Then she persuaded him to go out for a while to watch the fun. They walked for miles before they were recognised in the Boulevard des Capucines near the Opéra. The gendarmes rescued them from an enthusiastic crowd and bundled them into a hotel overlooking the Place de l'Opéra. Clemenceau was called to the balcony and spoke a few words to the crowd, although no one could hear him above all the noise. He wanted people to cry 'Vive la France!' instead of 'Vive Clemenceau!'

His daughter Madeleine arrived to join them. Clemenceau was subdued and miserable, unable to share the general enthusiasm for the Armistice.

'Papa, tell me you're happy,' pleaded Madeleine.

'I can't, because I'm not,' he told her. 'It won't have done any good.'

Clemenceau's friend Claude Monet wrote to him next day, suggesting some sort of painted tribute to the fallen. Weeping willows were the traditional symbol of mourning, but Monet thought water lilies might do instead.

At Amerongen, the Kaiser was settling in to his new quarters. He had been given a suite of four rooms at the back of the castle with a view of the shipping along the Rhine, a mile away. There was a bed for him and another for his wife, who was hoping to join him from Potsdam if she could escape the Bolshevists. The Kaiser's bed was a splendid old four-poster that had been slept in by King Louis XIV during the French occupation of 1672.

The Kaiser had some of his staff with him, as many as could be accommodated in the castle. The rest were staying in the village nearby. Count Bentinck had been preparing the castle for an influx of Belgian refugees, so the switch had been easy to make. He had arranged it with his housekeeper, a patriotic Scot, who kept her opinions about the sudden arrival of the Germans to herself. She had provided scones and shortbread for the Kaiser's tea, such as he had enjoyed at Balmoral as a child, staying with his grandmother, Queen Victoria.

Bentinck had almost as much English blood as the Kaiser. His father had served with the Coldstream Guards at Waterloo. His brother had served with the Coldstream too. His nephew had been killed with the Coldstream on the Somme. One of his sons, on the other hand, was in the German navy. It gave them something to talk about as he and the Kaiser sat down to dinner.

There were forty at table. They ate off silver plate bearing the arms of the Aldenburg family, into which one of the Kaiser's sons had married. The conversation was a little stiff, but the Kaiser did his best to put everyone at ease. He was angry about the part that Prince Max had played in his downfall, making it look as if he had deserted his people when he hadn't. Beyond that, though, he displayed little bitterness about what had happened. His staff remained deferential, still unable to believe that he was no longer the Kaiser. They were all rather dazed, struggling to catch up with everything that had gone wrong during the past few days. It was too much to take in, all at once.

Across the North Sea, the British Grand Fleet lay at anchor off the Scottish coast. The line of warships stretched unbroken for thirty miles, the most powerful display of naval might in the world. Battleships, cruisers, destroyers, torpedo boats, minelayers, every kind of ship for every kind of purpose. The fleet had known about the Armistice since morning, but it wasn't until after dark that the official celebrations began. The order had gone out to splice the mainbrace: naval talk for a free issue of rum. At a given signal, all the lights had come on and the foghorns had begun to sound. The bells had rung and the searchlights had swung through the sky, lighting up the darkness for miles around. From the decks of HMS *Tobago*, Petty Officer Henry Hill had never seen anything like it:

'We are engaged in making as much noise and commotion as possible. It is a magnificent sight to see the fleet as it is tonight. Every ship is ablaze with lights. The larger ships playing the searchlights around and the smaller ones firing Very lights and rockets. Every ship seems to be trying to outdo the others in showing their enthusiasm. Bells are ringing. Drums and bands are in full swing. Everyone is shouting himself hoarse.

'Admiral Beatty has just sent a signal around the fleet. "That's the stuff to give 'em." Officers and men are carried away by the increasing excitement. A motor boat has just passed decorated with flags and lights. The band is playing all the ragtime music. It is rumoured that Admiral Beatty is aboard the motor boat. He is game enough for anything. Thank God it is over, anyway.'

The Royal Navy had policed the oceans of the world for more than a century, fighting the slave trade, combating piracy, starving the Germans of the materials they needed to make war. But the navy's function would be taken over by the proposed League of Nations, if President Wilson had his way. He wanted the British to disarm their fleet now that the fighting had stopped, in order to guarantee the freedom of the seas for everyone else. Failing that, he wanted the United States to build a fleet of their own, laying two keels for every one laid by the British.

President Wilson was not much admired in the Royal Navy.

At 10 Downing Street, Lloyd George was having a quiet dinner with a few colleagues. Winston Churchill was there, his friend F. E. Smith, and General Sir Henry Wilson. Portraits of Pitt, Fox, Lord Nelson, the Duke of Wellington and George Washington looked down on them as they sat discussing the Kaiser, wondering what to do with him now that he had been overthrown. The question turned on whether or not the Kaiser was a war criminal.

He was certainly a bad man. He had behaved disgracefully before the war, bullying Germany's neighbours, rattling his sabre, always using the threat of military action to resolve disputes instead of quiet diplomacy. He had driven other countries in Europe to form defensive alliances against him. He had even forced the British, natural allies of the Germans, into the arms of the French – hardly a marriage made in heaven. And when the alliances had been formed, the Kaiser had complained that Germany was surrounded, that the rest of Europe was conspiring against him.

He hadn't wanted the war when it came, but he had done nothing to stop it either. German atrocities had been magnified out of all proportion by Allied propaganda, but it was not disputed that babies had been bayoneted when they marched into Belgium and women publicly raped in Liège marketplace. The Germans had invaded a neutral country, bombed civilians, shelled troops with poison gas and torpedoed non-combatant shipping without regard for the crews. They had broken the rules of war, and for that they must be called to account.

Lloyd George was for shooting the Kaiser. So was F. E. Smith. Wilson and Churchill disagreed. Wilson thought that the Kaiser ought to be exposed for the villain he was and then left to his own devices. Churchill was more worried about the future than the past:

'My own mood was divided between anxiety for the future and desire to help the fallen foe. The conversation ran on the great qualities of the German people, on the tremendous fight they had made against three-quarters of the world, on the impossibility of rebuilding Europe except with their aid.'

Churchill was worried, too, about the food shortages in Germany. The Germans would be easy prey for the Bolshevists if they were starving:

'I suggested that we should immediately, pending further news, rush a dozen great ships crammed with provisions into Hamburg.

Although the Armistice terms enforced the blockade till peace was signed, the Allies had promised to supply what was necessary, and the prime minister balanced the project with a favouring eye.'

As they sat discussing it, they could hear a dull roar outside as the rest of London continued to celebrate. From deep within the walls of No. 10, the roar sounded to Churchill 'like the surf on the shore'. To Alice Connor, in Trafalgar Square, 'the sound was like the waves crashing on to a beach.'

At the palace, the king was still on the balcony, still waving to the crowd. He went indoors every so often to continue work on the hundreds of telegrams he had received from around the world, but the crowd kept calling him back, kept wanting to see him again. Two stage reflectors had been rigged up to illuminate the balcony so that the people could see the king properly as he stood in the drizzle with the queen by his side. He was in khaki, she was in diamonds and pearls. The band of the Irish Guards was playing and the people were singing hymns and patriotic songs. They were going to be there for a few hours yet and would return again tomorrow.

Ex-king Manoel of Portugal was watching from a palace doorway, sheltering from the rain. He had been a refugee in England since the revolution of 1910. Margot Asquith bumped into him on her way to see Lord Stamfordham, King George's private secretary. She had a few words with Manoel, then went into the palace to look for Stamfordham.

She found him overwhelmed, exhausted with all the people coming in and out and the telegrams continuing to arrive from all over the world. One human being in every five was a subject of King George and an awful lot of them had decided to send him greetings on this happy occasion. Stamfordham himself was still grieving for his only son, killed in 1915. Margot Asquith kissed him on both cheeks and congratulated him on all the hard work he had put in during the war years. Then they both fell silent, not trusting themselves to say another word.

*

The lights were back on in London, in part at least. There hadn't been time to clean the black shading from all the street lamps, but most were on and Big Ben was lit up. Trafalgar Square was ablaze with bonfires. 'The sound of cheering and singing still drifts into my room where I sit with the light on and the BLIND UP!' wrote Winifred Kenyon in her diary. 'Our first tangible proof on this side of the water that hostilities are over.'

Arnold Bennett was in Piccadilly as the lights shone. His friend John Buchan had come in to his office at the Ministry of Information that morning to shake hands when the Armistice was announced. Buchan went to bed early on Armistice night, but Bennett stayed up and was there to see the lights go back on:

'Great struggling to cross Piccadilly Circus twice ... Vehicles passed festooned with shouting human beings. Others, dark, with only one or two occupants. Much light in Piccadilly up to Ritz corner, and in Piccadilly Circus. It seemed most brilliant. Some theatres had lights on their facades too. The enterprising Trocadero had hung a row of temporary lights under one of its porticoes.'

The Ritz was a blaze of light for its long-awaited Armistice dinner. Lady Diana Manners was there with her fiancé Duff Cooper. They were doing their best to enjoy themselves, but neither of them really felt like it when so many of their friends were no longer alive to see it. Cooper was ill with Spanish flu and went home early. Diana Manners followed soon afterwards, unable to bear the jollity. 'After so much bitter loss it was unnatural to be jubilant. The dead were in our minds to the exclusion of the survivors'. She broke down and cried when she got home.

Oswald Mosley was passing the Ritz when he heard the sound of laughter and looked in to see what was happening. Invalided out of the front line, Mosley shared Diana Manners's disgust at the festivities:

'Smooth, smug people, who had never fought or suffered, seemed to the eyes of youth – at that moment age-old with sadness, weariness and bitterness – to be eating, drinking, laughing on the graves of our companions. I stood aside from the delirious throng, silent and alone, ravaged by memory.'

Monday, 11 November 1918, evening

The only bright spot for Mosley was Cimmie Curzon, Lord Curzon's daughter, who was at the Ritz with a Union Jack around her shoulders, singing patriotic songs. Later that night, she tore around Trafalgar Square setting fire to old cars and trucks, to the horror of her father. It was another eighteen months before Mosley married her, but he always remembered the night he had seen her at the Ritz.

Siegfried Sassoon was in Chelsea, at a dinner party full of strangers. He had been in Oxford that morning, walking in the water meadows near Cuddesdon when the bells began to ring. Full of distaste for the celebrations, he had nevertheless been unable to keep away. He had caught the train to London and was staying with the friend of a friend, who had invited him to the dinner at Chelsea.

Sassoon's companion was in the RAF, but they were the only ones at the dinner who had been in the war. They were in no mood for celebration and found it hard to share the exuberance of the other guests:

'The chorus was led by an effusive American woman journalist, who confided to me that she had never before known such a sense of high-plane emotion-release. This was probably an accurate description of her feelings, but I accepted the statement rather glumly. Now it so happened that my friend and I were the only members of the party who had seen any active service, while two of the others were of an age which suggested that they might likewise have done so, had their now exuberant patriotism prompted them to the adventure. Towards the end of an excellent dinner this unfortunate cleavage became conspicuous.'

Sassoon and his companion picked a quarrel with a 'youngish gentleman' of military age. They were adamant that the war had been a loathsome tragedy that no amount of flag-waving could change. They didn't hide their contempt for their fellow guest and had made themselves thoroughly unpopular by the time the party broke up. Sassoon learned afterwards that the man had spent the war working for the Central Liquor Control Board. He probably had a medal for it.

*

At the Adelphi, Monty Shearman was throwing a party. It had begun after lunch and was to continue intermittently for several days. Most of the Bloomsbury set looked in at one time or another, although they had trouble afterwards remembering exactly who had been there with whom.

D. H. Lawrence was certainly there with his wife Frieda von Richthofen, cousin of the German air ace. Lady Mond was there, naturalised German wife of a government minister. Augustus John was there, accompanied by some land girls still in their breeches and leggings. Osbert Sitwell came with Sergei Diaghilev, David Garnett with Duncan Grant. Lady Ottoline Morell came too, and Clive Bell, Roger Fry, Mark Gertler. So did Carrington and Lydia Lopokova, Maynard Keynes and Lytton Strachey.

Almost everyone was dancing, even Lytton Strachey. It was a sight not often seen. Strachey had come up from Sussex for the night. Famous for telling the draft board that he would try to come between them if a German soldier attempted to rape his sister, Strachey had spent much of the war in a deckchair, calling for lemonade and contemplating the lissom youth who had replaced the postman when he went to war. Sometimes he had heard the guns across the Channel as he sat reading his book. He was pioneering a new form of biography in which the subject's every defect was mercilessly examined in print.

Among the few not dancing was Diaghilev. He had enough of it in his work at the Ballets Russes. On their way to the party, his principal dancer, Léonide Massine, had stopped to watch the dancing in the street for a moment to see if they could pick up any new ideas, but had not been impressed. The British were better at war than ballet.

After a while, the party moved on via Trafalgar Square to Maynard Keynes's flat in Gordon Square. Strachey was going to stay the night there, since it was too late to return to Sussex. Keynes was an affable host, telling Garnett that there could be no resumption of the war because everyone would refuse to fight again now that they had stopped. Whatever happened at the peace conference, they had certainly seen the last of the war.

Monday, 11 November 1918, evening

It was the peace that worried Keynes. As a Cambridge don and Treasury economist, he was already planning ahead for the reconstruction of Europe after the war. He was worried about the reparations to be demanded of Germany. He was afraid the Germans would be pushed beyond their ability to pay. Keynes understood the desire to make the Germans pay every last penny for all the damage they had done, but as an economist he knew it could never happen. The Germans should be encouraged instead to get back on their feet as quickly as possible. It was in everyone's interest that they did.

The peace conference was the key. Would the politicians go for a sensible solution along the lines that Keynes had already suggested, or would they pursue their own agenda, reducing the Germans to rubble because they knew it would play well back home? Keynes was not optimistic. Clemenceau was determined on revenge and Lloyd George always played to the gallery. Wilson was far too high-minded, with little understanding of the world outside the United States. Charlatans all, in Keynes's opinion. The peace was far too important to be left to politicians. They were bound to make a mess of it if they didn't listen carefully to what he had to tell them.

Noël Coward was in Trafalgar Square. It was still full of people, happily swaying backwards and forwards 'like a field of golden corn moving in a dark wind'. Eighteen-year-old Coward had recently been discharged from the army after a miserable few months in which he had singularly failed to impress as a soldier. He had been made to go on route marches and stab sacks of straw with a bayonet, tasks for which his previous employment in the theatre had not prepared him. Diagnosed with acute neurasthenia, he had returned to civilian life with relief. His idea of camping had never been the same as the army's.

He had spent Armistice day wandering the streets with everyone else. Later, he had dined with a rich, gay Chilean diplomat and his wife. The Chileans belonged to a louche and glamorous world far removed from Coward's own:

'After dinner we drove in a dark-red Rolls-Royce through the

Park and into Trafalgar Square, where we stuck, while hordes of screaming people climbed on to the roof of the car, the footboards and the radiator. We screamed with them, and shook hands with as many as we could, and I felt ignobly delighted, in this moment of national rejoicing, to be in a tail coat, a Rolls-Royce, and obviously aristocratic company. After a couple of hours in Trafalgar Square, we managed to get to the Savoy, where everybody wore paper caps, and threw streamers, and drank champagne, and Delysia, in a glittering pink dress, stood on a table and sang the "Marseillaise" over and over again to wild applause. It was a thrilling night.'

Just back from Arabia, T. E. Lawrence was in Trafalgar Square, dining quietly with friends at the Union Club. Lady Mond was dancing in the Square after Monty Shearman's party. Some Canadian soldiers had torn down a row of hoardings covered in war slogans and were throwing them on to a bonfire at the base of Nelson's column. The flames lit up the crowd's faces as they sang 'Keep the Home Fires Burning'. Everyone was cheerful and good-humoured, glad the war was over rather than exulting in the victory. Osbert Sitwell had watched the crowd 'cheering for its own death' outside Buckingham Palace in 1914. He watched it again now:

'A long nightmare was over: and there were many soldiers, sailors and airmen in the crowd which, sometimes joining up, linking hands, dashed like the waves of the sea against the sides of the Square, against the railings of the National Gallery, sweeping up so far even as beyond the shallow stone steps of St Martin-in-the-Fields. The succeeding waves flowed back, gathered impetus and broke again ... It was an honest, happy crowd, good-natured, possessed of a kind of wisdom or philosophy, as well as of a perseverance which few races knew: but it had nothing of Latin grace.'

Vera Brittain was in Whitehall, just off Trafalgar Square. She had been with a crowd of nurses until they were ambushed by some soldiers:

'Outside the Admiralty a crazy group of convalescent Tommies were collecting specimens of different uniforms and bundling their wearers into flag-strewn taxis; with a shout they seized two of my companions and disappeared into the clamorous crowd, waving flags and shaking rattles. Wherever we went a burst of enthusiastic cheering greeted our Red Cross uniform, and complete strangers adorned with wound stripes rushed up and shook me warmly by the hand. After the long, long blackness, it seemed like a fairy tale to see the street lamps shining through the chill November gloom.'

Vera broke away from the others and walked down Whitehall by herself. She felt dreadfully out of place in this new, brightly lit world. Everyone she had ever been close to was dead. There was nobody left to share her memories, and as she grew older even her remembrance of the dead would grow dim. An ever-deeper darkness would engulf the young men who had once been her boon companions:

'For the first time I realised, with all that full realisation meant, how completely everything that had hitherto made up my life had vanished with Edward and Roland, with Victor and Geoffrey. The war was over; a new age was beginning; but the dead were dead and would never return.'

In the East End, they were marking the Armistice in their own quiet way. In Canning Town, down by London's docks, the children of the Freemasons Road council school had heard the sirens at eleven that morning and had assumed at first that it meant another air raid on the docks. The children knew about air raids because they had already been bombed once at school. A huge crater had appeared in the playground one day, while Dora Dewar, the infants' teacher, got them all clapping their hands and singing 'The Grand Old Duke of York' to distract them from the noise of the anti-aircraft guns going off all around.

But the sirens had heralded good news this time. Teachers from the upper school had rushed in to announce the Armistice and the children had been given the rest of the day off to join the celebrations. A corner shop on Dora's road had opened for the first time since the beginning of the war to give away free fireworks for the children to enjoy that night.

Unfortunately, the children had never seen fireworks before. They decided, after due consideration on Armistice night, that they didn't like fireworks either. 'Them bomb things' reminded them too much of the Germans.

Across the Atlantic, the party was still going on. The Italian embassy was having a ball. It was the king of Italy's birthday and everyone who was anyone in Washington had flocked to the embassy to help the Italians celebrate it.

Even the president was there. It was not strictly proper for the president to visit a foreign embassy, but he felt he had to go somewhere on a night like this. Splendid in white tie and tails, he had arrived unannounced with Mrs Wilson, while the ambassador hurried down to receive them. It was just after eleven and the ball was already in full swing. There were uniforms everywhere as the president accepted a glass and drank to the health of the king.

He and Edith stayed for an hour. They were too excited to sleep when they got back to the White House. They sat on the sofa in Edith's room instead, warming themselves by the fire and talking until the early hours of the morning. Then the president read a chapter of the Bible before bed. He had promised a delegation of soldiers going to the war that he would read a chapter every night, no matter how busy he was. It was the last thing he did before turning out the light.

In France, Harry Truman was in bed too. He had gone at ten, exhausted after all the excitement. It had been Very pistols and rockets after dark, just like everywhere else. The French artillerymen behind him had got hold of some wine and were having a party. Truman tried to sleep, but the French wouldn't allow it:

'The French battery became intoxicated as a result of a load of wine which came up on the ammunition narrow gauge. Every single one of them had to march by my bed and salute and yell, "Vive President Wilson, vive le capitaine d'artillerie américaine!" No sleep all night, the infantry fired Very pistols, sent up all the flares they could lay their hands on, fired rifles, pistols and whatever else would make noise, all night long.' It seemed more like the Fourth of July than the front line.

In the Vosges, Corporal Teilhard de Chardin had been celebrating with equal vigour, drinking with the officers of his regiment. There had been toasts, songs, tears and then more toasts. Teilhard was glad to get away at length, back to the room he had been given in the Docelles presbytery. Searching for his door in the small hours, he tried to put his key into the lock, but found that the key had apparently turned to rubber. He couldn't get it in at all. Exasperated, he gave up trying after a while and went out to the barn instead. France's foremost philosopher-theologian toppled over on to the straw and was asleep within minutes.

On the way to Mons, US officer Howard Vincent O'Brien and his driver had slid off the road in the dark and were perched on top of a mine. Fortunately for them, it had failed to explode. Extricating themselves gingerly, they drove on until they were stopped by a party of Scottish soldiers in the rain, outraged that they were driving with their lights on.

O'Brien told them the war was over.

'Aye', one replied sceptically. 'We've heard that before.'

Pressing on, O'Brien found shelter for the night at Grandéglise. He and his driver shared a room with two soldiers of the Northumberland Fusiliers. They prepared for bed. As they settled down, one of the Tommies ventured the opinion that the United States had come criminally late to the war.

'Yeah,' O'Brien's driver agreed. 'Lucky for youse guys the Canucks held 'em off till we got here.'

The conversation languished. They fell asleep.

Adolf Hitler couldn't sleep. In hospital at Pasewalk, he was still wide awake, turning the day's calamitous events over in his mind. He still couldn't believe what had happened:

'So it had all been in vain. In vain all the sacrifices and privations; in vain the hunger and thirst of months which were often endless; in vain the hours in which, with mortal fear clutching at our hearts, we nevertheless did our duty; and in vain the death of two millions who died ... Was it for this that those boys of seventeen sank into the Flanders mud? Was this the meaning of the sacrifice the German mother made for the Fatherland when with anguished heart she let her dearly loved boys march away, never to see them again? Did all this happen only so that a gang of wretched criminals could lay their hands on the Fatherland?'

The Germans had been stabbed in the back. That much was clear. The traitors at home had done it, the profiteers and speculators, the Marxist revolutionaries, the Jews. They had betrayed the soldiers at the front just when the German army was on the point of victory.

It was all the Jews' fault. They were the ones to blame. The Jews had been behind it from the start. Lying in bed in Pasewalk, Adolf Hitler decided then and there that he would have to go into politics when he got out of hospital. It was his duty to do so. He owed it to the Fatherland. He owed it to the German people.

Those wretched Jews. They would have to pay for what they had done ...

BIBLIOGRAPHY

Adam Smith, Janet, *John Buchan*, Hart-Davis, 1965

Adam, H. Pearl, *Paris Sees it Through*, Hodder and Stoughton, 1919

Arthur, Max, *Forgotten Voices of the Great War*, Ebury, 2002

Asquith, Margot, *The Autobiography of Margot Asquith*, Butterworth, 1920

Aston, Sir George, *The Biography of Marshal Foch*, Hutchinson, 1929

Aubry, Octave, *Eugénie*, Cobden-Sanderson, 1939

Baker, Carlos, *Ernest Hemingway*, Collins, 1969

Baumont, Maurice, *The Fall of the Kaiser*, Allen and Unwin, 1931

Bennett, Arnold, *The Journals of Arnold Bennett*, Cassell, 1932

Bentinck, Lady Norah, *The Ex-Kaiser in Exile*, George Doran, 1921

Birdwood, Lord, *Khaki and Gown*, Ward, Lock, 1941

Blackburne, Harry, *This Also Happened*, Hodder and Stoughton, 1932

Blücher, Princess Evelyn, *An English Wife in Berlin*, Constable, 1920

Boyden, Matthew, *Richard Strauss*, Weidenfeld, 1999

Brittain, Vera, *Testament of Youth*, Gollancz, 1933

Buchan, John, *The History of the South African Forces in France*, Imperial War Museum, 1920

Bucher, Georg, *In the Line*, Jonathan Cape, 1932

Chandos, Viscount, *The Memoirs of Lord Chandos*, Bodley Head, 1962

Christie, Agatha, *An Autobiography*, Collins, 1977

Churchill, Winston, *The World Crisis*, Butterworth, 1923

Clark, Stanley, *The Man who is France*, Harrap, 1960

Conan Doyle, Arthur, *Memories and Adventures*, John Murray, 1930

Cooper, Caroline Ethel, *Behind the Lines*, Collins, 1982

Cooper, Lady Diana, *The Rainbow Comes and Goes*, Hart-Davis, 1958

Coper, Rudolf, *Failure of a Revolution*, Cambridge UP, 1955

Coward, Noël, *Autobiography*, Methuen, 1986

Crawley, Aidan, *De Gaulle*, Collins, 1969

Crozier, Brian, *De Gaulle*, Eyre Methuen, 1973

Emslie Hutton, Isabel, *With a Woman's Unit in Serbia*, Williams and Norgate, 1928

Erzberger, Matthias, *Erlebnisse im Weltkrieg*, Stuttgart, 1920

Evans, A. J., *The Escaping Club*, Bodley Head, 1931

Foch, Ferdinand, *The Memoirs of Marshal Foch*, Heinemann, 1931

Garnett, David, *The Flowers of the Forest*, Chatto & Windus, 1955

Gibbs, Sir Philip, *The War Dispatches*, A. Gibbs, Phillips and Times Press, no date

Gilliam, Brian, *The Life of Richard Strauss*, Cambridge UP, 1999

Glubb, John, *Into Battle*, Cassell, 1978

Graham, Stephen, *A Private in the Guards*, Macmillan, 1919

Gussow, Mel, *Zanuck*, W. H. Allen, 1971

Haffner, Sebastian, *Failure of a Revolution*, André Deutsch, 1973

Hindenburg, Gert, *Hindenburg*, Hutchinson, 1935

Hiscock, Eric, *The Bells of Hell Go Ting-a Ling-a Ling*, Corgi, 1977

Hitchcock, Captain F. C., *Stand To*, Hurst and Blackett, 1937

Hitler, Adolf, *Mein Kampf*, Hutchinson, 1969

Holroyd, Michael, *Lytton Strachey*, Heinemann, 1967

Horn, Daniel, *Mutiny on the High Seas*, Rutgers UP, 1969

Houston, David, *Eight Years with Wilson's Cabinet*, Doubleday, 1926

Lloyd George, David, *War Memories of David Lloyd George*, Nicholson and Watson, 1936

Longford, Earl of, *Eamon de Valera*, Hutchinson, 1970

Ludendorff, Erich, *My War Memories 1914–1918*, Hutchinson, 1919

Ludendorff, Margarethe, *My Married Life with Ludendorff*, Hutchinson, 1930

MacArthur, Douglas, *Reminiscences*, Heinemann, 1964

Bibliography

MacDonogh, Giles, *The Last Kaiser*, Weidenfeld & Nicolson, 2000

McGuinness, Brian, *Wittgenstein*, Duckworth, 1988

Mann, Thomas, *Diaries*, André Deutsch, 1983

Masur, Gerhard, *Imperial Berlin*, Basic Books, 1970

Matthias, Erich, *Die Regierung des Prinzen Max von Baden*, Droste, 1962

Maurois, André, *The Silence of Colonel Bramble*, Bodley Head, 1965

Max von Baden, *Memoirs of Prince Max of Baden*, Constable, 1928

Millard, Oscar, and Vierset, Auguste, *Burgomaster Max*, Hutchinson, 1936

Miller, Webb, *I Found No Peace*, Gollancz, 1937

Mosley, Sir Oswald, *My Life*, Nelson, 1968

Muggeridge, Malcolm, *Chronicles of Wasted Time*, Collins, 1972

Nicolson, Harold, *Peacemaking*, Constable, 1933

Niemann, Alfred, *Revolution von Oben*, Verlag für Kulturpolitik, 1928

Noakes, F. E., *The Distant Drum*, privately printed, 1952

Norwich, John Julius, *The Duff Cooper Diaries*, Weidenfeld, 2005

O'Brien, Howard Vincent, *Wine, Women and War*, J. H. Sears, 1926

Onions, Maude, *A Woman at War*, privately printed, 1928

Owen, Harold, *Journey from Obscurity*, Oxford UP, 1965

Pershing, John, *My Experiences in the World War*, Hodder and Stoughton, 1931

Priestley, J. B., *Margin Released*, Heinemann, 1966

Quinn, Susan, *Marie Curie*, Heinemann, 1995

Rawlinson, Lord, *The Life of General Lord Rawlinson of Trent*, Cassell, 1928

Reitz, Deneys, *Trekking On*, Faber & Faber, 1933

Rickenbacker, Eddie, *Fighting the Flying Circus*, Frederick Stokes, 1919

Rider Haggard, Lilias, *The Cloak that I Left*, Hodder and Stoughton, 1951

Riva, Maria, *Marlene Dietrich*, Bloomsbury, 1992

Rogers, Bogart, *A Yankee Ace in the RAF*, University Press of Kansas, 1996

Russell, Bertrand, *The Autobiography of Bertrand Russell*, George Allen and Unwin, 1967

Sandes, Flora, *The Autobiography of a Woman Soldier*, Witherby, 1927

Sassoon, Siegfried, *Diaries*, Faber, 1983

Schebera, Jürgen, *Kurt Weill*, Deutscher Verlag für Musik, 1983

Schubert, Paul, and Gibson, Langhorne, *Death of a Fleet*, Hutchinson, 1933

Schultze-Pfaelzer, Gerhard, *Hindenburg*, Philip Allan, 1931

Scott, Michael, *The Great Caruso*, Hamish Hamilton, 1987

Seth, Ronald, *The Spy Who Wasn't Caught*, Robert Hale, 1966

Sitwell, Osbert, *Laughter in the Next Room*, Macmillan, 1975

Smith, Aubrey, *Four Years on the Western Front*, Odhams, 1922

Stallworthy, Jon, *Wilfred Owen*, Chatto and Windus, 1974

Stephens, D. Owen, *With Quakers in France*, C. W. Daniel, 1921

Stumpf, Richard, *The Private War of Seaman Stumpf*, Leslie Frewen, 1969

Sulzbach, Herbert, *With the German Guns: Four Years on the Western Front*, Leo Cooper, 1973

Teilhard de Chardin, Pierre, *The Making of a Mind*, London, 1965

Terraine, John, *Douglas Haig*, Hutchinson, 1963

Tims, Hilton, *Erich Maria Remarque*, Constable, 2003

Townley, Lady Susan, *Indiscretions of Lady Susan*, Butterworth, 1922

Truman, Harry, *Dear Bess*, W. W. Norton, 1983

Tschuppik, Karl, *Ludendorff*, George Allen and Unwin, 1932

Tumulty, Joseph, *Woodrow Wilson as I Knew Him*, Heinemann, 1922

Von Ilsemann, Sigurd, *Der Kaiser in Holland*, München, 1968

Von Lettow-Vorbeck, Paul, *My Reminiscences of East Africa*, Hurst and Blackett, 1920

Walker, Roy, *Sword of Gold*, Indian Independence Union, 1945

Weizmann, Chaim, *Trial and Error*, East and West Library, 1950

Wemyss, Lady Wester, *The Life and Letters of Lord Wester Wemyss*, Eyre and Spottiswoode, 1935

Westman, Stephen, *Surgeon with the Kaiser's Army*, William Kimber, 1962

Bibliography

Weygand, Maxime, *Memoires*, Flammarion, 1953
Wilhelm, Kaiser, *My Memoirs*, Cassell, 1922
Wilson, Edith, *Memoirs of Mrs Woodrow Wilson*, Putnam, 1939
Woolf, Virginia, *The Question of Things Happening*, Hogarth Press, 1976

Imperial War Museum Department of Documents
Almack, Miss T. F. (05/61/1)
Bickerton, T. A. (80/43/1)
Coles, Second Lieutenant G. T. (03/58/1)
Cooper, E. R. (P121)
Cox, C. H. (88/11/1)
Dixon, Lieutenant R. G. (92/36/1)
Foot, Brigadier R. C. (86/57/1)
Gifford, Miss J. H. (93/22/1)
Hamilton, Major A. S. (93/31/1)
Hill, H. A. (87/20/1)
House, Major H. W. (88/56/1)
Hulme, H. (01/60/1)
Johnstone Wilson, Captain W. W. (97/5/1)
Kirkpatrick, Sir Ivone (79/50/1)
McGrigor, Captain A. M. (P399)
McGuire, Misses A. & R. (96/31/1)
Mascall, Mrs E. M. (P121 & PP/MCR/284)
Mullineaux, Mrs A. (78/36/1)
Rees, Brigadier H. C. (77/179/1)
Sauter, R. (Con Shelf)
Wells, Miss O. (91/5/1)
Wilson, Commander H. M. (04/1/1)
Wilson, J. (84/52/1)
Wrench, A. E. (85/51/1)

Liddle Collection, Leeds University
Major S. C. Marriott. Letter 11.11.18
Julian Pease Fox CO 036

Royal Archives
RA GV/CC9/3 November 1918
RA GV/CC9/10 November 1918
RA GV/CC9/11 November 1918
RA GV/GVD/11 November 1918

INDEX

Abbeville 272–3
Adenauer, Konrad 65–6
air raids 143, 144, 219–20, 285–6
Aix-la-Chapelle 100, 118, 143, 257
Albania 48–9
Aldershot 222
Alexander, Lieutenant Colonel Harold 230–1
Almack, T. F. 251–2
Alsace 62
Alsace-Lorraine 235
Amazon, HMS 207
Amerongen 158–9, 175–6, 275–6
Amiens 250
Arabs 262
Arc-Ainières 138–9
Argentina 73
Argonne, the 4, 23
Armistice commission
  leader appointed 53–4
  credentials 54–5
  membership 55
  departure 55–6
  safe passage arranged 57–8
  leadership 58
  arrival in Spa 58–9

crosses French lines 77–9
journey to Compiègne 80–1
conditions spelled out to 81–7
train 81
waiting 110–11
learns whereabouts 137–8
Foch demands answer from 156
authorised to accept terms 160–1
signs Armistice 162–5
Armistice, the 17–18
  Pershing's opposition to 19–20
  Allies agree terms 38
  Max von Baden discusses 40–2
  terms 41, 129–31, 162–3
  signing rumour 69–77
  conditions 84–5
  reparations clause 111
  Hindenburg's address to the troops 152
  Hitler's reaction to news of 152–3
  conditions accepted 156–7

signed 162–5
fighting continues 165–72, 184–90, 197–9, 223–4
news of spreads 166
reaction to 173–5, 181–4, 191–6, 200–7, 225–30
last fatalities 198–9, 223–4
celebrations 203–24, 234–7, 242–6, 265–6, 269–75, 276–7, 279–87
news spreads around world 222–3
casualties and losses, 11 November 224
Arthur of Connaught, Prince 231
Asquith, Henry 181–3, 243
Asquith, Margot 182–3, 243, 279
Astraea, HMS 263–5
atrocities 24, 49, 148, 171–3, 278
Australia 71, 222, 263
Australian forces 250–2
Austria-Hungary 17, 48, 91, 93

Index

Index

Index

Nicholas Best grew up in Kenya and was educated there, in England, and at Trinity College, Dublin. He served in the Grenadier Guards and worked in London as a journalist before becoming a full-time author. His many other books include *Happy Valley: The Story of the English in Kenya*, *Tennis and the Masai*, and the widely praised *Trafalgar*. Nicholas Best was the *Financial Times*'s fiction critic for ten years and has written for many other national publications. He lives in Cambridge, England.

PublicAffairs is a publishing house founded in 1997. It is a tribute to the standards, values, and flair of three persons who have served as mentors to countless reporters, writers, editors, and book people of all kinds, including me.

I. F. STONE, proprietor of *I. F. Stone's Weekly*, combined a commitment to the First Amendment with entrepreneurial zeal and reporting skill and became one of the great independent journalists in American history. At the age of eighty, Izzy published *The Trial of Socrates*, which was a national bestseller. He wrote the book after he taught himself ancient Greek.

BENJAMIN C. BRADLEE was for nearly thirty years the charismatic editorial leader of *The Washington Post*. It was Ben who gave the *Post* the range and courage to pursue such historic issues as Watergate. He supported his reporters with a tenacity that made them fearless and it is no accident that so many became authors of influential, best-selling books.

ROBERT L. BERNSTEIN, the chief executive of Random House for more than a quarter century, guided one of the nation's premier publishing houses. Bob was personally responsible for many books of political dissent and argument that challenged tyranny around the globe. He is also the founder and longtime chair of Human Rights Watch, one of the most respected human rights organizations in the world.

·   ·   ·

For fifty years, the banner of Public Affairs Press was carried by its owner Morris B. Schnapper, who published Gandhi, Nasser, Toynbee, Truman, and about 1,500 other authors. In 1983, Schnapper was described by *The Washington Post* as "a redoubtable gadfly." His legacy will endure in the books to come.

Peter Osnos, *Founder and Editor-at-Large*